The Labour Market in Winter

The Labour Market in Winter

The State of Working Britain

Edited by
Paul Gregg and Jonathan Wadsworth

OXFORD
UNIVERSITY PRESS

OXFORD
UNIVERSITY PRESS

Great Clarendon Street, Oxford OX2 6DP

Oxford University Press is a department of the University of Oxford.
It furthers the University's objective of excellence in research, scholarship,
and education by publishing worldwide in

Oxford New York

Auckland Cape Town Dar es Salaam Hong Kong Karachi
Kuala Lumpur Madrid Melbourne Mexico City Nairobi
New Delhi Shanghai Taipei Toronto

With offices in

Argentina Austria Brazil Chile Czech Republic France Greece
Guatemala Hungary Italy Japan Poland Portugal Singapore
South Korea Switzerland Thailand Turkey Ukraine Vietnam

Oxford is a registered trade mark of Oxford University Press
in the UK and in certain other countries

Published in the United States
by Oxford University Press Inc., New York

British Library Cataloguing in Publication Data
Data available

Library of Congress Cataloging in Publication Data
Data available

Typeset by SPI Publisher Services, Pondicherry, India
Printed in Great Britain
on acid-free paper by
MPG Books Group, Bodmin and King's Lynn

ISBN 978–0–19–958737–7

1 3 5 7 9 10 8 6 4 2

Preface

- How did the UK labour market cope with recession?
- What were the trends that emerged in the latest downturn?
- Which policies worked and which didn't?

The Labour Market in Winter is the third book in the important *State of Working Britain* series. The aim of this latest volume is to give an overview of key issues concerning the performance of the labour market and policy, with the focus this time around on the latest recession and its aftermath. The intention is to provide something that is an indispensable reference source on contemporary labour market developments in the UK that will be of lasting use to academics, students, practitioners and policy makers.

Topics covered include:

- employment and unemployment trends in the downturn;
- immigration;
- an assessment of the efficacy of family-friendly work schemes;
- an evaluation of education reforms;
- wage inequality and intergenerational income mobility;
- happiness, well-being and job security over the economic cycle.

This book is an edited volume consisting of chapters from leading experts on the UK labour market, each summarising the key issues and trends in their particular area of expertise. The text is illustrated liberally with graphs and tables as the principal means of summarising the underlying analysis.

Paul Gregg is Professor of Economics at the University of Bristol and a senior research fellow at the Centre for Economic Performance, London School of Economics. Jonathan Wadsworth is Professor of Economics at Royal Holloway College, University of London and a senior research fellow at the LSE's Centre for Economic Performance.

Acknowledgements

The editors are extremely grateful to Helen Durrant for her tireless and excellent work in formatting the book and generally putting it together so effectively in such a short time. Giulia Faggio also provided invaluable and enthusiastic help with the data that underlie the figures and tables in several chapters. The editors are also grateful to the authors of each chapter who gave up their time to contribute. Lastly they would like to thank Jamie Jenkins and Debra Leaker of the Office for National Statistics, Newport, for invaluable help in preparing data and figures for Chapter 1 in this volume. Joanna K. Swaffield extends her thanks to the editor, Jonathan Wadsworth, for helpful comments on her chapter and also to Giulia Faggio for her research assistance.

The Crown Copyright LFS and BHPS data used in the chapters of the book have been made available by the Office for National Statistics through the ESRC Data Archive at the University of Essex. Neither the ONS nor the Data Archive bears any responsibility for the analysis or interpretation of the data reported here.

The data that underlie the figures in this book can be downloaded from the following website <http://cep.lse.ac.uk/state3/data.asp>.

Contents

Contents

List of Figures

List of Figures

List of Figures

List of Tables

Abbreviations and Acronyms

ALSPAC	Avon Longitudinal Survey of Adults and Children
APS	Annual Population Survey
ASHE	Annual Survey of Hours and Earnings
ATL	Association of Teachers and Lecturers
BCS	British Cohort Study
BGM	Britain's General Trade Union (Originally General Municipal Boilermakers)
BHPS	British Household Panel Survey
BMA	British Medical Association
BSA	British Social Attitudes Survey
CEPREMAP	CEntre Pour la Recherche EconoMique et ses APplications (Centre for economic research and its applications)
CLS	Centre for Longitudinal Studies
CMP	Condition Management Programme (NHS)
CWU	Communication Workers Union
DB	Defined benefit
DC	Defined contribution
DCSF	Department for Children, Schools and Families
DfES	Department for Education and Skills
DOT	Dictionary of Occupational Titles
DWP	Department of Work and Pensions
EiC	Excellence in Cities
ELSA	English Longitudinal Survey of Ageing
EMA	Education Maintenance Allowance
EPPE	Effective Provision of Pre-School Education
ERM	Exchange Rate Mechanism
ESA	Employment Support Allowance
ESDS	Economic and Social Data Service
ESRC	Economic and Social Research Council

FRS	Family Resources Survey
FSM	Free School Meals
GCSE	General Certificate of Secondary Education
GDP	Gross Domestic Product
GHQ	General Health Questionnaire
GHS	General Household Survey
HBAI	Households Below Average Income
HIM	High Involvement Management
ICB	Incapacity Benefit
ICT	Information Communications Technology
IFF	International Finance Facility
ILO	International Labour Organization
IPS	International Passenger Survey
IS	Income Support
ISER	Institute for Social and Economic Research
JSA	Job Seekers' Allowance
JUVOS	Joint Unemployment and Vacancies Operating Systems Cohort
LA	Local Authority
LEA	Local Education Authorities
LFS	Labour Force Survey
LSC	Learning and Skills Council
LSYPE	Longitudinal Survey of Young People in England
MCS	Millennium Cohort Survey
NAIRU	Non Accelerating Inflation Rate of Unemployment
NASUWT	National Association of Schoolmasters/Union of Women Teachers
NCA	National Curriculum Assessment
NCDS	National Child Development Survey
ND50+	New Deal 50 Plus
NDDP	New Deal for Disabled People
NDLP	New Deal for Lone Parents
NDYP	New Deal for Young People
NEET	Not in Employment, Education and Training
NEPA	National Equality Panel Analysis
NES	New Earnings Survey
NESS	National Evaluation of Sure Start
NHS	National Health Service

NMW	National Minimum Wage
NPD	National Pupil Database
NUT	National Union of Teachers
NVQ	National Vocational Qualification
OECD	Organisation for Economic Co-operation and Development
Ofsted	Office for Standards in Education
OLS	Ordinary Least Squares
ONS	Office for National Statistics
PAMs	Practices Allied to Medicine
PCS	Public and Commercial Services Union
PIRLS	Progress in International Reading Literacy
PISA	Programme for the International Student Assessment
PLASC	Pupil Level Annual School Census
PRBs	Pay Review Bodies
QLFS	Quarterly Labour Force Survey
RCN	Royal College of Nursing
RTWC	Return To Work Credit
SBTC	Skill-Biased Technology Change
SSCs	Sector Skills Councils
TBTC	Task-Biased Technical Change
TIMSS	Trends in International Mathematics and Science Study
UCATT	Union of Construction, Allied Trades and Technicians
UKCES	UK Commission for Employment and Skills
UNISON	UK Trade Union, representing public sector workers and volunteers
Unite	UK Trade Union
USDAW	Union of Shop, Distributive and Allied Workers
WERS	Workplace Employment Relations Survey
WFIs	Work Focused Interviews
WFTC	Working Families Tax Credit
WTC	Working Tax Credit
WTR	Working Time Regulations
YCS	Youth Cohort Studies

Notes on Contributors

Jo Blanden is a lecturer in the Economics Department at the University of Surrey. She is also a research associate at the Centre for Economic Performance (CEP) where she worked as a full-time researcher from 2000–5. Her published work has focused on intergenerational economic mobility; in particular, on comparisons of mobility across time and between nations. She has also worked on child poverty, the transmission of social disadvantage and the economics of education.

Alex Bryson is a senior research fellow at the National Institute of Economic and Social Research (NIESR) and a visiting research fellow at the Centre for Economic Performance (CEP), London School of Economics. His research interests are labour economics and industrial relations.

Andrew E. Clark holds a Ph.D. from the London School of Economics. He is currently a CNRS Research Professor at the Paris School of Economics (PSE), and previously held posts at Dartmouth, Essex, CEPREMAP, DELTA, the OECD and the University of Orléans. His work has largely focused on the interface between psychology, sociology and economics, using job and life satisfaction scores, and other psychological indices, as proxy measures of utility. One research field has been that of utility comparisons, finding evidence of comparisons to others with respect to both income and unemployment. Another has involved collaboration with psychologists to map out habituation to life events (such as job loss, marriage and divorce) using long-run panel data. A third project has taken subjective measures such as job satisfaction as indicators of job quality.

Richard Dickens is a Professor of Economics at the University of Sussex and a senior research fellow with the Labour Markets Programme at the Centre for Economic Performance, LSE. He has written extensively on the National Minimum Wage and on poverty in the UK.

Richard Disney is Professor of Labour Economics at the University of Nottingham having previously been a Professor of Economics at Queen Mary College, University of London, and at the University of Kent at Canterbury. His research interests lie largely in the field of applied microeconomics, including tax policy, social welfare reform and pensions policy, in both developed and developing countries, and the economics of labour markets, including retirement behaviour and wage structure. He has published numerous articles in academic journals and several books in these fields of public policy. He was a member of the NHS Pay Review Body (NHSPRB) from 2003–9 and is currently a member of the Senior Salaries Review Body 2009–11. He was conference chair for the 2005 Royal Economic Society annual conference held at the University of Nottingham and on the Council of the Royal Economic Society from 2002–6.

Peter Dolton is a Professor of Economics at Royal Holloway College, University of London and Senior Research Fellow at CEP. His research interests are in the economics of education, the labour market and applied econometrics. He has published many articles in leading economics journals on topics such as: the teacher labour market, gender discrimination, the rate of return to education, public sector pay, unemployment duration and aspects of labour supply. Recently he has served on the Doctors and Dentists Pay Review Body and now serves on the School Teachers Pay Review Body.

Christian Dustmann is the Director of the Centre for Research and Analysis of Migration (CReAM) based at University College London (UCL) in the Department of Economics where he is also Professor of Economics. In 1992 he received his Ph.D. in Economics at the European University Institute and in 1997 received his 'Habilitation' from the University of Bielefeld. He is the editor of the *Journal of Population Economics*, and research fellow of the Centre for Economic Policy Research (CEPR), London, at the Institute for the Study of Labor (IZA) and a research associate of the Institute for Fiscal Studies (IFS), London. His main research interests are: Population Economics (migration, economics of the family), Labour Economics (education, wage structures, and earnings mobility), and Microeconometrics. He has also directed recent research for the British Home Office on the labour market performance of immigrants and the effect of migration on local labour markets in the UK and on the effects of EU enlargement on East–West migration.

Giulia Faggio is a research economist at the Spatial Economic Research Centre (SERC) at LSE. She previously worked as a senior economist at Citigroup Global Market Ltd. and as a full-time researcher at CEP. Her work has focused on wage inequality and productivity dispersion in the UK, patterns of work and unemployment in OECD countries and the rise in inactivity and disability among prime-age Britons. She has also analysed the economic and political transformation of countries of Central and Eastern Europe.

John Forth is a Research Fellow at NIESR, working on labour market issues. He has a particular interest in the study of employment relations. His work in this area has included a substantial involvement in the design and analysis of the series of Workplace Employment Relations Surveys. Major publications from this work include *All Change at Work?* (with N. Millward and A. Bryson; Routledge, 2000) and *The Evolution of the Modern Workplace* (with W. Brown, A. Bryson and K. Whitfield; Cambridge University Press, 2009), both of which trace the development of workplace employment relations in Britain since 1980. Other publications in the area of employment relations have focused on trade union effectiveness, the methods and outcomes of wage setting, and aspects of unfair treatment at work.

Tommaso Frattini is Franco Modigliani Research Fellow at the University of Milan, and a Research Fellow at CReAM at UCL. His main research interests are in Labour Economics, Applied Microeconometrics and the Economics of Migration. In particular his current research focuses on the economic consequences of immigration for host and sending countries and on the economic and non-economic integration of immigrants.

Antoine Goujard is a research assistant in the Labour Markets programme at the CEP and a Ph.D. student in Economics at LSE.

Francis Green is Professor of Skills Development and Labour Economics at the Institute of Education, London. After graduating in Physics at Oxford University, he studied Economics at the London School of Economics, before writing his Ph.D. thesis at Birkbeck College. His research focuses on skills, training, work quality and industrial relations issues. He has published many articles and nine books, including his recent work *Demanding Work: The Paradox of Job Quality in the Affluent Economy* (Princeton University Press, 2006). He has served on several advisory committees for UK government departments and now sits on the academic experts' panel of the UK Skills and Employment Commission.

Paul Gregg is a Professor in the Department of Economics, University of Bristol. He recently completed a review of personalised support and conditionality in the welfare system for the UK Department of Work and Pensions. He is also a member of the London Child Poverty Commission and a programme director at the Centre for Market and Public Organisation (CMPO). He was formerly a member of the Council of Economic Advisors at HM Treasury 1997–2006, where he worked on welfare reform and child poverty. His research has covered youth unemployment, workless households, child poverty, intergenerational mobility and the drivers of social disadvantage.

Stephen Machin is Professor of Economics at University College London and Research Director of CEP. He is one of the editors of the *Economic Journal*. Previously he has been Visiting Professor at Harvard University (1993–4) and at the Massachusetts Institute of Technology (2001–2). He is an elected fellow of the British Academy (since 2006), President of the European Association of Labour Economists (from 2008) and is an independent member of the Low Pay Commission (since 2007).

Lindsey Macmillan is a postgraduate research student in the Department of Economics, University of Bristol and CMPO, University of Bristol. She is also currently a Visiting Research Fellow at the Saguaro Seminar in the Harvard Kennedy School of Government, Harvard University. Her research focuses on intergenerational mobility, intergenerational worklessness and educational inequality in the UK. She is also working on comparative studies in educational inequality and family income volatility in the UK and the US.

Gerry Makepeace is a Professor of Labour Economics at Cardiff Business School. He is also a member of the Economic and Social Research Council's Birth Cohort Studies Scientific Committee and a research fellow at the Institute for the Study of Labor (IZA), University of Bonn. His research interests are applied labour economics, comparing labour market outcomes for different groups and applied micro-econometrics.

Sandra McNally is Director of the Education and Skills Programme and a Senior Research Fellow at CEP. Current research interests include: economic evaluation of government policies; the effect of careers-related information on educational decisions;

returns to education; the effects of 'ability tracking' within school systems; special educational needs; and education and mental health. She received her Ph.D. from University College London in 2003.

Stephen Nickell is currently Warden of Nuffield College, Oxford. He is also Chairman of The Advisory Committee on Civil Costs (Ministry of Justice) and a Board Member of the UK Statistics Authority. Previously he has held Economics Professorships at both LSE and Oxford and was President of the Royal Economic Society 2000–2003. He was a member of the Bank of England Monetary Policy Committee 2000–2006. He is a Fellow of both the Econometric Society and the British Academy as well as being a foreign honorary member of the American Economic Association and the American Academy of Arts and Sciences.

Barbara Petrongolo is a Senior Lecturer in Economics at the London School of Economics (LSE). She is currently a research affiliate of Paris School of Economics, CEPR and IZA, and a research associate at CEP. Her main area of interest is applied labour economics. The focus of some of her recent contributions is the performance of labour markets with search frictions, with applications to unemployment dynamics, welfare policy and geographic spillovers. She is also carrying out research into the causes and characteristics of gender earnings inequality across countries, with emphasis on the role of employment selection mechanisms and structural transformation.

Anita Ratcliffe is a Ph.D. student in the Department of Economics at the University of Bristol. She has previously worked as a researcher at CMPO.

Chiara Rosazza-Bondibene is a full-time researcher at Royal Holloway College, University of London. Most of her work is on the impact of the minimum wage and the spatial aspects of labour markets.

Jumana Saleheen is a Senior Economist at the Bank of England, where she has worked since 1996. Prior to that, she completed her Ph.D. at University College London. Her research has been in the field of unemployment and more recently on immigration. She has also worked on inflation expectation and forecasting inflation using the Bank of England model.

Sarah Smith is a Reader in the Department of Economics, University of Bristol. Her research interests are in the analysis of public policy, focusing on retirement and pension incentives and pro-social behaviour. She has previously worked at the London School of Economics, the Financial Services Authority and the Institute for Fiscal Studies.

Joanna K. Swaffield is Professor of Economics at the University of York. Her research interests lie in the field of labour economics, with particular interest in the gender wage gap and the national minimum wage. Joanna was a member of the Royal Economic Society's Conference Programme Committee, 2006–8 and the Royal Economic Society's Committee for Women in Economics (April 2001–March 2005). Joanna is currently also a Research Fellow at the ESRC-funded research centre, Administrative Data: Methods Inference and Network, at the Institute of Education, University of London.

Nikolaos Theodoropoulos is a lecturer in Economics at the University of Cyprus. He is also an external Research Fellow of CReAM at University College London. His research focuses on immigration, discrimination, human capital and personnel economics. He received his Ph.D. in 2006 from Leicester University.

John Van Reenen is the Director of CEP, Europe's leading applied economics research centre (<http://cep.lse.ac.uk/>). He is also a Professor of Economics at the London School of Economics and Political Science. He has been a senior policy advisor to the Secretary of State for Health, Downing Street and many international organizations. In 2008–9 he was the Denning Visiting Professor of Global Business and Economics at Stanford University. He has published widely on the economics of innovation, labour markets and productivity. Professor Van Reenen received his BA from the University of Cambridge, his MSc from the London School of Economics and his Ph.D. from University College London. He has written over 100 articles and book chapters and frequently appears in the media. He has been a CEPR Research Fellow since 1997. In 2009 he was awarded (jointly with Fabrizio Zilibotti) the Yrjö Jahnsson Award.

Jonathan Wadsworth is Professor of Economics at Royal Holloway College, University of London. He is also a senior research fellow at CEP, deputy director of CReAM and a research associate at IZA, Bonn.

Jane Waldfogel is Professor of Social Work and Public Affairs, Columbia University School of Social Work. Waldfogel received her Ph.D. in public policy from the Kennedy School of Government at Harvard University. She has written extensively on the impact of public policies on child and family well-being, poverty, inequality, and social mobility.

Introduction

The 15 years of output expansion from 1993 to 2008, the longest period of continuous growth in modern times, helped ease many of the labour market problems that had emerged on the backs of the deep recessions of the 1980s and 1990s. Yet growth alone was not responsible for the improvement. Policy too needed impetus and direction and the 1997 Labour administration undoubtedly devoted a considerable amount of energy and attention to the labour market. It is almost inconceivable that institutions that are now seemingly well-established and accepted, such as the National Minimum Wage, the New Deals or the expanded Working Tax Credits, would have been introduced under an administration with a more laissez-faire view. The undoubted labour market progress during this time was however brought to a grinding halt with the collapse of the speculative financial bubble that pushed the UK and much of the industrialised world into the deepest recession seen for 80 years.

This book is about the performance of the UK labour market before, during and after the 2008–9 recession. It is the third volume in the State of Working Britain series and comes, unlike its predecessors, at a period in the economic cycle when the UK economy is just beginning to emerge from the downturn. In some ways, politicians, policy makers and academics were better prepared this time round. There had, after all, been two severe recessions well within memory of most adults over the age of 30. The understandings that were gained during these periods undoubtedly helped frame a policy response in the latest downturn.

Yet there was more to it this time round. Economic orthodoxy had ventured for 30 years that the only way for a country to achieve economic success was to pursue 'labour-market flexibility' and the UK was sometimes held up as an exemplar of this approach. While the meaning of this phrase is, in truth, somewhat nebulous, it is sometimes taken as shorthand for weak employment protection legislation; weak union power; low levels of, and short-lived, unemployment benefits; a low or non-existent minimum wage and extensive opportunities for employment at relatively low wages. Yet the UK now has institutions—such as minimum wages, family-friendly work policies or in-work welfare payments—that stray far from the orthodoxy. It is also true that, for the past decade, the UK enjoyed lower unemployment rates relative to most of the rest of the OECD.

Just before the recession, however, there were significant shifts in thinking amongst several influential international institutions, recognising that there could be more than one way of achieving a given level of labour market performance. Indeed, going into the recession, policy makers in the UK and elsewhere have dusted off interventionist economic policy tools that for 30 years had been seemingly discredited. This, we believe, has helped make the labour market consequences of the recession more benign than they otherwise would have been.

Economic fashions are rather capricious. No one currently sees Ireland as the economic success story it was held up to be in the middle of this decade. Germany, Sweden, Japan and the US, along with the UK, have all in their turn been held up as economic paragons and no doubt a new champion will emerge from the current downturn and recovery. The real debate is whether minimal regulations and limited institutions are the key to economic success or whether targeted, costed interventions can help alleviate labour market failures. The aim of this book is to try and help make an assessment of it all, bringing together the thoughts and appraisals of key labour market analysts on the trends, policies and impacts on the labour market over the past ten years. The result is a serious comprehensive analysis of the record of the Labour government in the field of employment spanning its entire time in office.

Labour market performance can be judged along many different criteria. No one should ever judge labour market performance by recourse to a single indicator like the unemployment rate. Different institutional criteria across countries and within countries across time mean that success (or otherwise) needs to be assessed by use of more than one performance indicator. The more criteria in which a country does well, the easier it is to declare the overall performance to be a success. In order to support these claims it is essential that there be empirical verification. This book attempts to provide some evidence across a range of labour market issues.

The book is divided into three parts. The first part deals with jobs, the second looks at the characteristics of jobs and the final section looks at labour market inequality across various dimensions. The theme that runs through the first part is that, on aggregate, the performance of the labour market before the recession was good and that during the recession the aggregate outcomes were not as bad as some feared (see Gregg and Wadsworth, Chapters 1 and 2). This is to be welcomed. The unprecedented increase in the number of immigrants appears to have been absorbed without large-scale effects on the wages and employment of UK-born individuals. Also, unlike in previous recessions, immigrants have not borne the brunt of the downturn (see Nickell and Saleheen, Chapter 6). Older workers, on average, have done relatively well unlike in previous downturns, (see Disney et al., Chapter 4) and younger workers have not been disproportionately hit this time round (Goujard et al., Chapter 3). It is not all good news with regard to jobs however. Youth unemployment and in particular inactivity were rather high going into the recession. As a result, joblessness among youth has ratcheted up to levels not seen for a very long time. It was also, once again, a male-centric recession (Swaffield, Chapter 12). Likewise, inactivity among men, particularly older less skilled men, remains stubbornly high (Gregg and Wadsworth, Chapter 2). Workless household rates have also ratcheted up once again after failing to fall much during the recovery (Gregg and Wadsworth, Chapter 5).

The quality and nature of jobs is also an ongoing cause for concern. While comments about the end of a job for life have been exaggerated, it is true that stability in average job tenure over time disguises a sharp fall in average job tenure among men and an equally sharp rise in job tenure among women (Faggio et al., Chapter 7). Hours of work have fallen and paid holiday rights extended almost throughout the workforce (Green, Chapter 8). Practices to improve employees' work–life balance have become more widely available, but while the work intensification of the early 1990s has levelled off since 1997, there has been no reduction in work intensity and workplace stress remains a serious problem (Green, Chapter 8). It seems that the mental well-being of workers is pro-cyclical (Clark, Chapter 9). Well-being is significantly higher in booms than in busts. However, satisfaction with work itself is counter-cyclical, being higher in busts. The same is true of overall job satisfaction. Nevertheless, the past decade has seen a sea change in the support available for working parents (Waldfogel, Chapter 10). Paid maternity leave has doubled. Paid paternity leave has been introduced. Preschool is now universal for 3 and 4 year olds. Support for child care has been greatly expanded and parents now have the right to request part-time or flexible hours. This expansion in support has not come cheap. Government spending on early learning and childcare quadrupled between 1997–8 and 2007–8, but in addition to promoting better child health and development, the policies also provide an important boost to parental employment and family incomes.

It would be a mistake, however, to think that the period just before the latest recession was as good as the UK labour market could get. One problem that has dogged the labour market for three decades now and that so far has not been tackled satisfactorily, is the degree of inequality within the labour market. This is not only inequality in wages but also inequality in terms of employment chances and educational opportunities. This is the theme of the third part of the book. Despite welcome levels of performance on average across a range of labour market measures, there is a huge variation in performance around this average. For example, at the height of the boom in 2007 the unemployment rate had fallen to just under 5%. At the same time, the unemployment rate was 1.7% in Rutland and the unemployment rate in Hartlepool was 10.5%, five times larger. The spread of employment rates around the 72% average was 22 percentage points (60% in Ceredigion and 82% in West Berkshire). One in two men without qualifications was not in work and two in every three men over 50, without qualifications and living in Tyne and Wear were jobless. And all this at the height of a boom.

The key thing to note here is that it was not always thus. The UK in the past has managed to combine good aggregate performance with much lower levels of inequality and opportunity. Yet, for the last 30 years, wage inequality has first grown rapidly and then stubbornly refused to fall, despite the undoubted effects of the Minimum Wage in shoring up the bottom of the wage distribution (Machin, Chapter 11). Moreover, the ability of individuals to move through the wage distribution over time, so offsetting any wage inequality, is much lower now than in periods when wage inequality was much lower. Job prospects continue to vary considerably across the familiar dimensions of education, region, (Dolton et al., Chapter 19), age, gender (Swaffield, Chapter 12) and ethnicity. There have been important changes in the rate of both inequality and inter-generational mobility (Blanden and Macmillan, Chapter 13) that suggest it has become harder to move up an increasingly widening income distribution. It does seem though that inter-generational mobility among the UK's ethnic minority population has improved (Dustmann et al., Chapter 15). The ability of trade unions to act as a voice for concerns over inequality is now almost confined to the public sector (Bryson and Forth, Chapter 17). Despite apparent 'sector envy', with more private sector workers thinking their public sector counterparts are better off, over the last ten years the rate of growth in private sector earnings settlements has, on average, matched—more or less exactly—the rate of growth in the public sector (Dolton and Makepeace, Chapter 18). The relative buoyancy of public sector employment during the latest downturn, undoubtedly helped maintain higher levels of consumer demand.

Yet despite widening inequality making the task much harder, there are positive outcomes to report. It does seem that after a decade of the 1997 Labour government, about half a million children were lifted out of relative poverty; short of their target, but certainly reversing the previous record increases under the Conservatives (Dickens, Chapter 16). By far the largest impact on child poverty has come about through the increased generosity of both in-work and out-of-work benefits. Without these reforms, there would be an extra 1 million children living in poverty in the UK today. It also seems that over the last ten years, educational attainment has improved dramatically and that the pace of improvement has been greater in economically disadvantaged areas (McNally, Chapter 14).

Clearly the immediate task following a recession is to ensure that recovery in output is accompanied by recovery in employment. This book is, in part, a record of the issues in need of attention. In our view, the level of inequality in the UK labour market, along several dimensions, is the outstanding area of concern. In the last edition of *The State of Working Britain* we worried that progress was neither sustained enough nor balanced enough to bring many marginalised groups back into the labour force without inducing widening levels of wage inequality. This time round, the basis for targeted, costed, policy intervention that may help address these concerns is in place. All that is needed is the willingness to direct policy accordingly.

Part I
Employment and Unemployment

1

The Labour Market in Winter—The 2008–2009 Recession

Paul Gregg and Jonathan Wadsworth

Key findings

- The deep recession of 2008–9 inflicted a larger cumulative loss of UK output than any of the other post-war recessions. Nevertheless, employment rates have remained higher and unemployment rates lower than would have been expected given the experience of previous recessions.
- The preservation of relatively high employment through the recession is in contrast with some other countries such as the US and Ireland with similarly low levels of labour market regulation and has not come about through hours reductions as has happened in Germany and a number of other mainland European countries.
- The main reasons for the relatively positive jobs picture appears to be related to a combination of high profitability levels among firms going into the recession, supportive monetary and fiscal policies of the government and Bank of England during the recession, reductions in real wage costs to producers but relatively buoyant real consumer wages facilitated by mortgage rate and VAT cuts.
- The downside from maintenance of relatively high employment is that productivity has fallen sharply. As government support for the economy is reduced, there remains a likelihood that it will take a long time for employment to begin to get back to levels last seen before the recession.
- A number of vulnerable groups, who are typically hard hit in a recession, have performed in line with or better than the average. These include the disabled, ethnic minorities and lone parents.

Introduction

After some 15 years of near continuous job growth, the employment rate in the UK in 2008 stood at around 75% of the working age population, a level which was broadly in line with previous employment peaks observed in 1968, 1978 or 1989. In 2005, the (OECD-based) unemployment rate fell below 5% for the first time since the 1970s. Since then, the UK has experienced the worst recession since World War II, in terms of output lost. However the impact on the UK labour market has been rather surprising given the experience of previous recessions and the contemporaneous experience of other industrialised countries. This chapter aims to chart the performance of employment over the recession and offers some explanations for the surprising patterns that have emerged. It also tries to assess the prospects for the next few years.

Employment in the recession

This recession has seen a GDP fall of over 6%, far worse than in the recessions of the 1980s or 1990s (see Figure 1.1). The recession, with a full six quarters of falling output, has been both longer and deeper than the previous two. In the previous two recessions, the percentage fall in employment was broadly in line with the percentage fall in GDP (indeed the employment rate fall was somewhat larger than the percentage decline in GDP in the 1990s—Figure 1.1). Moreover, in the previous two recessions (see Figure 1.2), the fall in employment was only

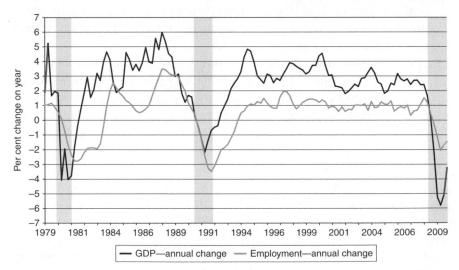

Figure 1.1: Annual change in LFS employment and GDP, 1979–2009
Source: LFS, ONS.

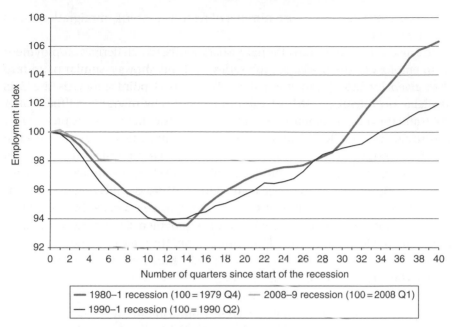

Figure 1.2: Employment levels from the start of recession for the 1980s, 1990s and 2008–9 recessions
Source: ONS.

halted some 12 to 14 quarters after the onset of recession. Employment also remained below before-recession levels for 18 months or so after the recovery in output started. Typically GDP growth of 2% seems to be needed before employment starts to rise, or unemployment starts to fall. Employers are thought to be rather cautious at the start of any recovery and prefer to increase hours initially, taking on extra staff only when recovery is assured.

However, this recession is strikingly different. Whilst the GDP fall has been markedly worse than in past recessions, the loss of employment has been rather benign, with a smaller employment fall, 900,000 on the workforce jobs series, and an earlier flattening of employment loss than in the past (Figure 1.2), limited to just over 2% of the initial employment level. This is notable, but could it be misleading?

One potential problem concerns the monitoring of recent migrants, mainly from the accession countries in Eastern Europe, often called the A8. If A8 workers in the UK were underestimated in the official employment numbers and A8 migrants returned home in large numbers in response to the recession, this could, conceivably, generate a smaller decline in employment in the official data. The employment numbers in Figure 1.1 derive from the Labour Force Survey (LFS), a survey of households. It is possible that recent migrants living in temporary accommodation on building sites or farms may not be surveyed. However, there are a number of reasons to think immigration is not a major factor here.

The first is that there is an alternative data source which derives employment from employers, the workforce job series, and this shows a similar pattern to that given by LFS employment data. The second point concerns the data available on migration. Whilst the numbers of new migrants fell back after 2006 and the number of returnees to the A8 countries has risen, the picture is of continuing but smaller net *in-migration* rather than a mass exodus (see Nickell and Saleheen, Chapter 6). It is also not obvious why immigrants to the UK would return to the source country if job prospects there are worse, as they currently appear to be in many A8 countries. The third is a question of scale. The number of jobs saved so far relative to what might be expected by the drop in GDP, amounts to just over 1 million (4% of employment). If, however, 1 million jobs had been lost, but obscured by immigration, the scale of hidden migration would have to be huge and this is very unlikely. Moreover, the recession would have to be centred on sectors that employ migrants and there is little evidence that this is the case. In short, it is unlikely that mis-measurement of immigration underlies the smaller than expected fall in employment.

So if an estimated net 1 million jobs appear to have been preserved, how has it happened? The first point to consider is how widespread across countries this pattern has been and whether it is related to institutional differences across countries. Table 1.1 shows that countries like France have escaped

Table 1.1: 2008–2009 recession—percentage change in GDP and unemployment across selection countries

	% change in GDP	% point change in unemployment
	2008 Q1–2009 Q2	2008 Q1–2009 Q4
Countries with small employment fall relative to decline in GDP		
UK	−5.9	2.7
Sweden	−6.1	2.9
Countries with small employment fall relative to GDP and with employment subsidies		
Italy	−6.5	1.8
Germany	−6.3	−0.1
Netherlands	−5.8	1.2
Japan	−7.1	1.3
Countries with similar employment and GDP falls		
France	−3.1	2.4
Countries with larger employment falls than GDP		
US	−3.5	5.0
Spain	−4.3	9.7
Ireland	−9.6	8.2
Countries with little GDP fall		
Australia	+1.5	1.5

Source: OECD (2009).

relatively lightly from the recession, with around a 3% fall in GDP and a similar rise in unemployment, in line with past norms, whilst in the US, Spain and Ireland, the rise in unemployment exceeded the fall in output. However, there are a large number of countries with smaller than expected employment falls. Some of these countries adopted a deliberate strategy to encourage short-time working rather than lose jobs. Hence, in Germany, the government has supported a policy of 'Kurzarbeit', or short-time working. Firms that face a decrease in demand avoid shedding employees by cutting hours instead. If hours and wages are reduced by 10% or more, the government pays 60% of lost salaries. Similar employment subsidy schemes are operating in Italy, the Netherlands and Japan.

The UK is one of a smaller number of countries which have experienced relatively small employment losses without a deliberate government-funded strategy of short hours working. Does this mean then that the putative flexible labour market in the UK is helping by creating adjustment in hours or wages instead of jobs? It is important to note that the low employment loss countries are far from obviously those with flexible labour markets. The US is held to be the prime example of the flexible model and Ireland is also a relatively less regulated country. Spain has strong labour protection but also has a large share of temporary jobs, which are weakly protected and have been very vulnerable in the downturn. By contrast, Sweden, Italy, Germany and the Netherlands have relatively high employment protection levels. In short, there is no relationship between a country's degree of labour market flexibility and employment losses in this recession.

Hours of work

We can also explore whether adjustment is falling on hours or wages rather than employment. Figure 1.3 gives the annual change in employment across the last three recessions (as in Figure 1.1) and adds the change in total hours worked. It is typical in recessions for total hours to fall faster than employment as overtime working is cut, some workers are placed on short-time working and people move into part-time work when they struggle to find full-time jobs. The difference between the fall in total hours and employment then reflects what is happening to average hours. The figure makes clear that hours have fallen in this recession but the picture is less marked than in the last two recessions, especially the 1980s recession when the government did subsidise short-time working in many major manufacturing plants. So, in the 1990s recession and in the latest recession, average hours amongst workers have fallen by around 2%, but in the 1980s this peaked at 4% with the policy of short-time working.

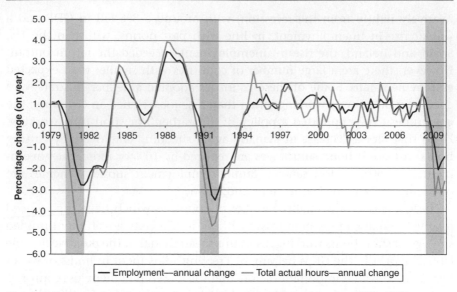

Figure 1.3: Annual percentage change in employment and hours, 1979–2009
Source: LFS, ONS.

Figure 1.4 tracks the long-term trend in part-time working in the UK. Part-time working rose from around 16% of employment in 1980 (excluding students) to 22% in 1995, after which it has been broadly stable. The share of part-time working has risen during this recession, consistent with the fall in hours above. However, this pattern is not unique to this recession. Similar or

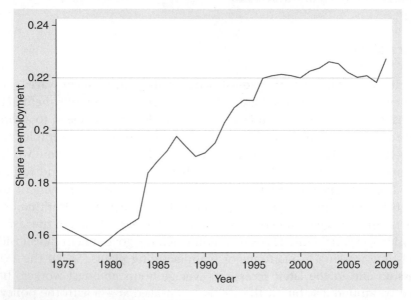

Figure 1.4: Part-time working in the UK
Source: LFS. Authors' calculations.

Table 1.2: Sectoral trends in employment

Total	1979–1983	1983–1990	1990–1993	1993–2007	2008 Q2–2009 Q4
% Δ Employment	−7.3	+15.0	−6.3	+15.6	−2.9
% Δ Manufacturing	−21.5	−5.6	−16.7	−27.8	−9.7
% Δ Finance	+3.7	+45.4	−1.5	+51.7	−4.3
% Δ Construction	−9.2	+35.2	−20.6	+18.9	−8.2
% Δ Retail, hospitality	−3.9	+20.7	−3.6	+12.8	−3.9
% Δ Public admin.	0	+13.8	+1.5	+21.9	+3.5

Source: Workforce jobs series, ONS. Authors' calculations.

sharper rises in the share of part-time work can be found during the last two recessions. The part-time job share tends to stabilise when employment recovers to before-recession levels.

Since output fell much faster than employment or hours worked, then productivity also fell sharply. This contrasts with the US where productivity levels were maintained by aggressive job cuts. So in contrast again with previous recessions, the lack of jobs being lost in the UK allied to relatively small hours reductions means that productivity has fallen (Figure 1.5).

One explanation for differential employment performance across countries over the recession is that the shock of the recession hit sectors with different

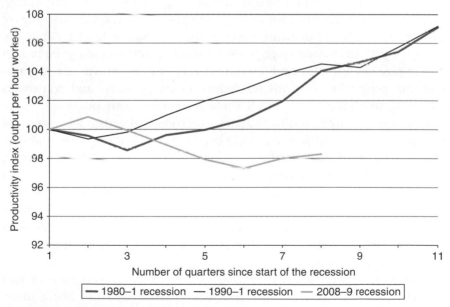

Figure 1.5: Productivity levels across recessions

Note: Index at start of recession = 100 for 1979 Q4, 1990 Q2 and 2008 Q1 respectively.

Source: ONS.

capital intensities or productivity differentials by differing amounts across countries. A high productivity, high capital intensity sector, subject to a negative shock is likely to experience a sharper fall in output than employment. Table 1.2 indicates that, in the UK, the manufacturing sector once again experienced the sharpest percentage fall in employment over the latest and indeed over previous recessions (in contrast to the financial sector, the source of the recession). Manufacturing and construction have been hardest hit, with 8–10% of employment lost compared to services at under 2%. Since high productivity manufacturing experienced the largest employment loss, it is unlikely that the simple shock to a high productivity story explains much of what we have observed in the UK. However, within the service sector there is considerable variation. In the public services of education, health and administration, employment has grown by 4%, and fallen by around 4% in finance, retail and transport. While these rates are well below construction and manufacturing as proportionate declines, because these latter sectors are larger, they account for around half of the total jobs lost.

Other things equal, any fall in productivity will put upward pressure on firm costs and reduce demand unless offset by an adjustment of wages. Over the last 50 years, productivity growth has allowed real wages to grow by around 2% a year, on average. Squeezing *real* wage costs during a recession is not as straightforward as it seems, as pointed out by Keynes. Prices also tend to fall during downturns, so offsetting any *nominal* wage moderation. Furthermore, wages are a major driver of consumer spending, and squeezing the earnings of consumers, and hence demand, makes stabilising output harder. Figure 1.6 shows the patterns for real wage growth, including and excluding the impact of mortgage interest rates, and thus aims to capture the growth of real wages from the perspective of firms (excluding mortgage rates) and consumers (including mortgage rates). In all three recessions, both prices and wage growth slowed sharply, but in the latest recession real consumer wages rose quite markedly as mortgage rates were cut. However, real wages to producers have been more subdued this time compared to past recessions. The reduction in wage growth has resulted in real wage cost falls *to firms* of the order of 3% or so. This gap between consumer wage growth and that faced by producers is perhaps made even more marked by the temporary 2% cut in VAT rates, since reversed in early 2010. This will undoubtedly have helped firms cope with cash flow, sustain demand and ultimately will have helped them to survive the immediate downturn.

To understand the factors that have influenced the preservation of jobs through the recession it is worth considering what we know about firms' workforce strategies. Staff are valuable to firms, they have firm-specific knowledge and productive experience. Losing valuable staff knowledge is costly,

Figure 1.6: Annual percentage change in real wages, 1979–2009
Source: LFS, ONS.

particularly if it will be needed again in the near future (see Geroski and Gregg, 1997, on the evidence for this over the 1990s recession). So firms will hold labour where possible through a recession, preferring instead to take short-term hits on profitability. However, if a firm is in deep financial trouble, such longer-term planning is discounted and the firm will take emergency measures to cut costs and improve cash flow. This means job cuts, as equivalent cost reductions made through dramatic wage cuts are difficult to implement quickly. So a large part of the story of employment through the recession is shaped by the extent to which firms are in a battle for survival rather than adjusting to lower demand. However, firms are also engaged in medium-term planning for employment needs over the near future. If the medium-term trading conditions continue to look difficult, then firms engage in job shedding on a slower, but more sustained basis. This usually continues after the recession is over. There remains the risk that firms will revise down these expectations if the recovery proves weak and the prospects now, given the financial position of the government, are for a sustained period of flat or gradually falling employment over the next two years or so.

Figure 1.7 looks at profitability through the latest recession as a guide to the potential for further job shedding. In the 1990s recession profitability was already being squeezed ahead of the recession proper, as interest rates were set high to bear down on inflation. By contrast, profits were much higher immediately prior to the 2008–9 recession. This means that the immediate pressure

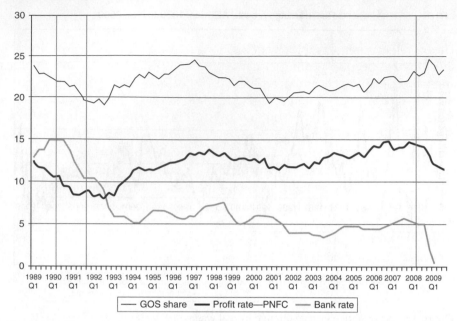

Figure 1.7: Rate of return on capital (profit rate), profits as a share of GDP and Bank of England base interest rate, 1989–2009
Source: ONS.

on firms to cuts jobs in order to survive was reduced. Since then, profitability held up well through the recession and indeed rose as a share of GDP. This is in part due to lower interest rates making financing debt easier; partly due to the fall in the exchange rate, unlike in the 1990s when membership of the Exchange Rate Mechanism (ERM) precluded devaluation; partly due to rapid falls in real wages and partly due to the maintenance of spending in the economy.

It seems that the explanation of how Britain got away with a smaller fall in employment in 2008–9 consists of three elements. Policy makers did the right thing in saving the banks, cutting interest rates and inducing a fiscal stimulus. Workers did the right thing in accepting lower nominal wage growth, although real growth was sustained by cuts in interest rates. Firms did the right thing in, wherever possible, holding onto valuable labour in the face of the pressure on profits and the severe nature of the crisis. However, the recession means that firms have under-used labour at the moment and this will allow them to grow without the need for extra jobs in the short to medium term. However, if demand continues to be weak, then job shedding will continue on a slow but sustained basis. Employment took eight to nine years to get back to before-recession levels after the last two recessions. This time it might be less if a second wave of job shedding is avoided.

Employment across different groups

The overall picture for employment has been surprisingly good, but whilst job shedding has been less common than before, firms have frozen recruitment and vacancies have become scarcer. Cutting back on hiring doesn't involve the loss of experienced staff and any natural outflows caused by quits and retirements are a relatively costless way of reducing employment numbers. This does, however, create acute problems for those trying to enter the labour market. This affects younger workers enormously. Youth employment has fallen sharply once again, but unemployment rises have muted a little by increased numbers staying on in full-time education (see Goujard et al., Chapter 3, on the youth labour market). In previous recessions older workers have also seen greater employment falls than most. This pattern is notably absent in this recession (see Disney et al., Chapter 4).

Chapter 12 (Swaffield) shows how past recessions have hit male employment more than female employment. The latest downturn was similar in this respect. It was, once again, a male recession.

This recession has also shown substantial variation in its impact across groups with traditionally low employment rates, who are typically more vulnerable to downturns. Figure 1.8 shows that employment rates in the most deprived wards in the UK and among the lowest educated have indeed fallen sharply through the recession, from a depressingly low base that 15 years of recovery had not managed to resolve fully. Employment

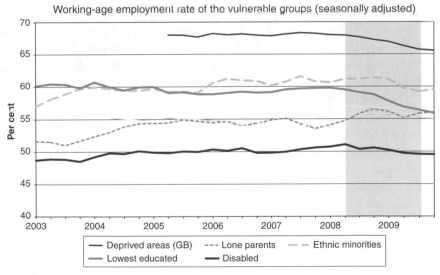

Figure 1.8: Employment rates for vulnerable groups since 2003
Source: LFS, ONS.

19

rates for the less educated had stabilised at 60% through the long period of growth prior to the recession, but have fallen by 4 percentage points, almost double the national average, in the recession. Employment in the most deprived wards has also fallen by twice the national average. However, employment rates for those with long-term limiting illnesses or disabilities and ethnic minorities have fallen in line with the national average. For lone parents, employment rates have risen (see Gregg and Wadsworth, Chapter 5).

Conclusions

This recession has been remarkable for the depth of the fall in GDP and the lengthy duration of falling output, but also for the relatively low loss of employment, at least so far. Lower redundancy rates seem to reflect a combination of three saving influences. First, employers entered the recession in good financial shape and this has helped avoid the level of job shedding that occurs when firms get into deep financial trouble. Second, the rapid reduction in interest rates, bank rescues and the fiscal stimulus from the government have all helped maintain demand and firm cash flow and helped avoid a more serious employment meltdown. Third, workers have accepted wage moderation early in this recession. Lower than expected levels of unemployment make it relatively easier to move back to work than in previous downturns, sometimes into part-time jobs when full-time jobs can't be found. To put it bluntly, the system as a whole has worked quite well. The government did the right thing in trying to keep demand going. Firms have avoided heavy redundancies, instead taking a reduction in what were high levels of profits going into the recession. Workers have accepted a degree of wage moderation and some seem willing to move to new, often lower quality, jobs. The cost has been huge for the public finances and in terms of productivity, which will hit cost competitiveness going forward. There are also serious jobless concentrations among more marginal groups that will need to be addressed when the economy recovers. Yet, overall, it seems that the labour market has performed relatively better than expected. Whether this generally good news will be sustained when the focus shifts to cuts in public spending and employers begin to assess their longer-term employment needs is also less than clear.

References

Disney, R., Ratcliffe, A. and Smith, S. (2011) The baby-boomers at 50: employment prospects for older workers. In: Gregg, P. and Wadsworth, J. (eds.) *The Labour Market in Winter: The State of Working Britain*. Oxford: Oxford University Press.

Geroski, P. and Gregg, P. (1997) *Coping with Recession: Company Performance in Adversity*. Cambridge: Cambridge University Press.

Goujard, A., Petrongolo, B. and Van Reenen, J. (2011) The labour market for young people. In: Gregg, P. and Wadsworth, J. (eds.) *The Labour Market in Winter: The State of Working Britain*. Oxford: Oxford University Press.

Gregg, P. and Wadsworth, J. (2011) Workless households. In: Gregg, P. and Wadsworth, J. (eds.) *The Labour Market in Winter: The State of Working Britain*. Oxford: Oxford University Press.

Nickell, S. (2010) The European unemployment challenge. In: Marsden, D. (ed.) *Labour Market Policy for the 21st Century. Essays in Honor of David Metcalf*. Oxford: Oxford University Press.

—— and Saleheen, J. (2011) Immigration in the UK. In: Gregg, P. and Wadsworth, J. (eds.) *The Labour Market in Winter: The State of Working Britain*. Oxford: Oxford University Press.

OECD (2009) *OECD Employment Outlook*. Paris: OECD.

Swaffield, J. K. (2011) Gender and the labour market. In: Gregg, P. and Wadsworth, J. (eds.) *The Labour Market in Winter: The State of Working Britain*. Oxford: Oxford UmversIty Press.

2

Unemployment and Inactivity

Paul Gregg and Jonathan Wadsworth

Key findings

- Unemployment had reached its lowest levels for 30 years going into the latest recession and remained subdued through the latest downturn, certainly compared to previous recessions.
- This seems to be due to a combination of lower inflow rates into unemployment allied with a relatively higher outflow rate into employment than in previous recessions.
- Unemployment rates, however, remain stubbornly high among more marginalised groups, as measured by age, education or area, and these groups have, once again, experienced larger rises in unemployment during the downturn.
- Economic inactivity, excluding students, going into the recession was the lowest for over 30 years.
- However, this disguises the failure of inactivity rates among men to come down significantly prior to the latest downturn, particularly among less skilled men, where inactivity rates have ratcheted up over time.

Introduction

The UK experienced 12 years of near continuous decline in unemployment after 1993, following the double-digit rates experienced in the early 1990s (and before that, in the first half of the 1980s). Most of the decline had taken place by 2001. Thereafter, the unemployment rate, measured on the ILO/OECD basis, hovered around 5% until 2008, the lowest it had been for some 30 years. For 20 years, policy regarding unemployment had been inextricably linked to the performance of the inflation rate. While it was known that an expansion of real GDP growth, typically above 2%, would bring down unemployment, policy makers feared that too rapid expansion would ignite inflation and upward wage pressures. The focus instead was on supply-side improvements to the productivity of the workforce, job-search effectiveness of the unemployed and sometimes attacks on institutions that were seen as potential inflationary bottlenecks in the system come any expansion. The period after 2001, when both unemployment and inflation were low and relatively stable, led some commentators to speculate on whether what is often labelled the NAIRU—the Non-accelerating Inflation Rate of Unemployment—had settled at this level (the label is wrong because policy makers are concerned with the level of unemployment that keeps demand and wage pressures in check sufficiently for inflation to be stable rather than accelerating).

However, with the advent of the latest recession, unemployment rose once again and all talk of whether the NAIRU had been reached evaporated. This latest recession was notable in that it was not, unlike the previous two recessions, exacerbated by a deliberate policy attempt at fiscal and monetary tightening to squeeze demand out of the system in order to get inflation on track. Instead, unemployment rose because of an old-fashioned collapse in demand following the bursting of a speculative financial sector bubble. Policy also shifted dramatically compared with previous recessions. There was a deliberate larger and more rapid loosening of fiscal and monetary policy to try and offset the fall in demand. Moreover, this was the first recession in which there was a raft of schemes in place, centred around the various New Deals designed to help deal with job-search effectiveness, facilitating the return to work and to address the problems associated with long-term unemployment. In some ways, the recession was a real test of whether these schemes are able to cope when faced with a high volume of new claims.

While long-term unemployment had fallen considerably going into the recession, many of the problems that had emerged in previous downturns had not been rectified fully by the time the labour market turned. In particular, since the recession of the 1980s, economic inactivity, for some, was quite often another dimension of (long-term) unemployment. Policy was not focused on these inactive groups until the problem had become entrenched. A key test of recent policy making introduced before the latest recession started is whether it can help avoid the buildup of concentrations of unemployment among sections of the population and the drift toward long-term disconnection from work. This chapter aims to assess this important question.

As with employment (see Gregg and Wadsworth, Chapter 1), a number of less obvious and surprising patterns of worklessness emerged in the latest downturn. First, the rise in unemployment was small relative to the fall in GDP. More interestingly, patterns of worklessness showed marked differences from past recessions. Likewise, the major workless benefits other than unemployment, such as income support (IS) for lone parents and incapacity benefits, have not seen a large rise in claimant numbers. This is in sharp contrast to the previous two recessions, when dependency grew by between 0.75 and 1 million. With the 1980–1 recession, unemployment on the internationally agreed ILO basis rose from just over 5% of the workforce to 12%, with over half of the rise occurring after the recession had ended (see Figure 2.1).

After the 1980–1 recession, unemployment did not start to fall consistently until 1986, some five years after the recession ended. The unemployment rate peak following the 1990–1 recession was lower than in 1986, but still in excess of 10%. It peaked some two years after the end of the recession. The period from 1999 to 2007 was one of broadly stable low unemployment rates at, or slightly below, the levels of the late 1970s. In the aftermath of the 2008–9 recession, the rise in unemployment has been sharp but appears to have peaked much earlier, at around 8%, even before the recession had ended.

Figure 2.2 documents the flows that shape the stocks of unemployment, employment and inactivity, all measured on the ILO/OECD definition. The top left row gives the flow out of employment. It is clear that the employment outflows in the 2008–9 recession were lower than in previous recessions, with 96% of those in work staying in work through the year (meaning that 4% lost work), compared to 92% (8% lost work) in the previous two recessions. Similarly, the outflow from unemployment into employment remained

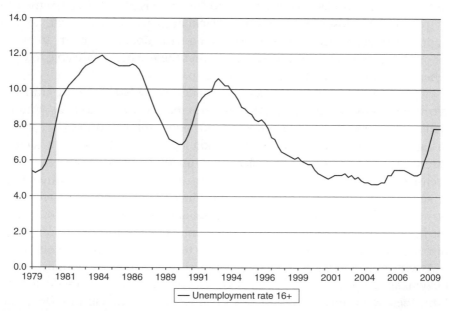

Figure 2.1: Internationally agreed ILO unemployment rate for UK, 1979–2009
Source: ONS.

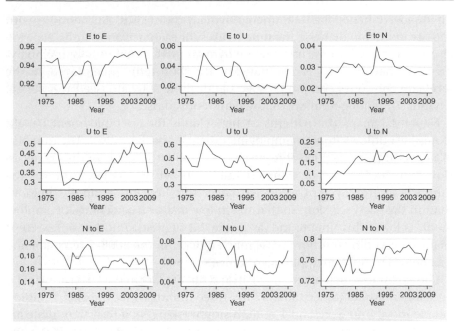

Figure 2.2: Inflows and outflow rates across employment, unemployment and inactivity

Note: Charts show annual transition rates between employment (E), unemployment (U) and inactivity (N), for population of working age excluding students.

Source: LFS. Authors' calculations.

higher this time round than in the past downturns, with 35% of those unemployed getting work compared to 30% in the previous recessions. As a result, the duration of unemployment, captured by the U-to-U flow, in row 2 of Figure 2.2, remained lower than in previous downturns. The numbers flowing into economic inactivity, E to N and U to N, have been falling or stable in recent years. Outflows from inactivity into unemployment have risen in recent years, perhaps as a result of schemes like the New Deals for Lone Parents, Disabled People and 50+, which are all aimed at bringing groups with high rates of economic inactivity back into the labour force. However, outflows from inactivity into employment were as low in the latest recession as in previous ones. The net result of all these flows is that lower unemployment in the 2008–9 recession has been driven by lower rates of job loss and slightly higher return rates to work than in past recessions, but that the low flows in and out of inactivity mean that the inactive population remains very marginalised.

In a downturn, the numbers becoming unemployed and the numbers who return to work both rise (see Figure 2.3). However, whilst the number finding new jobs rises, it does so more slowly than increases in the number of newly unemployed; hence the total unemployment count rises. Furthermore, with the rise in unemployment, the time it takes for each person to find a new job also starts to rise. Inflows into unemployment drive initial rises in unemployment, so that the stock is dominated by the short-term unemployed. As the recession continues and job prospects and hiring stagnate (see Faggio et al., Chapter 7), so long-term unemployment tends to rise.

Figure 2.3 maps the patterns of new claims for unemployment benefit alongside outflows from unemployment benefit, back to 1989. The numbers of new claims in the 2008–9 recession look similar to those in the last recession and the increase in claimant inflows is actually faster. However the numbers in employment are much larger this time (by around 3 million) than in the past recession, so that the inflow *rate*, as a percentage of employment, is lower this time round, as Figure 2.2 suggests. Another difference is that claims ending (outflows) rose much quicker in the 2008–9 recession and this helped to hold unemployment down.

The extent to which people move in and out of work in the UK at any time is probably not fully understood. In any three-month window, some 1 million people move into work and 1 million stop working. In a recession, there are small but important shifts in these patterns. An additional 100,000 more people lose work each quarter and 50,000 fewer individuals gain work, leading to unemployment rising by around 50,000 a month. What shifts more markedly is that vacancies are filled much faster. Indeed, the numbers of unfilled vacancies registered at Job Centres fell from around 700,000 to 430,000 during

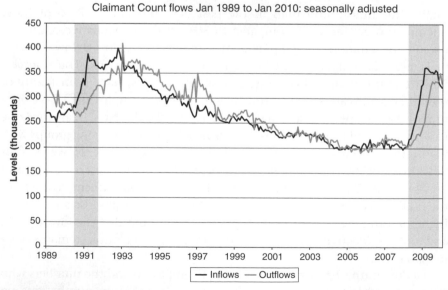

Figure 2.3: New claims for unemployment benefits and claim exits, 1989–2009
Source: ONS.

the latest recession. So whilst it is true that there are still some jobs available in a recession, the problem is that these jobs are scarcer and more competition for jobs means that it takes longer for any one person to get a job. Moreover, once a job is lost, there is the prospect that any new job will pay less well than the job lost. Faggio et al. (Chapter 7) show that the cost of job loss does appear to rise in a recession.

Long-term unemployment

Long-term unemployment typically begins to rise around one year after the initial rise in total unemployment and may often continue to rise even when total unemployment first starts to fall again. In previous recessions, LFS-based long-term unemployment (12 months spell or longer), reached 1.2 million, some 40% of the unemployed. Long-term unemployment is rising again and had reached 700,000 or 25% of the workforce by early 2010. The numbers of long-term claimants for unemployment benefits (Job Seekers' Allowance— JSA) tend to be lower than the numbers saying they have not worked in the last year (Labour Force Survey—LFS) (see Figure 2.4). Since the New Deal schemes were introduced, this gap has widened sharply. As a result, the numbers who had claimed JSA for over a year remained very low in the 2008–9 recession. With government intervention programmes in place, unlike in previous downturns, claims for JSA over a year should remain relatively low.

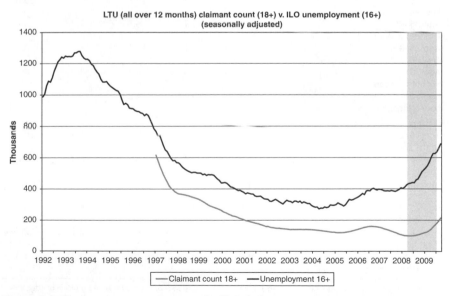

Figure 2.4: Long-term unemployment by ILO definition and claimant count
Source: ONS.

Unemployment across groups

The experience of unemployment is far from even in the population. Unemployment has always varied by factors like age, education, gender, ethnicity and region. Often the combination of these characteristics acts to make job prospects rather bleak for a significant minority. In good times, relative prospects tend to improve for these most disadvantaged groups. In bad times, relative prospects for the most disadvantaged worsen. Table 2.1 gives a flavour of how a combination of three factors, age, education and gender, interact to produce contrasting labour market performance over time.

It is clear that lower levels of education and youth combine to generate poor labour market prospects. Disadvantage amongst the young has been a long-standing feature of the labour market. As a general rule of thumb, the youth unemployment rate is always double the adult rate. However, younger workers, as Figure 2.5 shows, typically have much shorter spells of unemployment than others. So while the risk of unemployment is higher among the young, so are the chances of escaping it. There are, however, recent concerns that, for

Table 2.1: Unemployment rates by age, education and gender (%)

	1979	1986	1993	2007	2009
Men					
Age 16–24, High education	4.4	12.7	14.5	8.8	14.6
Age 16–24, Low education	14.1	26.4	24.6	21.0	26.4
Age 25–49, High education	2.4	5.1	6.8	2.7	3.8
Age 25–49, Low education	6.3	14.5	14.3	6.6	9.7
Age 50+ High education	2.4	5.6	9.1	3.0	4.5
Age 50+ Low education	4.4	10.0	14.5	5.2	7.5
Women					
Age 16–24, High education	5.3	10.4	9.0	7.2	10.8
Age 16–24, Low education	16.4	24.2	16.7	16.4	19.6
Age 25–49, High education	4.8	7.7	4.7	2.7	3.4
Age 25–49, Low education	6.4	10.3	8.5	6.2	8.1
Age 50+ High education	3.1	4.1	4.5	2.1	2.5
Age 50+ Low education	4.4	6.4	7.2	3.3	4.3

Notes: Population of working age, not including students. Low education is bottom 50% based on level of educational attainment.

Source: LFS. Authors' calculations.

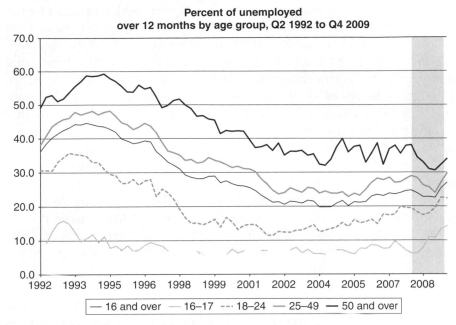

**Percent of unemployed
over 12 months by age group, Q2 1992 to Q4 2009**

Legend: — 16 and over — 16–17 --- 18–24 — 25–49 — 50 and over

Figure 2.5: Long-term unemployment by age
Source: LFS.

some youths, the chances of escaping unemployment are not that high. Unemployment rates among less educated young people in the latest recession were well above those of previous recessions, whilst the situation for older workers was much better. In the 2008–9 recession, the youth unemployment rate grew to nearly three times that for prime-age adults, rather than double as in past downturns. The failure of the labour market to absorb as much youth unemployment going into the recession meant that, by 2009, the share of long-term unemployed among younger workers was also much closer to the share among older workers than observed for a long time.

Scarring effects of unemployment

Over a five-year window, around one in three men will make a claim for unemployment benefit. Yet most days of unemployment are accounted for by a small number of individuals. This is because long-term unemployment ultimately affects only a minority, but also because some people experience a large number of repeat spells of unemployment, often moving frequently between employment and unemployment. Information on an individual's lifetime exposure to unemployment and inactivity can be determined from

29

data on birth cohorts where all those born in a given week are tracked for the rest of their lives. The National Child Development Survey (NCDS) of 1958 followed a group who were aged 21 at the onset of the 1980s recession. Research (Gregg, 2001 and Gregg and Tominey, 2005) has shown that many of the 1958 birth cohort made jobless in the 1980s recession went on, through to the age of 44, to experience much more time out of work, substantially lower wages and poorer health than others. Table 2.2 shows that around 9% of the male 1958 birth cohort had experienced a year or more out of work by the age of 23, but that more than half the cohort had experienced no unemployment at all. Those with lots of experience of unemployment often had more than one jobless spell, rather than being unemployed for a single long spell. The table then shows that those with long periods of unemployment went on to spend nearly 20% of their life between the age of 28 and 33 unemployed and another 20% of this interval economically inactive. Gregg (2001) suggests that around half of these scars are due to the long exposure to unemployment itself and the rest due to other factors like poor education, family background or residence in a depressed neighbourhood. For these groups there is a failure to connect to stable employment and jobs offering experience and training that can lead to higher wages. So the justification for intervention to prevent long or frequent periods out of work or education among young people does not rest just on current unemployment, but on the long-term scars that these young people experience and potentially pass on to the next generation. These scarring effects are not confined to young people (see Gregory and Jukes, 2001 for the UK) but they are more common for this age group.

Table 2.2: The effect of unemployment on later experience of unemployment

Group type at age 23	% of sample	Average percentage time spent unemployed, age 28–33 (% of group with any unemployment in this interval)	Average percentage time spent inactive, age 28–33 (% of group with any inactivity in this interval)
No spell of unemployment	58.6	1.4 (7.5)	2.3 (9.6)
1–5 months of unemployment	22.5	2.6 (13.8)	3.7 (15.6)
6–12 months of unemployment	10.1	5.3 (21.4)	7.1 (24.6)
13+ months of unemployment	8.7	18.5 (40.0)	22.9 (46.8)

Notes: JUVOS longitudinal data. Cohort is created by matching population by age range in 1983.
Source: NCDS Cohort, Men aged 23 in 1981.

Broader measures of unemployment

According to the international (ILO/OECD) measure of unemployment, an individual is deemed to be unemployed if they are not in work but have looked for work in the last four weeks and are ready to start any job within two weeks. This is quite restrictive in that when unemployment is high, many people give up looking for work and become economically inactive. Some of these individuals are known as 'discouraged workers' if they notify surveys that they are not searching for work because they believe that no jobs are available. Under-employment is also an issue in recessions, because some people will take part-time work if they can't find full-time work. Figure 2.6 shows the numbers of discouraged workers through from 1983. The numbers, never particularly high, have been in long-term decline, with brief interruptions in recession periods. Numbers rose in the latest downturn, but were well below those for the boom period in 1989, let alone the subsequent recession. The peak of discouraged workers has occurred typically about two years after the recession ends and so numbers are likely to continue rising in the near future. This is likely to be related to the intensification of required job search when claiming JSA and the Restart process which preceded it from 1986, but it may also reflect reclassification by jobless individuals themselves, allied to receipt of other welfare benefits.

Figure 2.7 shows that the numbers of under-employed grew to over 1 million in the 2008–9 recession. After the 1990–1 recession, under-employment, as

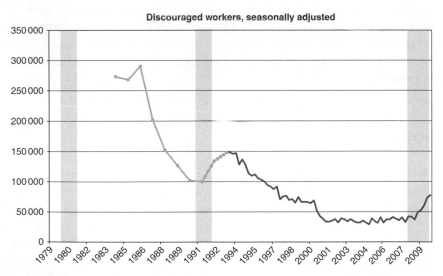

Figure 2.6: Discouraged workers, 1983–2009
Source: LFS, ONS.

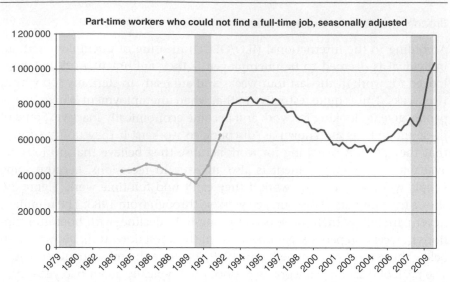

Part-time workers who could not find a full-time job, seasonally adjusted

Figure 2.7: Numbers of part-time workers reporting that they would like full-time work
Source: LFS, ONS.

measured by the fraction of part-time workers who would like a full-time job, peaked at 800,000, roughly a similar proportion of the then substantially smaller workforce. However, the numbers and workforce share of under-employment at the *onset* of the latest recession appear substantially higher than at the onset of the previous recession. This is perhaps indicative of a combination of relative buoyancy in job opportunities this time compared to last and individuals making greater use of more widely available and generous in-work benefits/tax credits combined with part-time work in order to maintain income.

Inactivity

Only a minority of those not working at any point in time are unemployed. It is more common for people not currently working not to be actively seeking a job. It is also true that unemployment can fall, both because individuals find work and because they become economically inactive. The main categories of inactivity are students, sickness, early retirement or looking after children. Inactivity normally rises in a recession, typically lagging behind movement in the unemployment rate by about a year. Some people losing work don't seek or are unable to find a fresh job. Others take early retirement because of this. For others, there is a move from what is often long-term unemployment into sickness-related inactivity. In some respects, for certain people, this latter movement has proved akin to an extended spell of what is effectively long-term unemployment. Figure 2.8 shows the proportion of the working-age population who have been economically inactive since 1979. The long-term average is for about 22% of the adult population to be neither working nor actively looking for work. In each of the last two recessions, the inactivity rate rose by around 2 percentage points. The rise in the latest recession has been more modest, but, on the basis of past experience, might be expected to increase later in the cycle.

One major development worthy of note is the increase in the number of young people staying on in both further and higher education. Staying-on rates have risen in past recessions and the latest downturn led to a substantial rise in those rates. The lower line in Figure 2.8 tracks the inactivity rate excluding full-time students. On this basis, economic inactivity has fallen steadily, by around 2 percentage points, since the aftermath of the 1990s recession. In 2009, just over 16% of the adult population was neither economically active nor in full-time education, the lowest rate for over thirty years. The figure also makes clear that the small rise in inactivity observed in the 2008–9 recession has, so far, been mainly due to increased participation in education (see Goujard et al., Chapter 3).

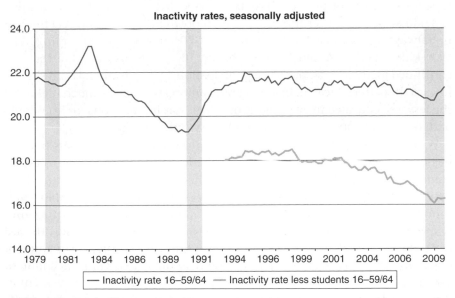

Inactivity rates, seasonally adjusted

— Inactivity rate 16–59/64   — Inactivity rate less students 16–59/64

Figure 2.8: Economic inactivity (%), 1975–2009, including and excluding full-time students

Source: LFS, ONS.

However the news is not all good. The composition of the (non-student) economically inactive has shifted markedly over time toward men. The gender ratio in favour of women fell from 87% in 1979 to 61% in late 2009. Back in 1979, around 40% of women aged 25+ were economically inactive compared to a rate of under 5% for men. Since then, the number of women entering the labour force has grown rapidly and shows little sign of halting (see Swaffield, Chapter 12). Rising inactivity for reasons of ill health and disability is concentrated on men. At around 2.3 million, there were almost twice as many inactive men as there were unemployed men (on the ILO/OECD definition), in the fourth quarter of 2009.

Policy changes on pensions, early retirement (see Disney et al., Chapter 4) and incapacity benefits have arrested the inflow of sickness-related inactivity recently, but the overall level of inactivity among men has been persistently high for 20 years. The net result is that inactivity among men is, at best, static and remains three times higher than the rates observed in the 1970s (Table 2.3). Indeed, more than half of the fall in the male unemployment rate from 1993 to 2008 can be accounted for by rising inactivity, though much of that rise in inactivity took place in the 1990s.

As Table 2.3 shows, the factors that help generate disadvantage among the unemployed are also present when inactivity is tracked across different subgroups. Inactivity rates are much higher for less skilled, older workers, particularly among men, and have been for some considerable time. It is here that the least inroads into the problem have been made. Inactivity levels among older, less skilled men have been around 30% for more than 20 years now. Yet this was not always so. As Table 2.3 shows, in the 1970s, inactivity rates among older less skilled men were much lower, below 10%. It is also notable that the continued increase in labour force participation among women is still skewed toward the better educated. Inactivity rates among women are much higher for the less well educated in every age group. This has implications for household patterns of joblessness (see Gregg and Wadsworth, Chapter 5).

With recovery, small inroads are made into the inactive numbers but this has never been enough, so far, to offset the initial problem. When recession comes, these individuals are at the back of the queue for jobs and so inactivity rises again. Figure 2.9 gives inactivity rates over time by gender and age. Among men, the ratcheting up of inactivity rates over time, for all age groups, is apparent, though an improvement has been made among men over the age of 50, back to levels last seen in the 1980s, but not the 1970s. For women, inactivity rates have declined significantly over time, for all but the youngest age group.

Figure 2.10 shows the numbers in receipt of the major welfare benefits available to those out of work and eligible to claim. In addition to the large cyclical fluctuations in unemployment benefit receipt, there were marked

Table 2.3: Inactivity rates by age and education

	1979	1986	1993	2007	2009
			Per cent		
Men					
All Men	4.3	9.5	11.3	12.2	12.0
Age 16–24, High education	0.5	3.2	4.4	4.9	4.6
Age 16–24, Low education	2.3	6.0	5.7	8.4	7.7
Age 25–49, High education	0.8	2.0	3.9	4.0	3.8
Age 25–49, Low education	3.2	7.0	9.1	12.7	11.8
Age 50+ High education	4.5	16.9	23.3	19.7	18.5
Age 50+ Low education	8.2	28.2	32.5	30.3	28.6
Women					
All Women	31.9	29.5	26.0	22.1	20.7
Age 16–24, High education	12.3	9.4	8.8	7.6	7.8
Age 16–24, Low education	33.2	27.0	20.8	21.5	20.3
Age 25–49, High education	32.7	24.6	16.5	13.2	12.1
Age 25–49, Low education	38.9	36.1	31.7	32.0	31.2
Age 50+ High education	33.0	30.8	28.7	18.3	17.5
Age 50+ Low education	42.0	44.2	40.8	34.8	33.5

Notes: Population of working age. Students are not classified as inactive.

Source: LFS. Authors' calculations.

increases in claims for IS by lone parents and for incapacity benefits. This amounted to around 0.75 million extra claims in the 1980s recession and 1 million in the 1990s. Unlike unemployment, claims for these benefits did not fall back after the recessions ended and represented structural increases in families reliant on welfare benefits. Numbers of claims for these inactive benefits only started to fall around 2001 and then mainly for lone parents. The government sought to use tax credits to make work more financially rewarding and welfare to work programmes were also focused on this latter group of the inactive. Lone parents with children aged 7 and over are now being moved from IS to unemployment benefits (JSA) that require active job search and the new Work Capability Assessment tests are also making claiming disability benefits much harder. These changes are pushing up the number of claims for JSA during the recession, making the small rise in JSA unemployment all the more remarkable. Yet claims for lone parent benefits did rise, once again during the latest recession. The uncertainty arises around how far,

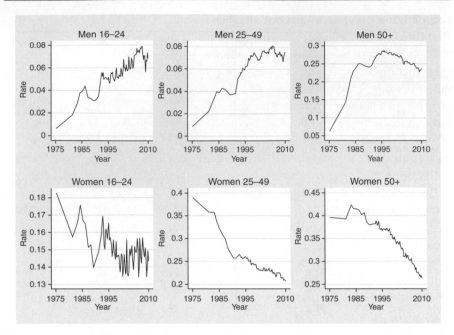

Figure 2.9: Inactivity rates by age and gender

Notes: Inactivity rates do not include students in numerator. Population of working age.

Source: LFS. Authors' calculations.

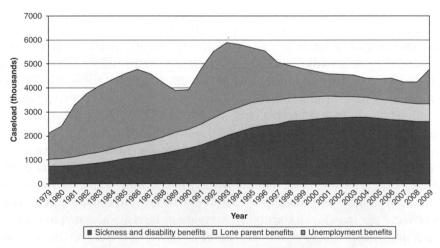

Figure 2.10: Number of claims for different workless benefits, 1979–2008

Source: DWP.

compared to previous recessions, they will rise this time. The expectation is that they will not because of the extra support now in place.

The tripling of the numbers of households reliant on benefits for most of their income lay at the heart of why the previous Conservative governments failed to cut taxation despite squeezing the generosity of benefits. The sheer number of claimants meant that the proportion of GDP going to support jobless, working-age families doubled. The subsequent period of Labour government reduced the numbers of unemployed claimants and lone parents, with some of the savings used to increase the generosity of support for families with children. However, despite this success, the number of claims at the end of the recovery in 2007 was still double that of 1979, mainly because of claims for incapacity benefits. Individuals claiming incapacity benefits for more than a year rarely return to work and most will claim until retirement or death. This means it takes a long time for changes in the numbers making new claims to affect the stock. The number claiming incapacity benefits for between one and two years has halved since 1999. This means that the numbers of claims may be set for a steady decline over the next decade or so, as this lower inflow eventually replaces those larger earlier cohorts flowing onto these benefits in the 1990s.

Conclusions

Unemployment has long blighted the UK labour market. There were signs that, prior to the recession, an unemployment rate of 5% was about as good as things were going to get without further changes in policy and performance on factors such as education, industrial policy, regional policy, export performance and productivity that furthered balanced and sustained growth. The recession represented the first serious test under fire of the labour market policies that have been put in place since 1996. Increased conditionality on welfare claimants to take active steps to secure work, an increased package of support services for job search, available to those claiming benefits, and use of outside providers to deliver these services rather than Job Centres are all innovations aimed at keeping individuals in the labour market and at maintaining search effectiveness. Reforms that increased the financial returns to working relative to not working, the National Minimum Wage and Working Tax Credit, should also continue to help make work pay through a downturn when job prospects may not be as good as in recovery.

The signs are that unemployment has not been as bad this time round as many people thought. This is to be welcomed, though the ability of the new policies to withstand a buildup of long-term unemployment that has in the past followed in the wake of a recession is still to be tested. However, the performance of the other scar that has blighted the UK labour market performance for 30 years, economic inactivity, is much more mixed. While (non-student) inactivity is the lowest for over 30 years, virtually all of this improvement has been among more educated women. For others, particularly less skilled men, 15 years of sustained recovery have failed to make major inroads into the legacy of high inactivity spawned by previous recessions. As a result, for some groups, there has been a ratchet upward in joblessness from the 1980s onward. It is toward these neglected groups that future labour market policy should be directed come the recovery.

References

Disney, R., Ratcliffe, A. and Smith, S. (2011) The baby-boomers at 50: employment prospects for older workers. In: Gregg, P. and Wadsworth, J. (eds.) *The Labour Market in Winter: The State of Working Britain*. Oxford: Oxford University Press.

Dorsett, R. (2006) The new deal for young people: effect on the labour market status of young men. *Labour Economics*, 13: 405–22.

Faggio, G., Gregg, P. and Wadsworth, J. (2011) Job tenure and job turnover. In: Gregg, P. and Wadsworth, J. (eds.) *The Labour Market in Winter: The State of Working Britain*. Oxford: Oxford University Press.

Goujard, A., Petrongolo, B. and Van Reenen, J. (2011) The labour market for young people. In: Gregg, P. and Wadsworth, J. (eds.) *The Labour Market in Winter: The State of Working Britain*. Oxford: Oxford University Press.

Gregg, P. (2001) The impact of youth unemployment on adult employment in the NCDS. *Economic Journal*, 111 (475): F623–53.

——and Wadsworth, J. (2011) The labour market in winter—the 2008–2009 recession. In: Gregg, P. and Wadsworth, J. (eds.) *The Labour Market in Winter: The State of Working Britain*. Oxford: Oxford University Press.

————(2011) Workless households. In: Gregg, P. and Wadsworth, J. (eds.) *The Labour Market in Winter: The State of Working Britain*. Oxford: Oxford University Press.

——(2008) Realising potential: a vision for personalised conditionality and support. London: Department for Work and Pensions, available at <<http://www.dwp.gov.uk/welfarereform/realisingpotential.asp>>.

——and Tominey, E. (2005) The wage scar from youth unemployment. *Labour Economics*, 12(4), August: 487–509.

Gregory, M. and Jukes, R. (2001) Unemployment and subsequent earnings: estimating scarring among British men 1984–94. *Economic Journal*, 111 (475): 607–25.

OECD (2009) *Employment Outlook: Tackling the Jobs Crisis*. Paris: OECD.

Van Reenen, J. (2004) Active labour market policies and the British New Deal for unemployed youth in context. In: Blundell, R., Card, D. and Freeman, R. (eds.) *Seeking a Premier Economy*. Chicago: University of Chicago Press.

3

The Labour Market for Young People

Antoine Goujard, Barbara Petrongolo and John Van Reenen

Key findings

- Young people have fared badly during the recession, with larger increases in their unemployment rates than for adults. However, young people always do worse in downturns (alongside other groups who are not well-connected to the labour market). There is no evidence that young people are doing worse relatively to older groups in this recession than in previous recessions.
- The youth labour market deteriorated during the 2004–7 period *prior* to the onset of the recession. The proportion of young people who are unemployed or 'NEET' (Not in Employment, Education and Training) fell from the early 1990s to the mid-2000s, but subsequently rose.
- The reason for the post-2004 deterioration is not well understood. There was some weakening of the adult labour market which accounts for some of the 2004–7 rise in youth unemployment. Increased immigration, minimum wages, skill demand changes and schooling are potential explanations, but there is little compelling evidence for any of these factors.
- Welfare reforms such as the New Deal for Young People introduced in 1998 have had a positive impact on jobs. The de-emphasis on the young unemployed relative to other disadvantaged groups (e.g. lone parents and those on incapacity benefits) by the employment service in the mid-2000s may be a factor in the post-2004 weakening of the youth labour market.
- The trends for 18–24 year olds not in employment, education or training (NEET) follow broadly the same pattern as for youth unemployment. NEET rates for 16–17 year olds are high (close to 20%) only if we include all part-time students. When these are removed, teenage NEET rates are halved.

Introduction

Unemployment is a perennial policy concern, but youth unemployment is a particular worry because of the scarring effects of joblessness which can persist for a long time in an individual's life (e.g. Gregg and Tominey, 2001). Additionally, large numbers of 'idle youth' can also cause serious issues of social disorder.

When Labour came to power in 1997, one of their five pre-election pledges was to 'get 250,000 under 25 year olds off benefits and into work'. Following on from the previous government, policies such as the New Deal for Young People (see Blundell et al., 2004) emphasised the importance of job search, but went beyond Job Seekers' Allowance (JSA) by guaranteeing some activity (either subsidised employment, a government job or education/training) for all young people (18–24 year olds) who were on JSA for more than six months.

Despite this policy activity, youth joblessness remains a problem. Before becoming Prime Minister, David Cameron pointed out that on some measures the level of youth ILO unemployed was higher than in 1997.[1] Youth joblessness has indeed risen dramatically since the recession began in 2008. But we will argue that this is expected, as 'marginal' groups almost always fare worse during recessions. The more surprising fact is that the youth labour market worsened between 2004 and 2007, *prior* to the start of the current downturn. This is harder to explain—it is partly linked to the sluggishness of the aggregate labour market, but may also be linked to changes in the policies of the Employment Service.

The youth labour market in the great recession of the late 2000s

The cumulative loss of GDP in the last recession has been around 6.5% peak to trough. Yet despite this being the worst recession since the war, unemployment is still under 8%, less than the peak of the 1990s and 1980s recessions.

Figure 3.1 plots the unemployment rates for the population of working age (16–64) and for three subgroups—prime age (25–49), young (18–24) and teenagers (16–17). The prime-age group follows the general pattern of the aggregate labour market, but it is clear that the young are much more sensitive to the state of the business cycle. The unemployment rate is higher for younger groups and the magnitude of this disadvantage widens during a recession. This is unsurprising as employers will be reluctant to lose more experienced workers who have firm-specific skills (and also greater redundancy costs), so

---

[1] <http://www.guardian.co.uk/politics/2009/nov/11/cameron-brown-pmqs-youth-unemployment>.

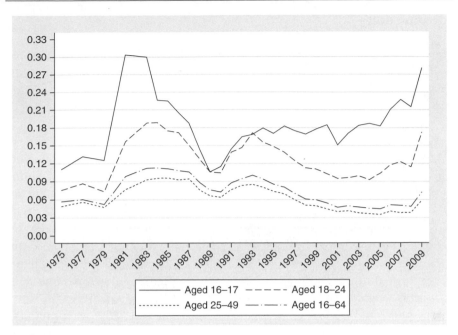

Figure 3.1: Unemployment rates by age group, 1975–2009

Source: Annual Labour Force Survey (LFS), 1975–1991 and calendar quarters 1992 Q2 to 2009 Q3. Unemployment rate (ILO) is measured yearly in March/April/May and linearly interpolated.

the burden of adjustment typically falls on low wage workers such as young people (minorities and the less educated also tend to fare worse during downturns). Teenagers do not appear to have experienced the same fall in unemployment after the 1990s recession as older groups, but this trend conceals important selection effects, as increasing numbers of non-employed teenagers stay in education. We will discuss this in more detail below.

Has the recent recession hit young people much worse than in the past? Figure 3.1 shows that the unemployment rate for the young has increased by more (in absolute terms) than the unemployment rate for older groups since the onset of the 2000s recession. This is the reason for the previously mentioned David Cameron statement regarding the large number of unemployed youth. (See again too, the *Guardian* link in footnote 1.)

Figure 3.2 plots the average hours worked for those who remain employed. There is a significant fall in hours worked for young people compared to older groups. Figure 3.3 plots the growth in hourly wages, which shows that (nominal) wages have flattened or are falling for younger workers. Both of these indicate that young people are faring worse during the downturn than other groups.

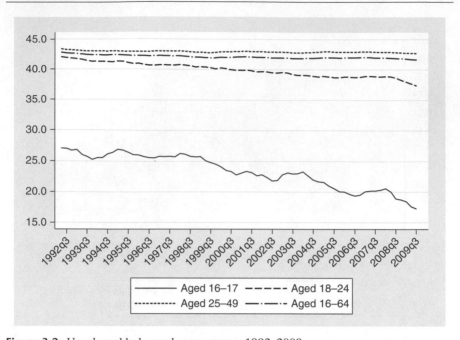

Figure 3.2: Usual weekly hours by age group, 1992–2009

Source: LFS calendar quarters 1992 Q2 to 2009 Q3. The series reported are averages of usual weekly hours, conditional on positive hours worked.

It could be said that this has been the general pattern in all recessions—in other words, 'twas ever thus. The unemployment rate for young people is about the same as its 1990s highpoint and better than the 1980s peak, despite the fall in GDP being deeper (the higher absolute number of young unemployed is due to the larger labour force and so is not really a relevant comparison). Figure 3.4 examines this more formally, breaking down the claimant count by age group in each recession (the Labour Force Survey (LFS) was only annual prior to 1992, so we cannot calculate ILO quarterly unemployment rates for earlier recessions). The growth of youth unemployment (relative to adult unemployment) in this recession looks no worse than in previous recessions. In fact it looks, if anything, slightly better.

We conclude that the available information does not suggest that there is a special problem of youth unemployment in this recession compared to past experience. The fact that young people suffer more during downturns is quite consistent with what has happened in previous recessions in the UK and elsewhere. A bigger problem is what was happening before the recession. We now turn to this issue.

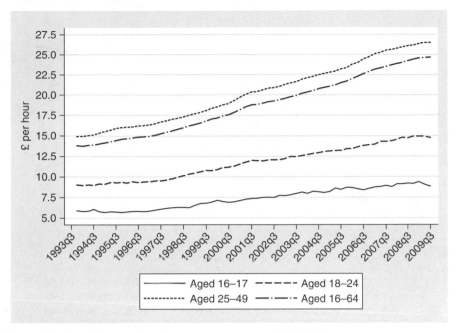

Figure 3.3: Average gross hourly pay by age group, 1993–2009

Source: LFS calendar quarters 1993 Q4 to 2009 Q3. The series reported are averages of hourly wages for those with positive hours worked.

The youth labour market in the years leading up to the great recession

Figure 3.1 showed that prime-age unemployment in the UK fell dramatically since the early 1990s, from nearly 9% in 1993 to 3% in 2005, after which it broadly stabilised and then rose again in 2008. Youth unemployment also fell after the early 1990s, and by 2004 it had dropped to about 9%, even below its 1989 level. But then it started rising in 2004, several years in advance of the current recession, until it reached 17% at the end of 2009. Thus there seems to be a component of the adult–youth unemployment differential that does not seem to be explained purely by the stronger impact of cyclical downturns on young people.

Despite several forces that may be (in theory) related to the poor performance of the youth labour market in recent years, the bulk of the rise in youth unemployment from 2004–8 remains largely unexplained. We will examine such potential forces below: rising immigration, unemployment benefit reform, the minimum wage and skill demand.

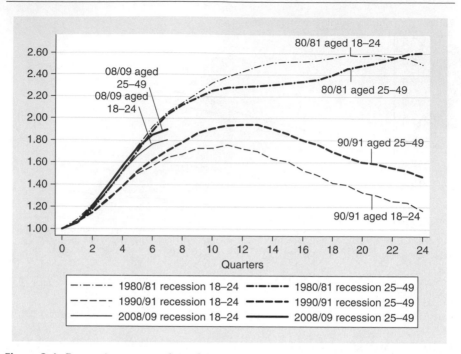

Figure 3.4: Proportionate growth in claimant count by age group in last three recessions

Source: ONS claimant count current data (1985–2009), historical data (1983–1985) and registrants (1979–1982), by age band. Data seasonally adjusted. The breakdown by age is not available for Northern Ireland before 1994, so the series covers Great Britain only. Reference quarters are 1979 Q4, 1990 Q2 and 2008 Q1 (first quarters before the fall in GDP). Historical data are for a given calendar month; a monthly time series has been created by linear interpolation, leading to the quarterly data.

Rising immigration

As the rise in youth unemployment dates back to 2004, the year of EU accession by eight Central and Eastern European countries (plus Cyprus and Malta), it would be natural to think that the increase in youth unemployment is related to stronger competition from immigrant labour.

The UK has experienced a record increase in immigration in the past few years. The proportion of foreign-born population was below 6% in the early 1990s, but is currently about 10%. In London, this proportion rose from 28% to the current level of around 40% (see also Nickell and Saleheen, Chapter 6). If immigration has a damaging effect on the labour market prospects of natives, it may hurt youths more strongly than adults. Immigrants who are less skilled than natives will be closer substitutes for inexperienced youths.

Table 3.1: Youth unemployment and migration

	Males	
	All 12 regions	Excluding London
Change in % of foreign born	0.431	0.263
Observations	817	748

	Females	
	All 12 regions	Excluding London
Change in % of foreign born	0.243	0.207
Observations	817	748

Notes: The table reports the effect of a 1 percentage point increase in the proportion of foreign born on youth unemployment (18–24 year olds). The coefficients are obtained from an ordinary least squares (OLS) regression of the change in the youth unemployment rate by gender, region and year, on the change in adult male unemployment and the change in the proportion of foreign born in the total population. Other regressors included are region and year fixed effects.
Source: Authors' analysis of LFS, 1992–2009.

Some simple evidence on this can be provided by looking at the correlation between youth unemployment and the migration rate across UK regions over time, having controlled for the state of the business cycle (proxied by adult unemployment). The figures reported in Table 3.1 show the effect of an increase in the proportion of foreign born on the youth unemployment rate for men and women separately.

For example, column (1) shows that a 1 percentage point increase in the proportion of foreign born is associated with an increase in youth unemployment of 0.43 percentage points, holding the state of the business cycle constant. Thus one could conclude that foreign migration harms the employment prospects of youths. However, column (2) shows this result is largely driven by differences between London and the rest of the country. If we drop London from the sample, the correlation between youth unemployment and the migration rate is greatly reduced (and, in statistical terms, one cannot exclude that the correlation is zero). Thus the appearance of an immigrant-driven rise in youth unemployment is driven solely by the contrast between London and the rest of the UK (as London experienced particularly high rates of immigration and a relatively higher increase in unemployment). Although it could be argued that the simple correlation underestimates the impact of migration, as immigrants will go to areas where the labour market is strong, we suspect that other factors may explain this correlation. A similar qualitative picture emerges from the lower panel of Table 3.1, where we report corresponding results for females.

Overall, we do not find compelling evidence that immigration causes higher youth unemployment, which is broadly consistent with the literature that finds that immigrants do not seem to have large harmful effects on the labour market outcomes of natives (e.g. Card, 2005).

Changing structure of welfare-to-work benefits

The poor showing of the youth labour market is particularly worrying given the considerable policy reform to the Employment Service (especially for young people) in the last two decades.

Job Seekers' Allowance (JSA) was introduced in 1996 as the main form of unemployment benefit and greatly increased the job search requirements for receiving benefits. It did appear to reduce the claimant count, but few of those leaving seemed to find sustainable jobs. JSA did not seem to significantly improve the overall employment rate (Manning, 2009) and may even have reduced it for the young (Petrongolo, 2009).

While the claimant count and LFS unemployment have been very close until October 1996 for the population over 18 years old, LFS unemployment remained well above the claimant count in the post-JSA period (see Figure 3.5).[2] Thus there is evidence of increasing numbers of workers who left the unemployment

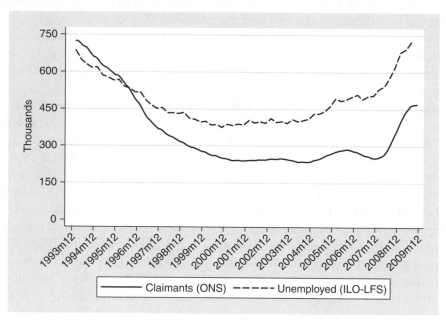

Figure 3.5: The difference between the number of young unemployed and young JSA claimants is now very large

Source: LFS calendar quarters 1992 Q2 to 2009 Q3 for ILO unemployed and ONS for the claimant count.

---

[2] One possible reading of these series is that the JSA removed from the register those who were not previously assiduous in their job search or were claiming fraudulently. Another interpretation is that the non-claimant unemployed simply have a level of search effort above the ILO/LFS threshold, but below the JSA threshold.

register but did not find jobs. About half of the 18–24 LFS unemployed do not claim JSA (compared to a third for 25–49 year olds). When dropping out of the welfare system, individuals may become more detached from the labour market and spend less effort on job search than while on unemployment benefits.

The New Deal for Young People was introduced in 1998 with the aim to improve the incentives and prospects for young workers seeking jobs. All 18–24 year olds on JSA for six months now receive help with job search from a dedicated personal adviser. So there is some 'carrot' of job search assistance as well as a tougher 'stick' of stricter monitoring. Rigorous evaluations have shown that job finding rates increased by about 20% as a result of the policy (Blundell et al., 2004; De Giorgi, 2005). These evaluations exploit the fact that there was a large difference in treatment between 24 years olds who were in the programme (the 'experimental group') and 25 year olds who were not (the 'control group'). Blundell et al. (2004) also compare youth unemployment in the areas where the New Deal was piloted to matched non-pilot areas. Using this alternative method, they again find that the New Deal caused job finding rates to rise by about a fifth.[3]

Around 2004 the Employment Service was incentivised to focus less on young people on JSA and relatively more on other groups such as lone parents and those on incapacity benefits through a system of 'job points'. This was because the problem of long-term youth unemployment was thought to have been broadly solved. Although there is no rigorous evaluation of this change, the timing does make one suspect that the introduction of incentive schemes at Employment Services may have affected the re-employment prospects of the youth unemployed.

A further problem is that the increasing numbers of LFS unemployed who are not claiming JSA (shown in Figure 3.5) separate them from any direct effect of the New Deal and the Employment Service in general. There is no way for the state to directly help those young unemployed who have little contact with the job finding agencies. An extreme example of this is 16–17 year olds who are ineligible for JSA, so will not need to have any direct contact with the employment service.

Minimum wage

The National Minimum Wage was introduced in the UK in April 1999, but 16–17 year olds were exempt. In October 2004 the minimum wage was

---

[3] In order to tackle the effect of the current recession on youth unemployment, in January 2010 the government introduced the Young Person's Guarantee, which extends the scope of the NDYP by providing every young person who is unemployed for six months with the guarantee of a job, training or work experience. It has been estimated that as many as 100,000 young unemployed would be eligible for this new scheme.

extended to also cover workers aged 16–17 who are not apprentices and this coincides with a strong increase in their unemployment rate in 2004.

Existing research in the UK has generally found few employment effects of minimum wages.[4] For example, Dickens and Draca (2005) find that the 2003 increase in the NMW had insignificant employment effects for all demographic groups including youths. Furthermore, if minimum wages were to blame, we would expect a positive jobs impact on teenage apprentices, who were exempt from the 2004 legislation. In fact the job rates of 16–17 year olds *fell* from 15% in 2003 Q1 to 13% in 2007 Q1,[5] casting doubt on explanations of youth unemployment based on minimum wages.

Cohort size

Increases in the size of the youth cohort can increase competition for jobs and, by placing downward pressure on wages, make employment less attractive. Table 3.2 shows the evolution of cohort size over time. Interestingly, when we focus on 18–24 year olds, their share in the working-age population fell through to 2000, but then rose from 13% to 14.6% by 2009. This roughly coincides with the fall and rise of unemployment.

Including relative cohort size in the simple model of Table 3.1 suggests that this 1.6 percentage point increase in cohort size could have increased male youth unemployment by about a quarter of a percentage point. So this is unlikely to be the major cause of the increase.

Falling demand for low skilled workers

There has been a large increase in wage inequality over the last three decades in the UK. The wage premium for being educated has risen despite a huge increase in the supply of college-educated workers which implies that there has been an increase in the demand for skills. This is probably due to new 'skill biased' technologies, but trade with less developed countries like China and India and falls in union power may also play some role in reducing demand for unskilled workers. There are similar rises in the relative demand for skills in the US and

---

[4] Machin et al. (2003) detect a mild reduction in employment in the care-home sector after NMW introduction. As the care-home sector is particularly vulnerable to NMW introduction, given the low starting level of wages, their estimates may be interpreted as an upper bound for the aggregate employment effects of the NMW. Stewart (2004a, 2004b) finds neither the minimum wage introduction nor the 2000 and 2001 upratings had significant employment effects for adults (aged 22+) or youths (18–21).

[5] The data source is the LFS individual record files.

Table 3.2: Change in the size of the youth cohort

	16–17 Population			18–24 Population		
	Millions	All age	Age 16–64	Millions	All age	Age 16–64
1992	1.311	2.4%	3.7%	5.541	10.0%	15.7%
1993	1.267	2.3%	3.6%	5.370	9.7%	15.2%
1994	1.257	2.3%	3.6%	5.166	9.3%	14.6%
1995	1.364	2.4%	3.7%	5.136	9.0%	14.1%
1996	1.436	2.5%	3.9%	4.949	8.6%	13.5%
1997	1.460	2.5%	4.0%	4.839	8.4%	13.2%
1998	1.448	2.5%	3.9%	4.804	8.3%	13.0%
1999	1.436	2.5%	3.9%	4.815	8.3%	13.0%
2000	1.442	2.5%	3.9%	4.839	8.3%	13.0%
2001	1.481	2.5%	3.9%	4.908	8.4%	13.1%
2002	1.511	2.6%	4.0%	5.006	8.5%	13.3%
2003	1.530	2.6%	4.0%	5.137	8.7%	13.5%
2004	1.559	2.6%	4.1%	5.272	8.9%	13.8%
2005	1.571	2.6%	4.1%	5.397	9.1%	14.0%
2006	1.525	2.6%	3.9%	5.343	8.9%	13.8%
2007	1.586	2.6%	4.0%	5.640	9.4%	14.3%
2008	1.578	2.6%	4.0%	5.733	9.5%	14.5%
2009	1.549	2.5%	3.9%	5.801	9.5%	14.6%

Source: LFS calendar quarters 1992 Q2 to 2009 Q3. Each cell contains the mean of the characteristics by quarter (weighted using LFS weights) and averaged by year.

other countries (e.g. Machin and Van Reenen, 2008). A rise in demand for human capital may disproportionately hurt the young because they have less experience.

This secular explanation is not so persuasive at explaining the post-2004 changes, as youth unemployment was falling from 1992–2004 (and for parts of the 1980s) even in the face of this rising demand for skill. Thus, although skill-biased technical change has a lot to do with longer-run trends in wage inequality, it is not a good explanation for the rise in youth unemployment after 2004.

Education and school to work transitions

Another issue is to do with schools. One possibility is that the quality of education for the type of young people likely to be unemployed may have declined. Although standards as a whole appeared to be rising, it is possible that targets have led schools to neglect some of the 'hard to reach' that may end up as non-employed.

Further, there is a rather chaotic school-to-work transition process which the recession has highlighted, although it is unclear whether such a process worsened in recent years. Improving the careers guidance service for school leavers could be an important way to improve the position of young people.

Idle youth? What about the young NEETS?

Unemployment rates may give a misleading impression of the labour market because of the large increase in the fraction of young people staying in full-time education and in training. Selection effects may raise the observed unemployment rate since those staying on longer in the education system will tend to be of higher ability and would have a lower unemployment rate than if they had left school earlier. The increase in staying-on rates at school would mechanically inflate the youth unemployment rate for a given level of unemployed individuals as the labour force is lower (although, as we would expect the job finding rate to adjust, this is unlikely to be a cause in the absence of selection effects).

An alternative indicator to the unemployment rate is the proportion of an age group who are NEET—not in employment, education and training. Reducing the number of young NEETS has been a priority of the Department for Children, Schools and Families. Figure 3.6 shows three alternative measures of NEET (explained below) for 18–24 year olds. Although the *levels* of NEET

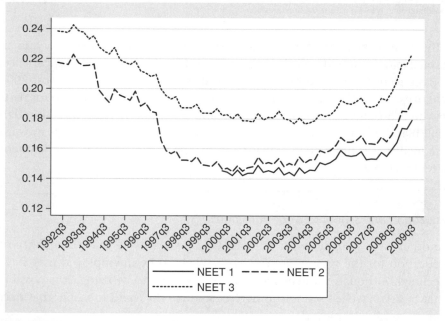

Figure 3.6: NEET rates, 1992–2009 (aged 18–24), smoothed time-series

Source: LFS calendar quarters 1992 Q2 to 2009 Q3. NEET1 defines as NEET (not in employment, education or training) all those who are not working, are not enrolled in either education or training, and declare that they are not working or studying towards a qualification. This latter information has only been available since 2000. NEET2 defines as NEET those who are not working or enrolled in either education or training. NEET3 defines as NEET those whose main economic activity is not education, training or work.

Table 3.3: Evolution of NEET rates by gender (youth 16–17)

Year	Men 16–17			Women 16–17		
	NEET1	NEET2	NEET3	NEET1	NEET2	NEET3
1992		13.0%	17.2%		11.7%	15.2%
1993		11.9%	16.8%		10.7%	15.3%
1994		8.3%	15.5%		8.8%	16.3%
1995		10.3%	16.0%		10.5%	15.5%
1996		11.7%	17.5%		10.3%	16.2%
1997		9.1%	17.0%		8.5%	16.3%
1998		9.2%	17.7%		7.9%	16.0%
1999		9.1%	18.5%		7.5%	15.6%
2000	9.1%	8.9%	18.2%	7.4%	7.6%	16.2%
2001	9.0%	9.5%	17.2%	7.7%	8.1%	14.9%
2002	10.3%	11.0%	18.0%	8.3%	8.8%	15.6%
2003	11.0%	11.9%	18.6%	8.2%	9.2%	15.5%
2004	10.6%	11.8%	18.3%	9.0%	9.8%	16.3%
2005	11.8%	12.9%	18.6%	8.6%	9.7%	16.4%
2006	11.2%	12.5%	19.8%	8.2%	9.4%	16.0%
2007	10.5%	12.0%	19.7%	8.5%	9.5%	17.9%
2008	9.7%	11.2%	18.5%	8.3%	9.5%	17.7%
2009	9.4%	10.9%	20.3%	8.4%	9.7%	18.4%

Source: LFS calendar quarters 1992 Q2 to 2009 Q3. NEET1 defines as NEET (not in employment, education or training) all those who are not working, are not enrolled in either education or training, and declare that they are not working or studying towards a qualification. This latter information is only available since 2000. NEET2 defines as NEET those who are not working or enrolled in either education or training. NEET3 defines as NEET those whose main economic activity is not education, training or work. Each cell displays the year average of the quarterly observations.

differ, across the three measures, they all show the same trends as the youth unemployment rates discussed above—a steady fall from the 1990s recession and then a rise, starting in 2004 and accelerating in 2008 as the recession began.

Even prior to the recession, however, several media reports have expressed worries that large proportions of 16–17 year olds were 'doing nothing' (i.e. NEETS). However, measuring the number of NEETS precisely is not straightforward because of the ambiguity of whether someone is 'really' in education or training (e.g. they might say they are at school but never turn up).

The 'narrow' definition (defined like the official rate) excludes from being NEET those who are in any type of education or training. According to this definition, at the end of 2009, about 9% of all 16 and 17 year old men were NEET (see Table 3.3, series NEET1). But if we include in the NEET count all those who say they are in education or training but would accept a job offer, this number leaps to 19% (series NEET3). The difference is mainly in the fact that there are a lot of students looking for part-time jobs—and thus it is incorrect to classify them all as NEET. At the same time, it is plausible that some of those who declare themselves to be receiving some kind of education, but are simultaneously looking for a job, have essentially dropped out of the education system. In this case, the 'narrow' 9% figure for NEET1 underesti-mates the NEET rate.

Figure 3.7 reports the evolution in alternative NEET over time. The 'narrow' definition (NEET1) has been available only since 2000, as it is based on a question of whether an individual is 'working or studying towards a qualifica-tion'. In order to obtain a longer time series, one can use information available since 1992 on school attendance and enrolment in training programmes (NEET2). For the time span when both measures are available, NEET2 is not more than a percentage point above NEET1 and trends in an identical way.

The true trends of teenage NEETs are hard to gauge. On the broad definition, the numbers have stayed high since the 1990s recession. The narrow series is only available for a shorter period of time, but here there does seem to be some improvement in the post-2005 period, with little effect in the recession. This suggests that many more teenagers are choosing to stay at school rather than face a hostile labour market. The planned extension of compulsory schooling will cement these trends.

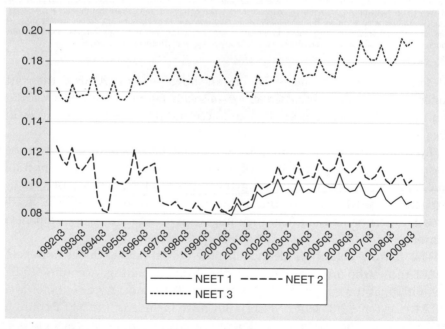

Figure 3.7: NEET rates, 1992–2009 (aged 16–17), smoothed time-series

Source: LFS calendar quarters 1992 Q2 to 2009 Q3. NEET1 defines as NEET (not in employment, education or training) all those who are not working, are not enrolled in either education or training, and declare that they are not working or studying towards a qualification. This latter information has only available been since 2000. NEET2 defines as NEET those who are not working or enrolled in either education or training. NEET3 defines as NEET those whose main economic activity is not education, training or work.

Conclusions

The UK labour market has held up surprisingly well so far, given the depth of the current recession. Young people, however, have fared much worse than other groups, with larger increases in their unemployment and bigger falls in hours and wages. We have argued that although this is, unfortunately, to be expected as young people always suffer worst during downturns, it does not seem that (relatively) they are doing particularly badly in the latest recession compared to the 1980s and 1990s recessions.

More worryingly, however, is that youth unemployment and NEET rates were bad going into the recession, having been rising since 2004. The existing evidence does not allow us to give a firm answer as to why, after over a decade of steady improvement, youth unemployment started rising in the mid-2000s. We think that part of it was due to some softening of the overall labour market and part of it to changes in the Employment Service, who targeted other 'at risk' groups with greater vigour. The other suspects—immigrants, the minimum wage and skill demand—do not seem to blame.

Finally, the refrain of 'idle youth' is overstated, as the young NEET numbers typically include a large number of students who are seeking part-time jobs.

References

Blundell, R., Costa Dias, M. Meghir, C. and Van Reenen, J. (2004) Evaluating the employment impact of a mandatory job search assistance programme. *Journal of the European Economics Association*, 2(4): 569–606.

Card, D. (2005) Is the new immigration really so bad?. *The Economic Journal*, 115: F300–23.

Dickens, R. and Draca, M. (2005) The employment effects of the October 2003 increase in the national minimum wage. CEP Discussion Paper No. 693.

De Giorgi, G. (2005) The New Deal for young people five years on. *Fiscal Studies*, 26(3): 371–83.

Gregg, P. and Tominey, E. (2001) The impact of youth unemployment on adult unemployment in the NCDS. *Economic Journal*, 111: F626–53.

Machin, S., Manning, A. and Rahman, L. (2003) Where the minimum wage bites hard: introduction of minimum wages to a low wage sector. *Journal of the European Economic Association*, 1: 1–154.

—— and Van Reenen, J. (2008) Changes in wage inequality. In: Weinberg, B. and Taber, C. (eds.) *New Palgrave Dictionary of Economics*. Basingstoke: Palgrave Macmillan.

Manning, A. (2009) You can't always get what you want: the impact of the UK Jobseekers' allowance. *Labour Economics*, 16: 230–50.

Nickell, S. and Saleheen, J. (2011) Immigration in the UK. In: Gregg, P. and Wadsworth, J. (eds.) *The Labour Market in Winter: The State of Working Britain*. Oxford: Oxford University Press.

Petrongolo, B. (2009) What are the long-term effects of UI? Evidence from the UK JSA reform. *Journal of Public Economics*, 93: 1234–53.

Stewart, M. (2004a) The Impact of the introduction of the U.K. minimum wage on the employment probabilities of low-wage workers. *Journal of the European Economic Association*, 2: 67–97.

—— (2004b) The employment effects of the national minimum wage. *The Economic Journal*, 114: C110–16.

4

The Baby-Boomers at 50: Employment Prospects for Older Workers

Richard Disney, Anita Ratcliffe and Sarah Smith

Key findings

- In contrast to younger workers, workers aged 50 and over have been relatively 'recession proof' since the credit crunch of 2007–8: older men have seen a slight rise in unemployment and fall in employment, but older women have seen little change. This is in contrast to the recessions of the early 1980s and 1990s, where older workers suffered.
- Several institutional changes have affected older workers—anti-age discrimination legislation, changes in state pensions and retirement rules, and changes in the nature of employer-provided pensions. While these have potentially offsetting effects on the timing of retirement, the overall effect is likely to be to cause workers to stay in work longer.
- The recession of 2008 onwards has had two broad effects on older workers: an adverse labour demand effect which might induce earlier retirement and an adverse shock to asset values which may have had the opposite effect. Using household panel data, and exploiting both time variation (pre-2008) and cross-section variation in asset ownership and in unemployment rates, we show that labour demand effects appear to be stronger.

Introduction

The baby-boomers born in the early 1960s are now approaching their fifties. Whilst their parents experienced a trend towards earlier retirement, this trend reversed in the early 1990s. As a result, the economic activity rate among older workers aged 50 and over is now at its highest rate for almost two decades. This rise in economic activity has affected workers both below and above state pension age. In 2009, almost three-quarters of men and women in the ten-year age band below state pension age (65 for men and 60 for women) were still economically active; in addition, one in four men aged 65–9 and more than 40% of women aged 60–4 were working. And while the recession from 2008 hit younger workers aged 18–24 hard, it appears to have had much less effect on older workers—in marked contrast to the experience of the previous two recessions in the early 1980s and early 1990s, both of which saw substantial falls in employment among older workers.

In this chapter we discuss a number of possible explanations for why employment among older workers has been rising—and why they now appear to be relatively 'recession proof'. A number of recent legislative changes have removed constraints on employment among older workers (such as the abolition of mandatory retirement ages before 65), while changes in pension provision, particularly those affecting private pensions, are likely to have reduced early retirement options. The key point, however, is that ex ante, the effect of a recession on retirement is unclear—it may encourage people to retire by reducing employment opportunities but may also be associated with a negative shock to wealth, which may delay retirement. We conclude by examining which of the two effects of recession—on employment opportunities and on retirement wealth—is likely to dominate, if any, using data on variations in assets across households and local unemployment rates from 1992 to 2007.

Employment trends

Figure 4.1, using Labour Force Survey (LFS) data, contrasts economic activity and unemployment rates since 1992 among men and women in their fifties with rates among men and women aged between 18 and 24.

The figures show a gradual fall in economic activity rates among men and women aged 18–24 over the period. For much of this time, this reflected the increased fraction of the cohort remaining in post-compulsory education. However, particularly since 2008, employment rates have declined more steeply among this group, coupled with a sharp rise in the unemployment rate, especially among young men (see Goujard et al., Chapter 3).

In contrast, economic activity rates among older workers, and especially among older women, have risen steadily since the early 1990s.[1] In part, this increase among men represents a recovery from the negative shocks to

---

[1] For a discussion of the factors behind the rise in economic activity rates among older workers up until the early 2000s, see Disney and Hawkes (2003).

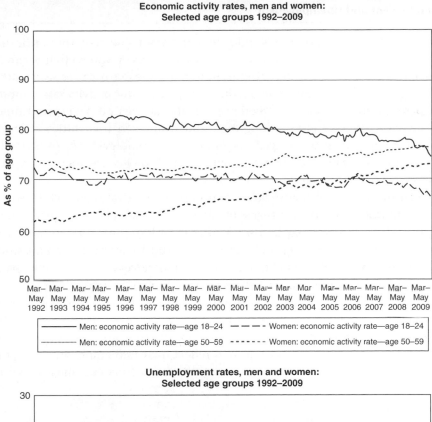

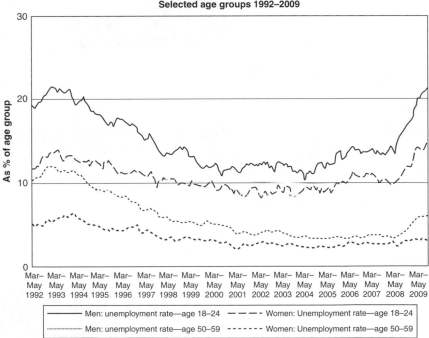

Figure 4.1: Economic activity and unemployment rates, by age and gender

Source: Labour Force Survey (LFS), 1992–2009.

employment in the early 1980s and 1990s, and among women, the continued higher labour force participation of successive cohorts of women that began in the late 1950s. But it is interesting to note that, unlike earlier recessions, the post-2008 period has not led to a reduction in economic activity rates among this group—indeed among women in particular, activity rates have continued to increase. Activity rates among men and women in their fifties are now higher than among those aged 18–24. There is some evidence of a rise in unemployment rates among older men, but nothing like the increase experienced by younger workers.

Even more striking upward trends in employment rates are exhibited by men and women in the five-year interval after the state pension age (i.e. men aged 65–9 and women aged 60–4). As shown in Figure 4.2, one in four men aged 65–9 are now working, an increase of around 10 percentage points since 1997. Underlying this overall trend have been increases across full-time, part-time and self-employment. The increase in employment among women over the state pension age has been even more dramatic. In 2009, 45% of women aged 60–64 were working, an increase of 15 percentage points since 1997. The majority of these women work part-time, but full-time and self-employment have been increasing. This may in part reflect increased employment opportunities for this age group, but also institutional factors encouraging work,

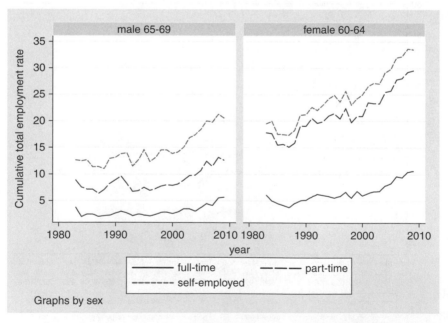

Figure 4.2: Employment rates (cumulative), men and women over state pension age
Source: LFS, 1989–2009.

such as the abolition of the 'earnings test' for older workers in 1989 (Disney and Smith, 2002), the increase in accrual rates associated with deferring the state pension, and the liberalisation of rules allowing individuals to continue to work even after drawing a pension from a private employer. This increase in employment among men aged 65+ and women aged 60+ predates the rise in state pension age from 60 to 65 that will be phased in for women between 2010 and 2020 and the proposed increase to 68 for both men and women that will be phased in between 2024 and 2046.

Determinants of employment among older workers

The timing of retirement is likely to reflect (among other things) individual preferences, employment opportunities, health, pension arrangements and levels of wealth. Since 1997, there have been a number of changes in these potential drivers of retirement that may have affected the timing of retirement. These potential drivers include:

- the ruling making mandatory retirement below age 65 illegal;
- changes to state and private pension arrangements;
- changing returns on assets held in household portfolios;
- tightening eligibility for individual health and disability benefits;
- welfare-to-work policies targeted at older workers.

We discuss each of these in this section. On balance, we would argue that the legislative changes designed to encourage later retirement (such as abolishing mandatory early retirement, raising incentives to defer state pension and allowing workers to carry on working and draw an employer's pension) are likely to have had little direct effect on employment but have succeeded in removing potential barriers to employment among older workers. Much of the drive to later working is likely to have come from reduced opportunities for early retirement through occupational pensions and disability benefits.

Mandatory retirement and age discrimination

Following a European Commission Directive, mandatory retirement before age 65 was made illegal from October 2006 under the Employment Equality (Age) Regulations. In addition, from this date, all employees had the right to request working beyond age 65 and age discrimination in recruitment, promotion and training has been banned.

Evidence from the US suggested that abolishing mandatory retirement raised employment among older workers by as much as 7 percentage points (Neumark and Stock, 1999). However, there is little evidence in the UK to suggest that the change had anywhere close to this effect. Prior to the reform, relatively few people appeared to be genuinely constrained by mandatory early retirement ages. Banks and Smith (2006), using data from the British Household Panel Survey (BHPS) and the English Longitudinal Survey of Ageing (ELSA), show that, prior to the change, at most 3% of employees aged 50 and above were forced to retire early by retirement ages below 65. The data in Figures 4.1 and 4.2 show a strong rise in employment among men aged 65–9 (who can still be subject to compulsory retirement) as well as among those aged 60–4. There may be a greater effect from the wider government initiatives aimed at promoting employment among older workers,[2] but the evidence suggests that outlawing mandatory retirement ages had little direct effect.

Changes to state and private pension arrangements

The timing of retirement is strongly influenced by an individual's pension arrangements, and by the availability of other benefits as alternative early retirement vehicles. In an influential study, Gruber and Wise (2004) brought together individual micro-econometric studies of retirement across a number of countries which, despite unique pension arrangements, cultures and labour market institutions, shared the following common findings on incentive effects: a positive wealth effect—that is, the higher someone's total pension wealth (and other financial wealth), the more likely that he or she would retire—and a negative accrual effect—that is, the more that someone could increase their total pension wealth by delaying their retirement, the less likely that he or she would retire.

From April 2005 the government improved the incentive for people to defer receipt of their state pension, for the first time offering an additional lump-sum payment to those who defer beyond the state pension age as well as an enhanced weekly income. The effective accrual rate on deferral was already 10.4% per annum; allowing the deferrer to commute the additional pension by deferral into a lump sum enhances the incentive still further. However, while this may make it more attractive to delay the start of a state pension, it will not necessarily encourage people to retire later if, for example, they have an additional source of income to finance retirement from an earlier date.[3] The option to defer will be more attractive to wealthier people (who are likely to live longer and thus benefit more from the enhanced weekly income); this is exactly the group who are likely to have alternative sources of pension income to draw on.

---

[2] For example, the Age Positive campaign, <http://www.agepositive.gov.uk/>.

[3] It is possible that it might actually encourage people to retire earlier by increasing the total amount of resources available in retirement and therefore reducing the incentive to carry on working.

Other changes to the state pension system may actually have created incentives to retire earlier through a wealth effect. In 1995 the government introduced the Minimum Income Guarantee, renamed the Pension Credit in 2003. The first component of the Pension Credit, the Guarantee Credit, is a means-tested benefit for those aged 60 and over that is set at a more generous rate than the basic state pension (the first age at which this guaranteed income can be paid will increase from 2010, as will state pension age for women). The second component, the Saving Credit, is an additional supplementary credit which is withdrawn against other retirement income and can be claimed by individuals aged 65 and over. In principle, Pension Credit could act as an early retirement vehicle for the low paid and those with limited private wealth.

For most people, however, the timing of retirement is likely to be affected not by the state pension system but by the incentives in their private pension—either a defined benefit (DB) employed-provided pension plan (also known as an occupational pension) or a defined contribution (DC) (employer-provided, personal or stakeholder) pension.

Historically, generous DB occupational pensions are likely to have encouraged early retirement (see Blundell et al., 2002). DB pensions typically 'guarantee' a final pension that depends on length of service and final salary.[4] By continuing to work, someone with a DB scheme can increase the value of their final pension and lump sum by increasing their years' service and increasing the final salary on which their pension is based.[5] But there is little incentive to carry on working beyond the normal or early retirement age, since deferral rates are typically not actuarially fair. In most schemes, accrual rates turn sharply negative after these retirement ages, creating clear incentives to start drawing the pension. Moreover, before April 2006, it was illegal to both draw a pension and work for the same employer, giving people a strong incentive to retire.

By contrast, DC schemes typically have much less strongly defined incentives to retire at particular ages than DB schemes—contracted-out rebates cease at age 65 and annuity rates and mortality rates both vary by age, but none of these will generate such sharp kinks in accrual profiles as are typically found in DB schemes. Although DB schemes typically have a stronger incentive to delay retirement—and stay in work—*until* the early/normal retirement age, in a DC scheme someone can continue to increase the value of their pension, even at older ages—and this reduces the incentive to retire, compared to most DB

---

[4] There is employment risk and, until 2005 and the introduction of a Pension Protection Fund, prudential risk, since there was no payout in the event of the employer going bankrupt.

[5] This second element matters more for workers with higher levels of education who experience more earnings growth over their lifetimes and in later years. Public sector workers also have trajectories of earnings that peak later than private sector workers, and it is no surprise that DB plans are therefore more common in the public sector. For further discussion, see Disney et al. (2009).

schemes. Several recent studies in the United States have found that DC plans have seen people delaying retirement by one or two years compared to DB schemes (see Friedberg and Webb, 2005).

This suggests that a shift in provision from DB to DC schemes, together with reduced provision for early retirement in occupational DB schemes, is likely to encourage later retirements. Figure 4.3 shows that membership of DB plans has increased in the public sector in the UK, reflecting in part the increase in the size of the public sector (now just over 20% of the workforce). In contrast, DB coverage has been falling sharply in the much larger private sector since the late 1980s, with that sector moving to either DC coverage or no pension coverage at all. Only around a quarter of private sector employees are now covered by some sort of DB plan and many existing DB plans are closed to new members or to permitting new accrued rights (Disney et al., 2009). Only among very high (and older) earners in the private sector does DB coverage remain an important driver towards early retirement in the UK, and even public sector DB plans, where retirement before state pension age was prevalent, are moving towards later normal retirement ages.

The *willingness* of employers to offer early retirement through a pension plan (i.e. below the scheme's normal age of retirement) depends in large part

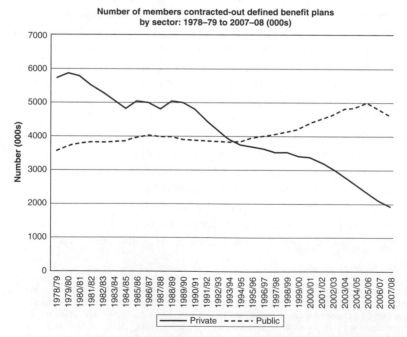

Figure 4.3: Members of contracted-out defined benefit plans (000s), by sector
Source: Department of Work and Pensions (DWP).

on the financial position of the pension fund. Through a combination of institutional factors and economic trends, the scope for pension funds in the UK to offer more generous discretionary early retirement packages has declined in recent years. The consultancy Mercer suggested that the 350 largest pension funds had a combined deficit of £170 billion at the end of 2009 (compared to £60 billion at the end of 2008), despite the rally in the equity market that occurred in 2009. The Association of Consulting Actuaries estimated that 91% of these funds were in deficit by the end of 2009. There are many reasons for these adverse trends. Pension funds themselves point to the reductions in the relatively favourable tax treatment of pension funds implemented in the early days of the Labour administration, and the general patchy performance of the equity market in the last decade. However, other factors include changes in accounting provisions, particularly the growing use of accounting practices to value fund assets at their current, rather than time-averaged, values and the general uncertainty of asset markets pushing up the premium on assets that have generally been used by pension funds to insure their liabilities—such as indexed-linked bonds.

Trends in household wealth

The timing of retirement may also have been be affected by what has happened to household wealth portfolios in recent years. As shown in Figure 4.4 (first panel), the value of the FTSE All Share index has fluctuated since the mid-1980s with peaks in 2000 and 2007. Overall, in contrast to the 1990s, the index ended the 2000s well below its starting value despite the fluctuations. Changes in the value of shares are likely to matter *directly* only for a small number of retirees. As shown in Figure 4.5, direct holdings of financial assets, including shares, represents a relatively small proportion of median wealth. Nevertheless, as mentioned in the previous sub-section, fluctuations in the value of equities matter for members of pension funds.

In contrast to the value of equities, the value of housing (Figure 4.4, lower left panel), which represents a much larger share of total household wealth, increased continuously from 1997 until 2007, effectively doubling over the decade. In general, such an increase in wealth would be expected to result in earlier retirement. Results from Blundell et al. (2002), for example, based on pension wealth, suggested that an additional £50,000 of wealth (in 1999 prices) would increase the probability of retirement by 3.5 percentage points. However, it is not necessarily the case that an increase in housing wealth would have exactly that effect—it relies on either people cashing in on their housing wealth by trading down when house prices are high (for which there is little evidence) and/or people believing that the increase in housing wealth

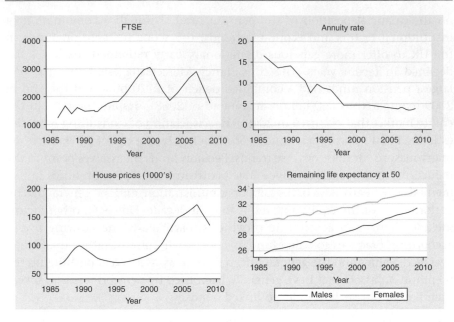

Figure 4.4: Asset returns and life expectancy

Notes: FTSE All Share price index, annuity rate proxied with 3.5% war loan (see Cannon and Tonks, 2004), UK house prices, period life expectancy tables. Asset indices are adjusted for inflation.

Source: Datastream, Halifax historic house prices, Office for National Statistics (ONS).

will not be reversed. In the next section, we present some regression results of the effect of housing wealth on retirement.

Figure 4.4 (upper right panel) also shows what has been happening to the annuity rate—that is, the rate at which people can convert their pension fund or other wealth into a flow of income in retirement. People with a defined contribution scheme are legally required to convert at least three-quarters of their pension fund into an annuity. The annuity rate, proxied here by the long-term rate on bonds, has been declining almost continuously over the last 20 years as life expectancy has been rising (Figure 4.4, lower right panel) and bond rates have remained low. A declining annuity rate effectively reduces the value of wealth held in DC pension plans, which would tend to encourage people to work later.

Individual health and disability benefits

Ill-health plays an important role in people's reported explanations for early retirement. It is the single most common reason people give for why they retire before the state pension age, cited by around one-quarter of early retirees (see Banks and Smith, 2006, and Banks and Casanova, 2004). Of course, this

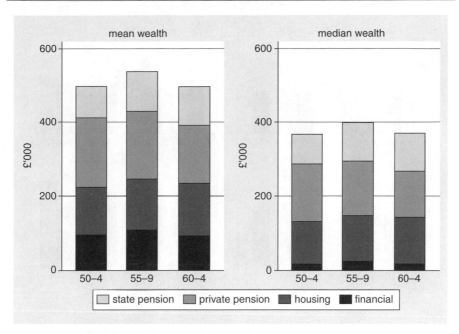

Figure 4.5: Composition of household wealth, by age
Source: English Longitudinal Study of Ageing, 2002–2003.

may reflect a degree of *post hoc* rationalization, particularly when early retirement is linked to receipt of disability and other ill-health benefits; nevertheless Disney et al. (2006) find that a more rapid deterioration in an individual's index of health after age 50, relative to households of similar age, is indeed associated with a higher probability of retirement in Britain.

There is very little evidence, however, to suggest that an overall *improvement* in health can account for rising levels of employment among older workers. While levels of life expectancy have been increasing, levels of health among those in their fifties and sixties do not appear to have improved. As shown in Figure 4.6, the average number of self-reported health problems (arguably a more objective indicator than general self-reported health status) has, if anything, increased since the early 1990s.

Reforms to the disability insurance regime

The government has made several attempts to tighten up the provision of the main benefit paid to the long-term sick and disabled, known as Incapacity Benefit (ICB). The key elements of these changes have been to reduce the generosity of the programme for all but the most severely disabled, to tighten

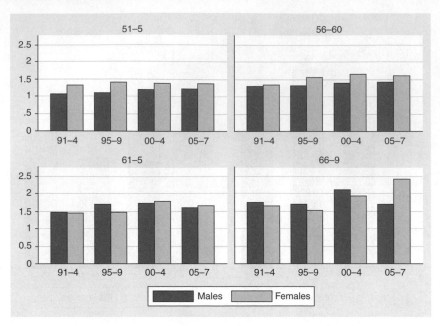

Figure 4.6: Number of self-reported health problems, by age and gender
Source: British Household Panel Survey (BHPS), 1991–2007.

the work-capacity 'hurdles' required to enter the programme, and to give claimants various incentives to leave the programme.

The 1999 Welfare Reform and Pensions Act replaced the existing work test with a new personal capability assessment which put an emphasis on the work that people might be able to do, as well as the work they are incapable of doing, which tightened the insurance contribution requirements required to move onto ICB and which also introduced an element of means-testing of ICB against private pension income.

In 2008 yet another new structure was introduced. In a reform in October 2008, Incapacity Benefit was replaced for new claimants by Employment Support Allowance (ESA). This reform involves more generous standard payments (but dependants' additions removed), a new and stricter health test and the national rolling out of Pathways to Work for disability claimants, which had been introduced on a trial basis in 2003.

Of these various reforms, Pathways to Work, as a strategy to induce claimants back into gainful employment, is perhaps of most interest in the context of retirement from the labour force. The programme contained several elements:

1. an intensive programme of Work Focused Interviews (WFIs), comprising an early WFI (eight weeks after the claim) and five further WFIs (roughly

every four weeks) except for the 'severely disabled' and 'those likely to return to work without help';

2. optional programmes to boost work prospects (Choices): the NHS Condition Management Program (CMP); the New Deal for Disabled People (NDDP), and other smaller programmes;

3. financial incentives: Return To Work Credit (RTWC) of £40 per week for the first year after moving into paid work of at least 16 hours a week for those expecting to earn no more than £15k p.a., as well as discretionary payments to help individuals find work.

Preliminary evidence from the trial evaluations suggested that these programmes had a significant effect on the outflow from disability insurance in the first six months of the spell, but little effect thereafter, and that the effect was focused more on some work disability conditions (mostly physical) than others (mostly mental).

Although there is evidence that some of these programmes have worked, in the sense of reducing inflows and increasing outflows among relatively short-duration claimants with physical disabilities, the net trend over time has been towards a claimant register dominated by older claimants for disability benefits, with longer benefit durations. The capacity of the programme to be a surrogate early retirement programme has probably been limited by these reforms, although the programme's use or otherwise in that respect would have been tested more stringently had the recession that began in 2008 been associated with the increase in exit from employment of older workers that was characteristic of earlier UK recessions (see the discussion above).

Welfare-to-work policies targeted at older workers

Following on the heels of employment programmes such as the New Deal for Young People, the New Deal 50 Plus (ND50+), introduced in April 2000, specifically targets older workers who have been unemployed for more than six months. This scheme provides participants with a personal adviser and with a training grant and earnings top-up (for low earners) upon employment. To date there is limited evidence about how this programme has changed employment amongst the over fifties. The official figures from the Department of Work and Pensions suggest that 97 740 participants have found jobs through the scheme since 2003, although the number finding jobs fell dramatically in 2009, which suggests that what really matters for the employment prospects of the over fifties is the economic climate. However, this says nothing about whether people would have found jobs (and stayed in them) in the absence of this programme. Grierson (2002) suggests the ND50+ may have had a positive effect on job retention, when comparing ND50+ participants to other job centre plus customers of the same age, although differential selection into these schemes and a lack of control variables are likely to be an issue here.

Impact of the recession

Ex ante, the effect of a recession on retirement timing is uncertain. Wages and employment prospects may be adversely hit, encouraging older workers to retire earlier. But the recession may also negatively impact on wealth through falling house prices and share values, which may cause people to delay retirement. An alternative viewpoint is that weaker stock market performance may lead to earlier retirement among people in defined contribution pension schemes owing to pension accrual effects. The increment to pension wealth from working an additional year, which is given by employee and employer contributions to the pension fund and the investment return on these contributions, is small when stock markets perform poorly, so the incentive to continue working is diminished. In Coile and Levine (2009), the US Current Population Survey is used to examine how retirement among the age group 62–9 is sensitive to local variations in unemployment, to state-wide variations in house prices, and to fluctuations in financial wealth which are not directly observable in the CPS and are matched from other data by educational group. They conclude that the local unemployment rate (the 'labour demand' effect) far outweighs in importance the 'asset effect' in its impact on retirement decisions.

In a similar vein, but with somewhat greater precision in matching asset ownership to households, we investigate which of these factors matters in practice—and how big the effects are likely to be in a UK context. Since household data are not yet available for the post-2007 period, we exploit variations in unemployment rates and asset values across a panel of households for the period 1992–2007 using data from the British Household Panel Survey (see Disney et al., 2010, for further details).

The results are summarised in Table 4.1. They show the estimated effect of changes in asset prices (housing and shares) and labour market conditions (wages and unemployment rates) on the retirement hazard (the probability that a person retires, given that they have not previously retired). Rising unemployment is estimated to have a positive and significant effect, suggesting that people retire earlier when facing tough labour markets. Further analysis (not reported) shows that this effect is uniform across education groups, so tough labour markets equally affect skilled and unskilled workers. Neither earnings, house prices or stock prices appear to have any effect on retirement timing but additional results (not shown) suggest that people with stock market investments tend to retire later *compared to others* when stock markets

Table 4.1: Factors affecting retirement

	Estimated increase in the probability of retirement (percentage points)
1 percentage point increase in the unemployment rate	0.30*
£10 increase in weekly earnings	−0.02
1 percentage point increase in house price growth (homeowners)	−0.03
1 percentage point increase in FTSE 500 share index (investors)	−0.02

Notes: * denotes that the effect is statistically significant. House price growth and share price growth are based on a one-year period. Analysis controls for homeowner, pension status (employer or private), public sector employee, stock market investor, age dummies interacted with gender, partnership status (partner, widowed or separated/divorced), whether 2 or 3+ adults live in household, whether children in household, number of health problems and year dummies.
Source: Regression analysis using BHPS, 1991–2007.

perform well. This suggests that accrual effects may be relevant to retirement decisions.

We can use the results to make some assessment of the likely effects of the current recession, which has caused unemployment to rise and stock prices to fall. We calculate that just over 60% of men and 40% of women retire before state pension age (64 for men and 59 for women). A permanent 1 percentage point increase in unemployment raises these percentages by about 2 percentage points. Between 2008 and 2009, the unemployment rate itself increased by about 2 percentage points and should this reflect a permanent increase in unemployment, our results imply that retirement could increase by 4 percentage points (to just over 64% for men and 44% for women).

Conclusions

At the start of the chapter, we noted that employment and economic activity rates had remained remarkably buoyant among age groups aged 50 and over since 2008 given the adverse shock that has hit the UK economy, and in contrast to, say, the increase in unemployment experienced by younger age groups.

A number of factors that might cause changes in retirement behaviour were discussed. Broadly, these could be separated into demand effects, changes in asset prices, in legislation governing employment practices, and changes in pension and disability benefit regimes. Each of these was discussed in turn.

Our analysis suggested that anti-age discrimination legislation has probably had limited effect, given how few workers reported that their retirement would have been affected by the legislative changes. Changes in asset prices would likely have led individuals to defer retirement, as would changes in employer-provided pension plans and the tightening of the disability regime. It was noted, however, that there had been an increase in generosity of the state pension, especially for poorer pensioners, and yet employment rates among people above state pension age had continued to increase sharply.

Following recent work for the United States, we combined several of these potential factors in a regression framework, using BHPS data. From these results, based on a fairly simple specification, we show that is important to consider the effect of both labour demand factors and asset values during periods of boom and bust.

References

Banks, J. and Casanova, M. (2004) Work and retirement. In: Marmot, M., Banks, J., Blundell, R., Lessof, C. and Nazroo, J. (eds.) *Health Wealth and Lifestyles of the Older Population in England: The 2002 English Longitudinal Study of Ageing*. London: IFS.

—— and Smith, S. (2006) Retirement in the UK. *Oxford Review of Economic Policy*, 22 (1): 40–56.

Blundell, R., Meghir, C. and Smith, S. (2002) Pension incentives and the patterns of early retirement. *Economic Journal*, 112, March: C153–70.

Cannon, E. and Tonks, I. (2004) UK Annuity price series 1957–2002. *Financial History Review*, 11(02): 165–96.

Coile, C. and Levine, P. (2009) The market crash and mass layoffs: how the current economic crisis may affect retirement. NBER Working Paper Series 15395.

Disney, R., Emmerson C. and Tetlow, G. (2009) What is a public sector pension worth? *Economic Journal*, 119, November: F517–35.

—— —— and Wakefield, M. (2006) Ill-health and retirement in Britain: a panel data-based analysis. *Journal of Health Economics*, 25(4): 621–49.

—— and Hawkes, D. (2003) Why has employment recently risen among older workers in Britain. In: Dickens, R., Gregg, P. and Wadsworth, J. (eds.) *The Labour Market Under New Labour. The State of Working Britain*. Basingstoke: Palgrave.

—— Ratcliffe, A. and Smith, S. (2010) Booms, busts and retirement transitions. CMPO Working Paper, 10/233.

—— and Smith, S. (2002) The labour supply effect of the abolition of the earnings rule for older workers in the United Kingdom. *Economic Journal*, 112, March: C136–52.

Friedberg, L. and Webb, A. (2005) Retirement and the evolution of pension structure. *Journal of Human Resources*, 40(2): 281–308.

Goujard, A., Petrongolo, B. and Van Reenen, J. (2011) The labour market for young people. In: Gregg, P. and Wadsworth, J. (eds) *The Labour Market in Winter: The State of Working Britain*. Oxford: Oxford University Press.

Grierson, K. (2002) New Deal 50 Plus: quantitative analysis of job retention. Working Age Internal Report 151. Leeds: Electronic Archive, available at <http://research.dwp.gov.uk/asd/asd5/working_age/wa2003/151_rep.pdf>.

Gruber, J. and Wise, D. (eds.) (2004) *Social Security Programs and Retirement around the World: Micro-estimation.* Chicago: University of Chicago Press.

Neumark, D. and Stock, W. (1999) Age discrimination laws and labor market efficiency. *Journal of Political Economy*, 107: 1081–125.

5

Workless Households

Paul Gregg and Jonathan Wadsworth

Key findings

- By 1997 the distribution of work across households (polarisation) was more unequal than at any time since records began in the mid-1970s.
- The years of subsequent economic recovery did reduce the share of households where no one is in work, but never back to the lower levels seen in the 1970s (or indeed the 1980s).
- Single-parent households have been the main beneficiaries of the recent improvement.
- The long-term increase in unequal allocation of work across households appears to have resumed following the latest recession.
- A steady increase in the number of people living on their own is pushing up the number of households without a worker, partially offsetting the reduction in the inequality in the distribution of work across households.

Introduction

In 1997 the incoming Labour government inherited an economy where nearly one in five of all households containing working-age adults had no one in employment. Some 5.2 million adults and 2.3 million children were living in these workless households, the majority of whom were dependent on welfare benefits. These workless numbers had been rising since the onset of the 1980s recession. Economic recovery during the late 1980s had tempered, but failed to offset, the rising trend. The subsequent recession of the 1990s ratcheted up the workless household numbers further still.

Two noticeable trends could help explain these patterns. First, there are more single-adult households. More single-adult households means households are either in work or not, so there is less chance that work can be shared within households. The Labour government of 1997 recognised the problem, began to compile and monitor workless household numbers and to introduce a raft of policy responses that could help address the issue. The New Deal programmes reached out to others than just the unemployed. The introduction of the Working Families Tax Credit, the National Minimum Wage, and the reduction in income taxes for the low paid, all stemmed from an understanding that many households with no earner had little incentive to work given the low wages on offer in the labour market. Hence the policy emphasis moved to raising the relative returns to working, tackling barriers on moving into work and to help to search for work. In what follows we assess developments in workless household numbers over the past ten years and assess whether any progress has been made.

The emerging problem

Figure 5.1 tracks movements in the workless household rate and the proportion of working-age individuals without a job (the non-employment rate), back to the mid-1970s.[1] It is apparent that the share of individuals without a job was approximately the same in 1997 as in 1975. However, this was not true for the jobless rate measured across households. Over the same period, subject to some cyclical variation, the proportion of households with no one in work grew steadily, reaching nearly 20% of all working-age households by the mid-1990s, with over one in five children living in a workless household (see Table 5.1).

Whilst employment recovered after each recession, two forces were keeping the number of workless households high. First, there are more single-adult households (see Figure 5.2). Young adults continue to leave the parental home earlier than in the past, but are also delaying the age at which they get married. Separation and divorce is now more frequent. More single-adult households means that households are either in work or not, so there is less chance that work can be shared within households. Among families with children, a rising share of lone-parent families, from 4 to 10% of all working-age households, also means an increased likelihood of observing a workless household, other

---

[1] We exclude full-time students and households where the head is above retirement age. This means we focus on households likely to be dependent on welfare payments aimed at working-age people. It is also why our numbers differ slightly from published sources.

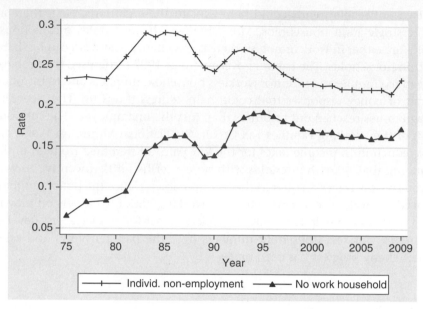

Figure 5.1: Distribution of work across households, 1975–2009
Source: LFS. Authors' calculations.

things equal. Since the mid-1990s the lone-parent household share has been broadly stable at around 10%, some one in five of all families with children.

The second major driver was that inequality in the distribution of work across households had increased, so that there were simultaneously more two-earner and more no-earner families. By 1995, as shown in Table 5.1, some 60% of households had all adults working, while the share of household with a mixture of working and non-working adults had fallen from 35% in 1977 to 20% in 1995.

In order to get a sense of how many workless households might be expected given the state of the economy, Gregg and Wadsworth (2008) suggest that it is possible to compare the actual household rate with the rate that would hold if everyone had the same chance of being in work (whilst allowing for any changes in the average number of adults who comprise a household). So if 25% of adults are out of work then we might expect that 25% of one-adult households and 6.2% of two-adult households would be workless (25% of 25% is 6.25%). If we observe rates higher than these, then work is not randomly distributed, rather there is 'polarisation' and this polarisation rate gives a measure of the excess numbers of workless households.

On this basis, Table 5.2 suggests that during the 1970s, the random allocation of work predicts the actual distribution of work across households quite well, so there were as many workless households as might be expected given

Table 5.1: Workless households in Britain

	Workless households (working age)		Households where all adults work		Working-age adults in workless households		Children <16 in workless households	
	(000s)	%	(000s)	%	(000s)	%	(000s)	%
1977	1200	8.2	8200	57.9	1600	5.7	1100	8.7
1987	2500	16.4	8100	53.6	3700	13.4	2000	18.0
1989	2100	13.8	9200	59.5	3000	10.7	1600	14.4
1995	3200	19.3	10 100	60.5	4400	16.0	2500	21.7
1997	3100	18.2	10 500	62.4	4200	15.2	2300	20.2
2006	2900	16.0	12 000	66.5	3800	12.7	1900	16.9
2009	3200	17.3	11 900	65.3	4100	13.9	2000	18.6

Notes: Child data not available before 1981. Employment rate excludes students and households with retired heads. Numbers rounded to nearest 100,000.

Source: LFS.

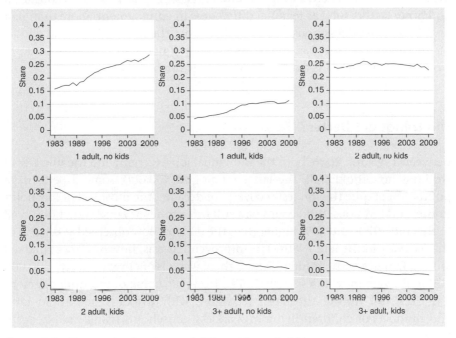

Figure 5.2: Changes in the shares of different household types
Source: LFS. Authors' calculations.

the prevailing employment rate and hence there was little polarisation. By the mid-1990s, however, the workless household rate had moved increasingly out of line with the benchmark predicted by an even distribution of work across households. In 1995, the excess of workless households stood at nearly 7 percentage points, some 1.2 million extra workless households.

Table 5.2: Excess workless household rates

	Workless household rate	Polarisation (% point excess)	Employment rate (%)
1977	8.2	− 0.2	76.5
1986	16.3	+ 4.9	71.0
1990	13.9	+ 5.0	75.6
1995	19.3	+ 6.7	73.9
1997	18.2	+ 6.5	75.9
2006	16.0	+ 5.2	77.9
2009	17.3	+ 5.0	76.7

Source: LFS, authors' calculations.

In part this pattern was influenced by women, especially married and better educated women, having gone out to work in increasing numbers, but not from households where male (largely older and less skilled) employment was lost. However, even accounting for differential work chances across education and other factors such as regional differences in employment, more than half of the rise in workless household numbers from the mid-1970s to the middle of the present decade was due to widening inequality in the distribution of work across households (see Gregg and Wadsworth, 2008).

Did things get better?

Between 1995 and 2006, both the individual jobless count and the number of workless households fell, the latter by around 300,000, some 3 percentage points. Yet despite the longest recovery for decades, the most recent low point in the workless household count was still three times as large as that observed in the mid-1970s and 50% higher than the previous low observed at the end of the recovery in the late 1980s. The improvement was, however, most marked among families with children, where there was a reduction of nearly 600,000 children living in workless households. However, some of that improvement has been lost during the latest recession, with workless household rates and numbers of children living in workless households rising sharply again (Table 5.1).

Table 5.2 shows that polarisation across households started to decline after 1997, returning to levels last seen in the late 1980s. Nevertheless the expected workless household rate in 2009, given the stage of the cycle, should have been around 12.3% rather than the observed 17.3%. This means that there are still around 900,000 more workless households now than would be the case in the absence of polarisation. Improvement in the inequality in the distribution of work across families has been partly offset by the continued move towards adults living alone rather than in couples or multi-adult family units. During

Table 5.3: Workless households, non-employment and polarisation across countries

	Australia	GB	US	Spain	Germany	France
Workless household rate						
1996	15.7	19.3	12.4	16.2	16.5	16.7
2000	16.1	16.9	10.7	12.3	16.3	16.9
2005	15.1	16.3	12.2	10.8	16.6	13.7
Non-employment Rate						
1996	26.5	25.4	24.2	44.0	29.8	31.5
2000	26.8	23.0	22.1	36.0	27.3	29.5
2005	22.7	22.1	23.1	31.7	27.9	32.6
Polarisation of work (% point excess workless household rate)						
1996	4.4	6.8	1.5	−3.0	−0.8	1.8
2000	4.6	6.1	1.0	−2.1	0.4	2.8
2005	4.4	5.5	1.2	−0.8	−0.3	−0.4

Notes: Earliest Australian data refer to 1998. Data exclude students and all households with head of working age.
Source: Gregg et al. (2010).

the recession, employment levels have fallen across most household types. Hence the workless household rate has risen, even though polarisation of work across households has not.

An excessive number of workless households is more a feature of the UK labour market than in many other OECD countries. Access to comparable data is not often as easy as in Britain, but we have obtained data that allow us to repeat these calculations for Australia, the US, Spain, France and Germany (Table 5.3). Britain had the highest workless household rate in 1996, despite having the second lowest non-employment rate. As a result Britain had the highest degree of polarisation. Australia was not far behind. Spain had fewer workless households than Britain despite only having just over half its adult population in work and hence, along with Germany, had negative polarization—fewer workless households than might be expected given the non-employment rate. Since 1996, the workless household rate in Britain fell and drew closer to the rates seen in Germany and France. However, polarisation in Britain remains much higher. The workless household rate in the US does not appear to move much over time and polarisation there is negligible, as it is in France and Germany. Note that the strong employment recovery in Spain between 1996 and 2005 helped reduce the numbers of workless households, but polarisation became less negative. This means that the recovery in Spain did not benefit workless households as much as other households. It remains to be seen how the recession affected the distribution of work across households in these and other OECD countries.

Families with children

The number of children living in workless households has been strongly linked to the incidence of child poverty (see Dickens, Chapter 16). The extent to which children are living in single-parent households and how work is distributed across families with children are key drivers of this. Table 5.4 gives workless household and polarisation rates in Britain according to number of adults and the presence of dependent children. The top panel (and Figure 5.2) give the shares of each household type over time. One of the notable trends in household formation is that the household with two adults and children is no longer the most common household type. Rather it is now the single-adult childless household that is the most common household type among the working-age population, at around 29% of working-age households. The

Table 5.4: Workless households and polarisation by presence of children and number of adults

	1 Adult		2 Adult		3 Adult	
	Child	No Child	Child	No Child	Child	No Child
% share of all households						
1983	4.3	15.8	36.6	23.8	9.1	10.4
1989	5.7	17.1	33.2	25.0	6.5	12.4
1996	9.5	23.2	30.7	24.4	4.2	7.9
2006	10.0	26.1	28.5	24.8	3.9	6.5
2009	11.2	28.6	28.0	22.7	3.5	6.0
Workless rate						
1983	54.8	34.1	9.7	9.6	4.3	3.1
1989	59.4	32.1	6.9	8.5	2.5	2.5
1996	56.9	26.8	9.2	5.5	5.7	1.5
2006	43.6	28.1	6.2	8.0	5.2	3.1
2009	43.8	30.0	7.2	7.8	5.6	3.2
Polarisation (% point excess)						
1983	25.8	5.1	1.3	1.1	1.9	0.7
1989	34.7	7.3	0.8	2.3	1.0	1.0
1996	31.5	9.5	2.8	4.2	4.1	1.3
2006	21.4	5.9	1.3	3.1	4.1	2.0
2009	20.4	6.7	1.7	2.3	4.3	1.9
Polarisation after age, gender, region, education (% point excess)						
1983	20.9	4.1	4.6	0.5	2.4	0.2
1989	30.1	5.3	3.2	1.5	1.4	0.5
1996	25.3	7.3	3.9	2.2	3.7	0.5
2006	15.8	6.1	2.1	2.3	3.4	1.5
2009	14.4	6.3	2.5	1.6	3.6	0.9

Source: LFS. Authors' calculations.

share of single-parent households has also continued to increase, albeit more slowly, in the last decade, after having risen sharply in the decade before.

Single parents have also been one of the big labour market success stories in recent years. Table 5.4 shows that the jobless rate fell from a peak of 61% in 1993 to a low of 46% in 2006. Single adults without dependent children and two adult households without children have also experienced relative improvements in performance, with workless household rates for both these groups in 2006 below the troughs seen in the 1980s. Once again, recession ended this advance and workless rates for both these groups are rising again. Two groups of potential concern are two adult and three adult households with dependent children (these are mostly couples with an adult child also in the home). Workless household rates for these groups in the 2000s never fell below the troughs seen in the late 1980s. Indeed workless rates appear to have been rising for these groups for some time now.

Jobless rates among single-parent households and single adults without children are much higher than we would expect if everyone in the population had the same chance of being in work. As a result, Table 5.4 shows that polarisation rates are much higher for these groups. Although polarisation amongst single adults without children is lower, this latter group is much larger than single parents and the high jobless rates perhaps more surprising. Since polarisation depends on both the workless rate *and* the share of each group in the population, increased absence of work in single adults without children has counteracted the larger improvements seen within single parents. Unlike single parents, the trends in workless households among couples have moved with the cycle in aggregate employment. There has been no policy-driven success among these households, for example in getting at least one adult into work.

As with unemployment (see Chapter 2, Gregg and Wadsworth), the incidence of employment varies across several dimensions, which, like age, gender, region, and skill, often combine together to reduce the chances of being in work. It may be that the share of these characteristics varies across household types and this may help explain differential workless household rates. The bottom panel of Table 5.4 gives a 'conditional' polarisation estimate which estimates the excess workless household rate after allowing for differences in age, gender, education and region across households. So the first column suggests that up to 40% of the workless household rate among single parents' children can be explained by the fact that they have characteristics such as low education or residence in economically depressed regions that make them more likely to experience joblessness than others. In contrast, accounting for these differences makes little difference to the expected workless household rates for all other household types. This suggests that their characteristics are closer to the average and that high levels of worklessness are not due to, say, less educated people having lower employment rates and living together.

The dynamics of workless households

One issue of which, as yet, we know little is which factors drive changes in the workless household rate. Just as an increase in the unemployment rate for individuals can be caused either by a rise in the number of people becoming unemployed or by a fall in the number of people leaving unemployment, so a rise in the workless household rate may be driven by increased inflow rate or a falling outflow rate, or both. As a first step toward assessing the flows that determine the workless household stocks, Figure 5.3 plots the inflow into workless households (the share of other households that become workless in a three-month interval), alongside the outflow from workless households (the share of households that were workless but are no longer three months later). The flows are constructed from LFS panel data and so are only available from 1992, a period when both the workless household rate and the all-work household rate rose and then fell back after 1996.

Figure 5.4 suggests that falling inflow rates were probably the main cause of the decline in workless household rates observed over much of this sample period. In bad times, around 5% of working households, one in 20, become workless in the course of three months. The outflow rate is much more volatile and shows less of a trend. This suggests that, during this period, the rate at

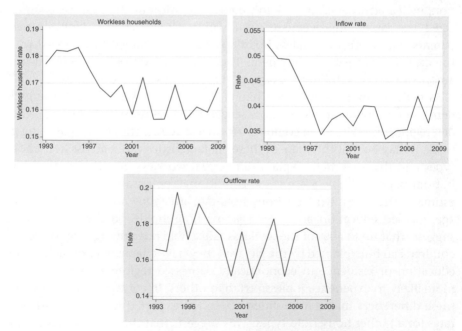

Figure 5.3: Movements in and out of worklessness over time (transition rates)
Source: LFS panel. Authors' calculations.

80

(a)   One-adult households

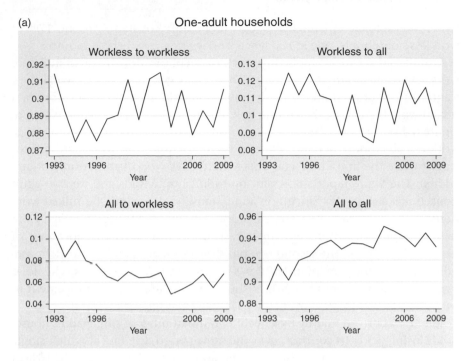

(b)   Two-adult households

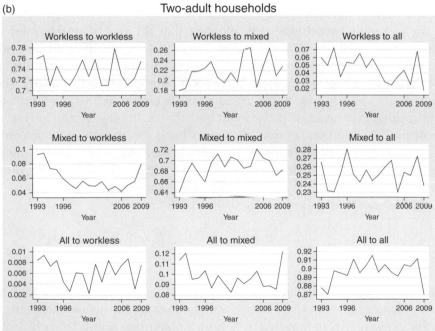

Figure 5.4: Household transition rates by number of adults (a) One-adult households (b) Two-adult households

Source: LFS Panel.

which households remained workless was broadly constant. Around 17% of workless households, one in six, leave worklessness every three months.

A similar idea can be applied to track the evolution of the distribution of work across all working households. Job loss may generate either a workless or a mixed-work household. Similarly, job gain could generate an all-work or a mixed-work household depending in which household type the job is found. Figure 5.4 outlines the inflow and outflows between three household states: workless, all-work (where everyone in the household is in work) and mixed-work (where the household contains a mixture of working and non-working adults). The figure reports flows for one-adult households and for two-adult households separately. Since one-adult households cannot be mixed-work households, there are only four transition windows for this group. Figure 5.4 is in the form of a transition matrix. The top row plots the flows out of workless household, the second row plots the flows out of mixed-work households and the final row plots the flows out of all-work households. The flows by household type seem to confirm the story for the aggregate movement in workless household rates over time. The fall in single-adult workless household rate was driven mainly by a decline in the number of single-adult households losing work. In contrast, over the same period, the rate at which single adults moved out of worklessness was broadly constant. Only around 10% of workless adults in single-adult households leave worklessness in one year.

For two-adult households, it is apparent that the end of worklessness is much more likely to generate a mixed-work household than an all-work household. In other words, it is much more likely that just one adult finds a job rather than that both adults find a job in a given period. Similarly, the most likely source of an inflow into a workless household is from a mixed-work, rather than an all-work two adult households. In other words, job loss is more likely to affect one person at a time. Changes in the *rate* of movements from mixed-work households to workless households, over time, is most obvious. When the workless household rate is falling, the inflow rate, from mixed to workless households, falls. When the workless household rate rises, the inflow rate from mixed work to workless also rises.

Conclusions

We concluded last time that a combination of economic recovery and government policy could help address the rise in the workless household rate. Indeed the workless household rate fell by around 3 percentage points between 1995 and 2006, affecting some 600,000 adults and some 600,000 children. Since then there has been stasis, with no prospect of improvement in the immediate future given the latest recession and weakness of any recovery. Once again, some one in six households of working age are workless and one in six children are living in a workless household. So the workless household rate remains much higher than in the 1970s and will continue to be so unless steps are taken to help make work more evenly distributed across households.

Despite improvements in the employment performance of lone parents over and above what the recovery would predict, there have been continued shifts in family composition toward single-adult households that have countered these improvements. Worklessness still disproportionately affects households with children to a much greater extent than in other countries. However, there has been less sign of any improvement among households without children, so it would seem that policy now also needs to be focused in this area. While changes in the rate of inflow into worklessness appear to drive changes in the stocks, the outflow rates from workless households are very low. This is yet another area of concern for policy makers.

References

Dickens, R. (2011) Child poverty in Britain: did work work? In Gregg, P. and Wadsworth, J. (eds.) *The Labour Market in Winter: The State of Working Britain*. Oxford: Oxford University Press.

Gregg, P., Scutella, R. and Wadsworth, J. (2010) Reconciling workless measures at the individual and household level: Theory and evidence from the United States, Britain, Germany, Spain and Australia. *Journal of Population Economics*, 23(1), January: 139–67.

—— and Wadsworth, J. (2008) Two sides to every story: measuring the polarisation of work. *Journal of the Royal Statistical Society, 2008*, Series A, 171(4): 857–75.

————(2011) Unemployment and inactivity. In: Gregg, P. and Wadsworth, J. (eds.) *The Labour Market in Winter: The State of Working Britain*. Oxford: Oxford University Press.

6

Immigration in the UK

Stephen Nickell and Jumana Saleheen

Key findings

- Net migration into Britain has been at an unprecedented level over the last decade and, while falling back recently, is expected to remain high.
- The general consensus is that immigrants have not had much of an effect on either unemployment or pay. However, we do find some evidence of a downward impact on wages in the low skill sector.
- This suggests that the focus should shift toward assessing the potential long-run effects of the high level of net migration on life in the UK via its impact on population growth.
- People in the UK appear to dislike the sort of rates of house building and infrastructure construction consistent with a high rate of population growth and it is this factor which is perhaps the most significant consequence of the current and projected levels of migration.

Introduction

Net migration into Britain has been at an unprecedented level over the last decade and is expected to remain so according to the projections of the Office of National Statistics. In this chapter, we look at the trends in migration and why net migration took off in 1998. We then consider where immigrants come from, what they are like and what they do. In particular, we note that those who work are located in a broad spread of occupations with no particular concentration at either the top or the bottom of the occupational distribution.

The next step is to focus on the impact of immigration on the labour market, the general consensus being that immigrants have not had much of an effect on either unemployment or pay. However, we do find some evidence of a downward impact on wages in the low skill sector. Finally, in the light of the apparently rather modest effects of immigration on the economy, we consider the potential long-run effects of the high level of net migration on life in the UK via its impact on population growth. People in the UK appear to dislike the sort of rates of house building and infrastructure construction consistent with a high rate of population growth and it is this factor which is perhaps the most significant consequence of the current and projected levels of migration.

Before moving on to the substance of the chapter, it is worth noting that throughout, a migrant is defined as someone who is foreign born, not someone who is foreign. In 2005, for example, around 45% of the immigrants in the UK labour force were UK citizens. Thus, while 10.1% of the UK labour force were foreign born, only 5.7% were foreign (i.e. non-UK citizens).[1]

Overall trends

Since the first edition of *The State of Working Britain*, net migration into the United Kingdom has been remarkably buoyant (see Figure 6.1). From 1965 to 1982, net migration was mostly negative, involving relatively small numbers. From 1982 to 1997, this was reversed, with net migration mostly small and positive. Over the entire period, net migration was never more than 100K in either direction. But from 1998, net migration has been positive, exceeding 130K in every year and 200K on a couple of occasions. As a consequence, immigrants as a proportion of the working-age population, having been around 8% for many years, have risen to around 14% since the mid-1990s (see Figure 6.2). Overall, there is some evidence of a slowdown in migration in the recent recession. Given existing regulations, this slowdown is only expected to be temporary.

By comparison with other countries, none of the UK figures is exceptional. For example, between 2003 and 2005 annual net migration into Spain exceeded 600K (see Blanchflower and Shadforth, 2009, table 3). And in both Australia and Switzerland, immigrants make up nearly one-quarter of the labour force. Nevertheless, the steady rise in the immigrant population in the UK in the last decade has generated a degree of consternation and lots of policies in the political arena, plenty of dramatic stories in the media and a significant increase in academic analysis.

[1] See OECD (2007), table I8.

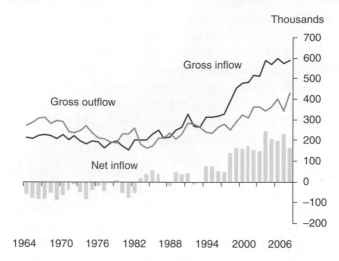

Figure 6.1: Immigration to and from the United Kingdom

Notes:
1. The number of people (all ages) entering/leaving the United Kingdom with the intention of staying/leaving for at least one year.

Source: Data are mainly from the IPS. From 1991, the ONS supplement the IPS with administrative data on asylum seekers and their dependants, and estimates of the migrant flow between the United Kingdom and the Irish Republic; the ONS also make other adjustments to account for those whose intended length of stay changes (from less than a year to more than a year, and vice versa). The IPS sampling methodology was also changed in 1999.

So why was there a dramatic increase in net migration from 1998? First, the UK labour market was exceptionally buoyant in the decade starting in 1998. Unemployment was below 6.1% (ILO measure) throughout the decade, having been above this level since 1980. Second, there has been an increasingly international market for skilled workers and the UK has been particularly active in this market. For example, almost uniquely in the world, both the UK Civil Service and the Bank of England have been recruiting in the international labour market for much of the decade. Third, in May 2004 there was a significant expansion of the European Union, including some of the larger countries of Eastern Europe, notably Poland; those countries collectively known as the 'A8 countries'. The UK allowed their citizens immediate access to the domestic labour market, leading to a dramatic increase in migration from these countries. Finally, there has been a steady rise in foreign students entering the UK as the UK higher education sector makes ever increasing use of overseas student fees to cross-subsidise the teaching of home undergraduates. We see, in Figure 6.3, the steady increase in the proportion of the migration inflow who are entering either to work or to study.

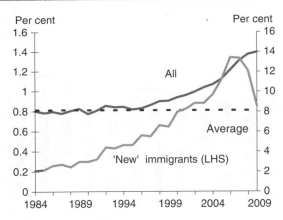

Figure 6.2: The foreign-born share of the population aged 16 to 64

Notes:
1. The number of 16–64 year olds born outside the United Kingdom as a proportion of the total population aged 16–64.
2. 'New' immigrants are those who entered the United Kingdom in the survey year or the year before the survey was carried out.
3. Dotted line is the average share of foreign-born individuals in the UK population between 1985 and 1995.
4. 2009 data capture data to 2009 Q3 only.

Source: LFS and authors' calculations.

What are migrants like and what do they do?

The relative proportions of migrants from different parts of the world have been broadly stable over the last decade (see Table 6.1). The exceptions are the dramatic rise in the A8 share following the 2004 EU expansion, the rise in the Africa share and the decline in the EU14 share. So what are these migrants like?

What are migrants like?

In Table 6.2, we see that the average age of migrants of working age is only marginally below that of natives (37.4 years relative to 39.9 years), but recent and new migrants are, on average, close to ten years younger. In recent years, the average migrant is somewhat better educated than the average native, with a significantly higher proportion of graduates. The proportion of graduates among migrants has risen significantly since the mid-1990s, in part because the immigration regulations have made it relatively easier for degree holders to enter and in part because a high proportion of A8 migrants have degrees.

Further down the table, we see that working-age migrants are less likely to work than natives, are more likely to be unemployed and to be inactive. But there

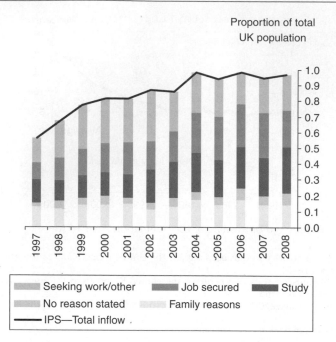

Figure 6.3: Reason for migrating to the UK
Notes:
1. Proportion of the entire UK population.
Source: IPS and ONS.

has been some degree of convergence, particularly among men, so that the employment rate of male migrants has been closing on that of natives so rapidly that they are now much the same. Composition is, of course, important here. A8 migrants, for example, have considerably higher employment rates than natives, so their rising proportion helps to explain this convergence. Other migrants with higher average employment rates than natives include those from the Old Commonwealth, the EU and the United States. These are more than offset by the lower employment rates of migrants from the New Commonwealth, particularly those from Pakistan and Bangladesh who have average employment rates of around 45% (excluding full-time students).[2]

What do migrants do?

In Figure 6.4, we see that migrants are broadly spread across all one-digit occupations with a very slight tendency to be crowded into the top and bottom of the

[2] See IPPR (2007), table 5.1.

Table 6.1: Share of immigrants in population: by country of birth

Per cent of population	All migrants			New migrants		
	2008	1997	*Change*	2008	1997	*Change*
Total	13.6	8.5	*5.1*	1.21	0.55	*0.66*
(of which)						
A8	1.5	0.1	*1.4*	0.33	0.02	*0.31*
Africa & Middle East	3.1	1.8	*1.3*	0.16	0.07	*0.10*
Indian Sub-Continent	2.8	1.8	*1.0*	0.21	0.05	*0.16*
EU14	2.2	2.3	*−0.1*	0.16	0.16	*0.00*
Americas	1.2	1.0	*0.2*	0.11	0.09	*0.02*
Rest of Asia	1.4	0.7	*0.7*	0.12	0.06	*0.06*
Rest of Europe	1.0	0.5	*0.5*	0.08	0.04	*0.05*
Australia & NZ	0.4	0.3	*0.1*	0.14	0.06	*−0.02*

Notes:
1. Based on individuals aged 16–64.
2. 'New' immigrants are those who entered the UK in the survey year or the year before the survey was carried out.
3. Country of birth data by all A8 countries is only available from 1998. For 1997, Poland, Hungary and Czechoslovakia (which account for 80% of those in the A8) are used to proxy the A8.
4. Those born in the Middle East are a tiny fraction of all and new immigrants.
5. Rest of Europe includes countries not in the EU15 and A8 and includes Cyprus, Malta, Gibraltar, Turkey, Russia, Yugoslavia, Norway, Switzerland, Romania, Albania and a whole host of other small countries.
Source: LFS.

occupational ladder. Were we to look in finer detail, we would find that there is an exceptional concentration of migrants among health professionals, emphasizing the reliance of the National Health Service on migrant labour. Otherwise, there are particularly low levels of migrants in protective services and skilled agricultural workers. Aside from these, the noticeable feature of these data is how evenly migrants are spread across the occupations. This reflects the wide variety of migrant types working in the UK. These range from managers in multinational companies, England cricket captains,[3] senior academics, hospital consultants and investment bankers at the higher end to care workers, flower pickers, waiters and bar staff at the lower end.

In Figures 6.5 and 6.6, we see how the migrant distribution across occupations has shifted over the last decade. The proportion of migrants across all occupation groups has risen significantly but the shift has been more marked at the lower end. In Figure 6.6, we see how rapidly the proportion of new immigrants has risen in the lowest two occupations, which is a direct consequence of the surge of A8 migrants since 2004. While a good proportion of these are well-qualified graduates, many are working in unskilled occupations, often while improving their spoken English, before either returning to their home country or attempting to move up the occupational ladder.

[3] In the 21st century, the England team has been captained by an immigrant in around half the test matches. The captains concerned are Nasser Hussein, Kevin Pietersen and Andrew Strauss.

Table 6.2: Educational attainment of natives and immigrants in the UK

	2008					1997				
	All	UK born	Immigrants			All	UK born	Immigrants		
			All	Recent	New			All	Recent	New
Weighted count (millions)	38.9	33.5	5.3	1.8	0.5	35.9	32.8	3.1	0.6	0.2
Sample size (thousands)	286.9	251.2	35.6	11.3	3.0	359.2	329.9	29.2	5.2	1.8
Immigrants (%)	13.7			4.6	1.2	8.6			1.6	0.6
Average age (working age pop.)	39.6	39.9	37.4	30.0	28.4	38.9	38.9	39.3	29.7	28.5
Distribution of workers										
By age left full-time education (%)										
<16 (*Incomplete schooling*)	15	16	11	6	5	27	28	20	9	6
16–20 (*Completed secondary school*)	64	66	51	48	48	60	61	53	47	45
21+ (*Completed a degree*)	21	18	37	46	46	13	12	27	43	48
Employment patterns										
Employed	72.9	73.6	68.4	69.1	62.6	71.0	71.9	62.1	52.4	53.2
Inactive	22.8	22.2	26.5	25.8	31.0	23.6	22.9	30.9	39.1	39.0
Unemployment rate	5.6	5.4	7.0	6.8	9.2	7.0	6.8	10.1	14.0	12.8
Average basic hours worked	34.7	34.6	36.1	36.7	36.7	35.2	35.1	36.5	36.0	36.7
Average paid overtime hours	6.5	6.5	7.1	7.6	7.9	7.2	7.2	7.6	8.6	8.8

Notes:

1. Based on individuals aged 16–64.

2. 'Recent' immigrants are those who entered the UK in the survey year or four years before the survey was carried out.

3. 'New' immigrants are those who entered the UK in the survey year or the year before the survey was carried out.

4. Overtime hours are measured on the subset of people who work overtime. Those who do not work overtime are excluded from this calculation.

Source: LFS.

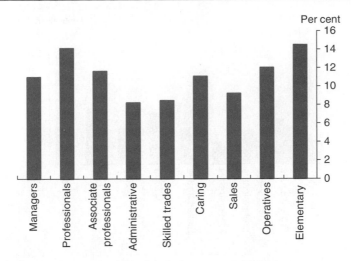

Figure 6.4: Immigrant–native ratio by occupation, one-digit classification (2004–2008)
Source: LFS and authors' calculations.

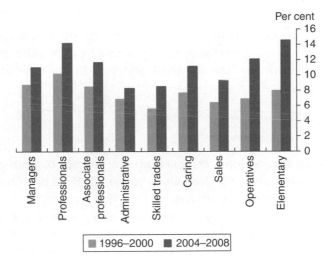

Figure 6.5: Immigrant–native ratio by occupation over time
Source: LFS and authors' calculations.

What does migration mean for the native born?

The rise in immigration over the last ten years is widely believed by the general public to have had large effects on the UK labour market. The stereotype of the Polish plumber—used widely as a symbol of cheap, but competent, labour—

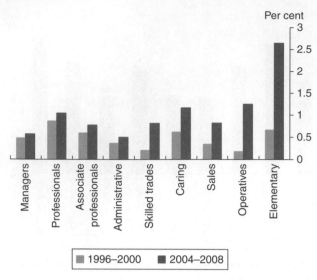

Figure 6.6: New immigrant–native ratio by occupation over time
Source: LFS and authors' calculations.

encapsulates the commonly held notion that immigrants are taking jobs from the native-born population, raising unemployment and holding down wages in the most affected jobs. The empirical evidence on this issue is, however, by no means clear cut.

Employment and unemployment

Comprehensive international evidence on the impact of immigration on unemployment is provided by Jean and Jimenez (2007). Based on panel data for 17 OECD economies, their analysis suggests that an increase in the number of immigrants equivalent to 1% of the labour force leads to the unemployment rate being, successively, 0.2, 0.3, 0.4 percentage points higher one, two and three years later, before fading away to a zero impact after around six years.

This is an average effect. Jean and Jimenez also find that the impact of strong employment protection laws is to slow down and extend the unemployment effects as a consequence of more sluggish employment adjustment. The extent of product market regulation is also important. A high degree of such regulation tends to magnify the unemployment effects throughout, essentially because the economy is slower to adjust to new sources of labour supply. By contrast, in the presence of very low levels of product market regulation, the unemployment effects of immigration are negligible. Since very low levels of such regulation rule in the UK, these results would lead us to expect little or no unemployment consequences of the surge in net migration over the last decade.

This is consistent with a number of more detailed UK studies. For example, Dustmann et al. (2005) find no significant impact of immigration on participation or unemployment and Lemos and Portes (2008) show that the surge of A8 migration from 2004 had no impact on claimant count unemployment, looking at the data by region, skill and age. This overall picture reflects that presented in the detailed survey in Blanchflower and Shadforth (2009).

Wage effects

The general consensus is that the wage effects of immigration in the UK are very small. (See the comprehensive summary in Lemos and Portes, 2008: 29.) Digging down a little, some negative effects of immigration on some wages have been noted. Manacorda et al. (2006) find negative wage effects for earlier migrants and Dustmann et al. (2007) present some adverse effects on the wages of those in unskilled jobs at the bottom of the pay distribution.

One important question is how is it that a surge of A8 migrants into unskilled jobs from 2004 appears to have had little impact on unemployment and wages. One possibility is that technology responds, so that there is a weaker adoption of advanced technology, which is complementary to skilled labour, in the presence of increasing numbers of unskilled. This would offset the wage effects of upward shifts in the proportion of workers competing for unskilled jobs. Beaudry et al. (2006) provide some US evidence in favour of this hypothesis.

Another possible explanation for the very small wage or unemployment effects of immigration is that migrants and natives are imperfect substitutes. This would attenuate the fall in demand for natives when the number of migrants rises. Manacorda et al. (2006) find that the elasticity of substitution between immigrants and natives in the UK is of the order of 5 to 7 which helps to explain the small wage effects of immigration on natives. The imperfect substitution model is based on the notion that firms, when facing native and immigrant wages in each education group, choose optimal numbers of natives and migrants to employ at each education level. As we noted in the Introduction, some 45% of UK migrants in the labour force in 2005 are UK citizens, having lived in the UK for many years, often since they were children. For this hypothesis and result to be valid, employers have to be able to distinguish between natives and migrants, and between UK citizens who are migrants and those who are not. If this is difficult, then any results generated by this model on the extent of substitution between natives and immigrants should be treated with some scepticism.[4]

Another problem with some of this work derives from the tendency to cut the data by education level. First, there is a problem of comparability and the difficulty of matching foreign and domestic qualifications. Second, for a variety of reasons, many recent immigrants work in occupations which are inconsistent with their apparent qualifications. For example, some 50% of A8 migrants with degrees work in unskilled occupations, compared with 2.8% of native born (see Wadsworth, 2009). A possible way around this problem is to focus on occupation rather than education level when searching for wage effects, though this approach itself may rely on testable assumptions.

A striking result, reported in Blanchflower and Shadforth (2009), is the relatively strong negative correlation across UK regions (–0.32) between the change in annual wage inflation from 2005 to 2006 and the change in the share of A8 migrants from 2004 to 2005 for those in unskilled occupations. Consistent with this is the finding in Nickell and Saleheen (2009) that while the overall impact of immigration on wages is very small, the effect of a 10 percentage point rise in the proportion of immigrants working in semi/ unskilled services (e.g. care homes, bars, shops, cleaning) leads to a 5.2% reduction in overall pay in this sector.

To summarise, the overall impact of the surge in immigration on the pay and employment of natives seems to have been relatively slight, although there is some evidence of a significant negative effect on the pay of natives in many unskilled occupations.[5]

The long-run effects of immigration

Given current immigration rules, it seems quite plausible that net migration into the UK will continue at an average rate in excess of 130K per annum once we emerge from the recession. Indeed the latest ONS projections are considerably higher than 130K, but these are mechanically based on the very strong recent trends. As we have seen, migrants are broadly spread across occupations with no particular bias in favour of high- or low-level occupations. Not surprisingly, therefore, the estimated impact on both GDP

---

[4] The same argument would appear to apply to the analysis of Ottaviano and Peri (2005) in the US, since around 40% of US immigrants were US citizens in 2005 and it would be difficult to distinguish between these and natives (of the same background). See OECD (2007, table I8).

[5] Immigrants in this sector earn around 6% less than natives, so a 10 percentage point rise in the proportion of immigrants will generate a 0.6% reduction in average wages solely because of the change in composition. So the vast majority of the 5.2% fall is not due to composition effects.

per capita and the government's budget tends to be very small and may be either positive or negative (see House of Lords, 2008, chapters 3 and 5).

So should we worry about continuing net migration at a historically high level? Since the direct long-term economic impact on the native or the existing population is relatively limited, whether or not we worry about immigration in the long run depends on whether or not we worry about the rate of increase in the population from whatever source. More people mean more houses, more schools, more roads, more power stations, more waste incinerators, more airport runways and so on. And the revealed preference of the existing population is that they dislike most of these things if they are built anywhere near where they live. There is, in fact, plenty of room, but this is not a view shared by many. For example, developed land in England occupies some 8.5% of the total land area. By contrast, some 54% of people surveyed in 2005 think that urban areas take up more than 50% of the land area![6] So, like it or not, the relatively high population density in England means that there will be serious problems generated by the rising housing and infrastructure requirements associated with the high rate of population growth generated by high rates of immigration. As a consequence, immigration policy will doubtless remain high on the political agenda for a long time to come.

References

Barker, K. (2006) *Barker Review of Land Use Planning*. London: The Stationary Office.

Beaudry, P., Davis, M. and Lewis, E. (2006) Endogenous skill bias in technology adoption: city level evidence from the IT revolution. Federal Reserve Bank of San Francisco Working Paper No. 06-24.

Blanchflower, D. G. and Shadforth, C. (2009) Fear, unemployment and migration. *Economic Journal, Features*, 119, February: F136–82.

Dustmann, C., Fabbri, F. and Preston, I. (2005) The impact of immigration on the British Labour Market. *Economic Journal, Features*, 115, November: F324–41.

—— Frattini, T. and Preston, I. (2007) A study of migrant workers and the National Minimum Wage and enforcement issues that arise. Low Pay Commission Report, available at <http://www.lowpay.gov.uk/lowpay/research/pdf/t0Z96GJX.pdf>.

House of Lords (2008) *The Economic Impact of Immigration, Volume I: Report*. Select Committee on Economic Affairs. London: The Stationery Office Limited.

IPPR (2007) *Britain's Immigrants: An Economic Profile*. London: Institute for Public Policy Research.

Jean, S. and Jimenez, M. (2007) The unemployment impact of immigration in OECD countries. OECD Economics Department Working Paper, No. 563.

---

[6] Ipsos Mori poll for the *Barker Review of Land Use Planning* (Barker, 2006).

Lemos, S. and Portes, J. (2008) New Labour? The impact of migration from central and eastern European countries on the UK labour market. IZA Discussion Paper No. 3756, October.

Manacorda, M., Manning, A. and Wadsworth, J. (2006) The impact of immigration on the structure of male wages: theory and evidence from Britain. IZA Discussion Paper No. 2352, October.

Nickell, S. and Saleheen, J. (2009) The impact of immigration on occupational wages: evidence from Britain. ESRC Spatial Economics Research Centre Discussion Paper No. 34.

OECD (2007) *International Migration Outlook*. Paris, OECD.

Ottaviano, G. and Peri, G. (2005) Rethinking the gains from immigration: theory and evidence from the US. NBER Working Paper No. 11672.

Wadsworth, J. (2009) Immigration and the labour market. Presented at the Workshop in honour of David Metcalf at LSE, 14 December 2009.

7

Job Tenure and Job Turnover

Giulia Faggio, Paul Gregg and Jonathan Wadsworth

Key findings

- Average job tenure has remained unchanged, subject to cyclical variation, for the last 25 years. The average duration of a job in progress is around five years. The average duration of a completed job is around ten years.
- Stability on aggregate disguises a significant fall in the long-term job share, which has been borne entirely by men.
- In contrast, average job tenure and the long-term job share among women has risen over time, concentrated on women with younger children. Maternity leave and other family-centred employment policies have facilitated these trends.
- While hiring rates and the short-term job share have fallen back recently, the evidence suggests that these movements are cyclical rather than secular.
- The chances of moving into work from non-employment have fallen considerably for men over time, but risen for woman. On this measure, the costs of job loss have worsened significantly for men.
- The cost of job loss as measured by the difference in wages before and after a job is lost also appears to have worsened in the recession.

Introduction

For some time now, the issue of job security has never remained far from the debate about labour market performance. Concerns are often aired about the end of the job for life, given increased use of outsourcing and competition from overseas. Measuring job security is problematic (see Green, Chapter 8). In this chapter, we take job tenure and job turnover as possible measures of job *stability*, since they are likely to be correlated with job security and look to see whether there is any evidence to suggest that the labour market has become more or less stable over time and if so why.

Figure 7.1 suggests that job stability has neither risen nor fallen over time. It traces the average (median) duration of jobs since 1985. While there may be a degree of cyclical variation, the average length of a job, at around five years, is little different now than 25 years ago. This is tenure of jobs in progress, so a simple extrapolation would indicate that the duration of all currently held jobs when completed will be approximately twice that of the duration of uncompleted tenure. This means that a job will last, on average, around ten years, much the same as it did in the early 1980s. Cyclical variation in job tenure means that job tenure tends to be shorter in good times, when there are more job opportunities around and individuals are willing and able to change jobs more frequently. As a result, average tenure falls. However, it is also clear from Figure 7.1 that job stability among men is much lower now than 20 years ago. Average job tenure for men has fallen by around 18 months, down by a third, since the mid-1980s. In contrast, among women job stability is rising, currently at nearly five years. Consequently the net result of these two opposing trends is that the average duration of a job has converged dramatically across the sexes over time. We return to the issue of job stability among different groups below.

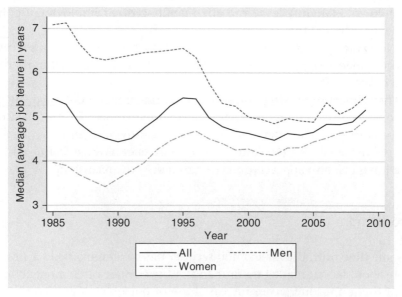

Figure 7.1: Trends in average job tenure
Source: LFS.

Long-term jobs

Since any changes in average job tenure will depend on a combination of changes in the share of both long-term and short-term jobs, we next look at the distribution of job tenure around this average. The distribution of job tenure reflects the history of engagements and separations and hence the timing of previous recessions or booms. In good times, there are lots of job opportunities, so hiring rates go up, voluntary job-to-job moves rise, whilst layoffs fall. As a result, the short-term job share rises. In bad times, hiring rates fall and there are more layoffs than quits among those with a job. So the short-term job share tends to fall and the long-term share tends to rise in bad times. Alongside these cyclical movements, the job distribution is also shaped by any secular trends that are changing the nature of work and hence the relative shares of short- and long-term jobs.

The share of long-term jobs (defined here as jobs that have lasted at least ten years) depends, in part, on the age distribution of the population. Since young people cannot be in long-term jobs then shifts in the age distribution can affect comparisons of long-term job tenure over time. In the UK the average age of employees has increased by around three years over time due to a combination of changes in the size of birth cohorts, increased immigration, increased staying-on rates in tertiary education and possible shifts in hiring rates against younger people (see Goujard et al., Chapter 3). To try to net these effects out, we calculate the long-term (ten years +) job share on the population aged 35 and over. Figure 7.2 and Table 7.1 show that the long-term job share appears to have been in steady decline for 25 years and that this is almost entirely concentrated on men. Over this period, the average long-term job share has fallen by around 8 points to 38% of those over 35 years of age and in work. The male long-term job share fell from 57% to 41% between 1985 and 2009. The female long-term job share grew from 32% to 35% over the same period.

Table 7.1 also shows that these trends appear to be broadly the same across different skill groups, as measured by educational attainment. While the long-term job share for men has fallen for all age groups, the share among men aged 35–44 appears to have fallen more in the last decade than the long-term job share among older men. Just 32% of men aged 35–44 are now in a job that has lasted for at least ten years, compared to 49% of men aged 55–64. So it would seem that the chances of younger (male) workers moving into a long-term job are much lower now than in the past. These trends are not unique. Farber (2008) suggests that similar trends can be found in the US labour market.

In contrast, the long-term job share among women is rising among younger women and women with young children and is, broadly, stable among older

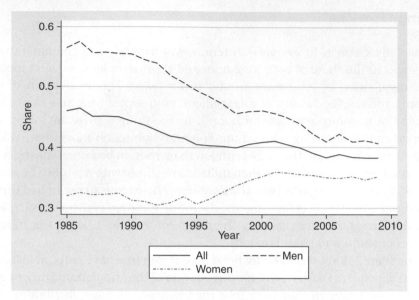

Figure 7.2: Long-term jobs over time
Source: LFS.

Table 7.1: Long-term jobs in the UK over time

	% share among all employees aged 35+				
	1985	1989	1993	2001	2009
All	46.1	45.1	41.9	41.1	38.3
Men	56.5	55.5	52.0	45.6	40.7
High Quals	57.1	56.1	51.6	45.6	40.6
Low Quals	55.6	55.4	52.3	45.9	41.9
Age 35–44	48.3	48.4	45.2	40.5	31.9
Age 45–54	60.7	59.2	57.4	50.2	45.3
Age 55–64	64.5	64.0	56.0	48.4	48.8
Women	32.1	32.5	30.9	35.9	35.2
High Quals	36.7	34.8	33.6	38.1	37.4
Low Quals	30.5	31.2	29.3	34.2	33.4
Age 35–44	18.4	19.1	21.3	26.7	27.3
Age 45–54	41.1	41.5	35.7	41.9	37.8
Age 55–64	53.8	57.4	51.7	51.7	50.8
Children <5	9.2	11.0	16.8	21.8	17.0

Source: LFS.

women. The trend toward increased stability among younger women may be linked to the increased use of maternity leave and family-friendly work practices (see Burgess et al., 2008). Certainly, as Table 7.1 shows, long-term job share has risen among women with young children, at least until the middle of the decade, since when it has fallen back somewhat. The right to extended maternity leave reduces any tension between a desire to stay at home with younger children and a desire to stay attached to the labour market. Job tenure rises as a result.

Short-term jobs

On average, every year around 4 million employees, one in seven, begin a new job. New jobs can be a path into a long-term job. Sometimes it takes several jobs before a good match is found and so the process of job shopping may take time. There might be concerns about the efficiency of the job-matching process, however, if the share of short-term jobs were to rise. This could suggest that it was taking longer to find a good match. Some care is needed here, because, as we show below, the short-term job share varies considerably over the cycle. Table 7.2 and Figure 7.3 show that there have been times when nearly one in five employees have been in jobs for less than one year. This was observed at the end of the 1980s upswing in 1989 and again in 2001. During labour market downturns, the share of short-term jobs falls below one in six. The most recent data for 2009 look very similar to the trough in hiring experienced at the end of the recession of the early 1990s. However, despite this cyclical variation, it is hard to say that there is any trend in the share of short-term jobs.

Table 7.2: Short-term jobs in the UK over time

	% share among all employees				
	1985	1989	1993	2001	2009
All	18.5	21.1	15.3	20.5	14.9
Men	15.4	17.8	13.4	19.4	14.2
High Quals	14.6	16.3	12.7	18.4	14.2
Low Quals	16.8	19.5	14.3	21.9	14.2
Age 16–24	37.2	37.5	30.6	45.6	35.6
Age 25–34	15.0	19.8	14.0	22.8	16.8
Age 35–44	8.9	12.0	9.8	14.4	10.6
Age 45–54	6.9	8.3	8.2	11.3	8.8
Age 55–64	4.5	7.4	7.5	10.4	7.8
UK-born	15.3	17.7	13.3	18.9	13.6
Women	22.8	25.2	17.4	21.6	15.7
High Quals	22.9	25.0	17.5	21.6	16.5
Low Quals	23.6	25.3	17.5	20.9	14.9
Age 16–24	40.0	42.3	33.1	48.6	37.7
Age 25–34	26.0	28.4	20.4	25.3	19.4
Age 35–44	19.1	21.9	14.9	17.9	12.6
Age 45–54	9.8	12.7	9.3	12.3	9.3
Age 55–64	5.7	8.4	6.5	8.3	6.1
Children <5	39.7	40.0	25.9	23.3	16.5

Source: LFS.

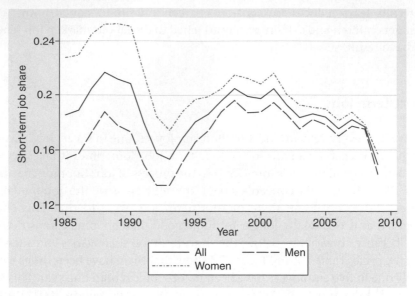

Figure 7.3: Short-term jobs over time
Source: LFS.

The share of short-term jobs among women has, since measurement became possible, always been higher than among men. As with long-term jobs, over time there has been a narrowing of the difference in the share of short-term jobs across gender. Again the decline in the short-term job share is particularly marked among women with younger children, down from 40% in 1985 to 17% in 2009. There is, perhaps surprisingly, little difference in short-term job shares by education. The short-term job share is much higher for younger workers. More than 40% of workers aged 16–24 have been in a job for less than one year, on average, compared to less than one in ten workers aged 55 and over. This decline by age is similar for men and women. The cyclical volatility in the short-term job share is also much more pronounced for younger workers, indicating that younger workers are often at the margin of hiring decisions. Again there is little evidence of any secular change in the short-term job pattern for younger workers, or indeed any age group, over time. Nor does this basic pattern change if we disaggregate by age and qualifications (results not shown).

Another issue is that rising immigration (see Nickell and Saleheen, Chapter 6) may have introduced increased competition for jobs and this will be reflected in a fall in the short-term job share among UK-born individuals if they are losing out to immigrants. In Table 7.1 there is no evidence to suggest that this is the case. The short-term job share for UK-born men has a similar cyclical variation in the period before immigration began rising as in the period after, but shows no evidence of any long-term trend.

Overall, the fact that, at a given stage in the cycle, the short-term job share does not appear to have changed much over time, suggests that workers may not be taking longer to find a good job match (if they were, the short-term job share may be rising at any given age).

It is sometimes argued that workers in temporary jobs are at the margin of labour market adjustment, since it is easier and cheaper for firms to fire workers on temporary contracts or supplied by an agency. So another proxy for job instability is the share of temporary jobs in the economy. As Figure 7.4 shows, there is very little evidence that the share of temporary jobs has changed much over the past 25 years. Around 5% of those in employment are in temporary work. There may be a cyclical element to some of the (small) changes observed over time. The share of temporary jobs appears to rise at the onset of any recovery in the labour market and fall at the end of recovery and onset of recession. This suggests that firms may offer more temporary jobs when the prospect of sustained recovery is still uncertain and then take on more permanent workers thereafter.

In 1998 the Labour government signed up to the European Social Chapter that increased protection from unfair dismissal for workers between one and two years in post. Economists have long debated the effects of employment protection legislation. On the one hand, the costs or difficulty in firing someone are increased. On the other hand, employers will be more wary in hiring staff because of the increased costs of any subsequent layoff. Marinescu (2009)

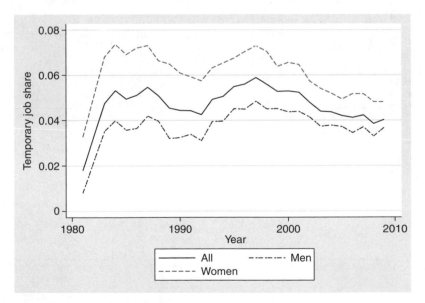

Figure 7.4: The share of temporary jobs
Source: LFS.

looks at the impact of the legislative change on firm behaviour. First, she demonstrates that the new legislation saw a sharp reduction in the layoff rate of staff with one to two years' tenure. Second, and more importantly, she shows that those with less than one year of job tenure also saw less frequent dismissal in the period after the legislation was in place. This suggests that firms took more care to improve the matching process, rather than sack more workers as they approached the one-year threshold that would trigger increased redundancy payoffs. She also suggests that the changes in behaviour were focused on less educated workers and that this did not lead to increased durations of unemployment.

Job flows

Another way to study job stability is to look at the flows into and out of work. This can be used to help judge whether there have been any changes in the cost of job loss. If it takes longer to get back into work following job loss then it may be argued that this aspect of the cost of job loss has risen, other things equal. Figure 7.5 graphs the annual flows between employment and

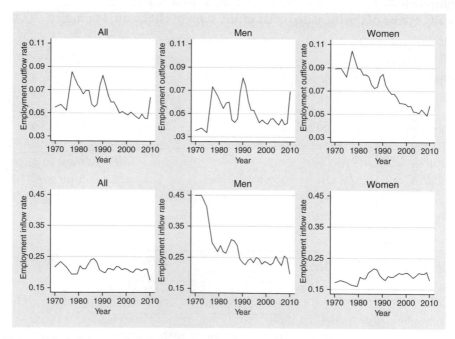

Figure 7.5: Labour market flows over time
Source: LFS.

non-employment over time. The top row records the yearly flows out of employment and the second row gives the flows into employment.

The first thing to notice is that the flows out of employment, proxying the rate of job loss, are lower than in the past, given the state of the cycle. The average annual outflow rate from employment is around 6%. So, on average, one in 17 of those in work will not be in work one year later. In a recession these outflows rise above 8%, to nearly one in 12. In the latest recession, the outflow rate remained well below 7%. Once again these aggregate patterns disguise contrasting patterns by gender. While outflows for men in the latest recession are similar to those in previous recessions, the outflow rate for women in the latest recession was much lower than in the past. In this aspect, the recession was centred on men.

The aggregate inflow into work (bottom panel of Figure 7.5) shows little change over time. While these flows do not capture moves made by individuals who lose work and find work within a year, this average pattern suggests that this aspect of the cost of job loss, capturing the speed at which individuals return to work, may have changed little over time.

The charts also help explain the convergence of job tenure between men and women over the last 30 years. For women, the chances of becoming workless have fallen markedly, from being sharply higher than for men to being lower in the latest recession. Job loss in the recession has been heavily focused on men. By contrast, job entry patterns for men and women are quite similar now, whereas in the past men secured employment far more quickly than women did. This represents the shift in economic inactivity away from women for reasons of looking after children, toward men, mainly for reasons of poor health and early retirement observed in Gregg and Wadsworth, Chapter 2. Since job loss among men has not changed much over time, the fall in male job tenure documented earlier in this chapter is due to more frequent job-to-job moves. However, once out of work, returning again has become more difficult for many men. For women job tenure is rising because of less frequent job loss, rather than fewer job-to-job moves. The rate as women enter work has remained the same over time. On this basis, the cost of job loss has risen for men and fallen for women.

Wage costs of job loss

Another way to assess the cost of job loss is to compare the average wage of those who leave work for a spell of non-employment (exit wage) and compare this to the average wage of those who move into work after a spell of non-employment (entry wage). If the typical exit wage is bigger than the typical entry wage, then this is one way to measure the cost of job loss. If the gap

Table 7.3: The wage cost of job loss

	Exit hourly wage (in 2009 £)	Exit wage as % of median wage	Entry hourly wage (in 2009 £)	Entry wage as % of median wage
All				
1998	5.70	22	5.50	18
2001	6.60	24	6.10	19
2005	7.10	25	6.70	22
2009	7.90	32	7.20	23
Men 25–54				
1998	8.00	45	5.60	30
2001	8.80	45	8.00	36
2005	8.70	39	7.50	27
2009	9.10	42	8.40	34

Source: LFS. Authors' calculations.

between the exit wage and entry wage rises over time, then it could be argued that the cost of job loss has increased. Table 7.3 shows that for most of the last decade, exit wages were a little higher than entry wages, suggesting only a small pecuniary cost of job loss, for those who managed to find work. The typical wage of those who move into work after a spell of non-employment, is around the 20th percentile of the wage distribution. The typical wage of those who leave a job and experience non-employment is around the 25th percentile of the wage distribution. For prime-age men, the cost of job loss is much higher. Wages lost are typically higher up in the wage distribution, but wages on offer are much lower in the wage distribution. There is, also, some indication that the cost of job loss may have risen during the latest recession. This is because the exit wage has risen, presumably because layoffs bite further up the wage distribution, while the entry wage has remained much the same as in the past. Hence the gap between exit and entry wages has grown.

Conclusions

It seems clear that jobs are much less stable and long lasting for men than they were in the past. While short-term job share or the rate of job loss have not changed much over time for men, the chances of moving into work from non-employment and the chances of moving into a long-term job have deteriorated. This is not a new development, rather it is the consequence of a series of underlying shifts that have changed the nature of jobs in which men work. In contrast, the stability of jobs for many women has risen over time. Recessions seem to reduce an individual's job survival chances higher up the wage distribution. Since wages on offer appear to be less affected by the cycle, the cost of job loss may also have risen during a recession.

References

Burgess, S., Gregg, P., Propper, C. and Washbrook, E. (2008) Maternity rights and mothers' return to work. *Labour Economics*, 15(2): 168–201.

Farber, H. (2008) Employment insecurity: the decline in worker–firm attachment in the United States. Princeton University Industrial Relations Section Working Paper No. 530.

Goujard, A., Petrongolo, B. and Van Reenen, J. (2011) The labour market for young people. In: Gregg, P. and Wadsworth, J. (eds.) *The Labour Market in Winter: The State of Working Britain*. Oxford: Oxford University Press.

Green, F. (2011) Job quality in Britain under the Labour government. In: Gregg, P. and Wadsworth, J. (eds.) *The Labour Market in Winter: The State of Working Britain*. Oxford: Oxford University Press.

Gregg, P. and Wadsworth, J. (2011) Unemployment and inactivity. In: Gregg, P. and Wadsworth, J. (eds.) *The Labour Market in Winter: The State of Working Britain*. Oxford: Oxford University Press.

Marinescu, I. (2009) Job security legislation and job duration: evidence from the United Kingdom. *Journal of Labor Economics*, 27(3): 465–86.

Nickell, S. and Saleheen, J. (2011) Immigration in the UK. In: Gregg, P. and Wadsworth, J. (3) (eds.) *The Labour Market in Winter: The State of Working Britain*. Oxford: Oxford University Press.

Part II
Job Quality

8

Job Quality in Britain under the Labour Government

Francis Green

Key findings

Extrinsic aspects of job quality have improved significantly since 1997 but there remains much still to be done to improve intrinsic job design.

The plus points are that:

- pay is higher in real terms;
- hours of work have fallen and paid holiday rights extended almost throughout the workforce;
- practices to improve employees' work–life balance have become more widely available.

However, on the negative side:

- while skills have been rising, neither the supply of nor the demand for skills are expanding fast enough to meet 2020 targets set for Britain's workplaces to be among the most skilled;
- managers have afforded lower discretion for employees to control the tasks they do;
- the work intensification of the early 1990s has levelled off since 1997, but there has been no reduction in work intensity and workplace stress remains a serious problem.

Introduction

Throughout the 1980s and for most of the 1990s, reducing unemployment and job insecurity was the most pressing labour market issue. In the late 1990s, however, a new agenda was added to the public discourse: the need for improved job quality. This change was already evident in the emphasis the new Labour government had given in its manifesto to introducing a national minimum wage. Yet job quality relies on much more than pay and the large majority of the workforce was not in any case directly affected by the minimum wage. By the start of the millennium both the government and international agencies such as the Organisation for Economic Cooperation and Development (OECD) had joined in a call for 'more and better jobs'. In this chapter I will review how job quality has fared in Britain since 1997.

One reason why policy makers thought that it was important to improve jobs was because they were aiming to raise the employment rate. Although unemployment had been falling for some time, there remained too many households where no one was in work. Economically inactive workers could more easily be persuaded to take up paid work if the available jobs were both intrinsically rewarding and paid well enough. There was also a wider concern with many aspects of job quality among the working public of Britain, which was essentially the product of increasing affluence. The country as a whole was much wealthier than in the 1970s, the last time that Labour had been in government. Yet, arguably, there was a sense in which this affluence had not resulted in better or more fulfilling work lives. Indeed, there were public pressure points awaiting attention, including the intensification of work and an accompanying rise in cases of stress, and the demands for an improved balance between work and personal lives.

Another reason why 'quality' came to the fore lies in the very ambiguity which the word denotes: it could be made to seem desirable from different perspectives. From the employers' viewpoint, the quality of work came to refer to how effectively their employees worked, in respect of their organisational objectives, virtually synonymous with 'productivity'. The quality of work therefore came to be integral to the competitiveness agenda. A key ingredient of quality in this interpretation is the worker's skill. Since more skilled work is generally intrinsically rewarding for the worker, training and other means of raising skills are important from everyone's point of view. But, from the employees' perspective a number of other aspects of working life are also relevant: fair pay, a reasonable pace of work, autonomy, a decent work-life balance, and security. Each of these aspects of working life is related to, and matters a lot for, human need; and there is substantial evidence demonstrating their links with well-being at the workplace.

The forces for change

What has job quality got to do with government? In Britain, the Labour government assumed a certain role for the state in the determination of several aspects of job quality, through the creation of employment rights and regulations, and through influencing the institutions that frame the labour market. However, it also adhered to the liberal maxim that the relationship between employer and employee is a private matter, and that government should intervene only where it is able to redress socially detrimental inequalities or differences between private and social costs or benefits.

Whatever the government does, the trajectory of job quality depends on developments in the economy and in the practices of employers. The key changes in the wider economy that ultimately affect job quality are the increasing extent of global competition, and the computer-driven technological revolution. The former drives employers based in Britain to seek ways of competing with the newly rising economies of China, India and Eastern Europe, as well as their older competitors. Innovation, creativity and moving to high value-added production are typically argued to be the only ways to compete in areas of intensive internationally driven competition and potential offshoring. This puts pressure on jobs to become more skilled, but perhaps also to be lower paid and with inferior working conditions. Technological changes also favour high-skilled workers.

Changes in work organisation are also found to be especially important for the quality of work life. For example, policies to make jobs more 'flexible' have been found to be associated with increments in work intensity. However, managers have considerable scope to choose how work is organised. One development in management culture affecting work organisation is the focus on 'high involvement work practices'—engaging the worker more closely with the organisation both psychologically with emotional and social bonds and economically with material incentives. Opening up new and effective channels for communication between workers and managers, and performance-related pay, are typical examples of this approach to management. While this approach has become more prevalent, it is not widespread. Although the evidence is not yet in that could convince an impartial jury, the approach is found in some studies, not all of the highest standard, to be highly beneficial for an organisation's performance. There remains much more controversy about whether it is beneficial for employees. If new practices raise their skills, employees benefit; however, 'high performance' may also be accompanied by work intensification. In part because of this ambivalence, and also because of the considerable leeway that managers have in how to run their businesses, there are no set imperatives about how work quality will change.

The Labour government stepped in to influence a number of key aspects of job quality since 1997. New employment regulations were enacted on several occasions, in most instances at the behest of directives from the European Commission, to which the government would consent through a process of political negotiation with EU partners. In addition to the National Minimum

113

Wage (see Machin, Chapter 11, this volume), key pieces of regulation have governed working time and holiday rights (1998), employees' entitlement to information about the organization they work for (2004), the fair treatment of part-time workers (2000) and the fair treatment of workers on fixed-term contracts (2002). Temporary agency work was also originally intended to be covered, but agreement for regulation of this type of work was held up several years. Eventually an accord was reached in 2008 between the Confederation of British Industry and the Trades Union Congress, paving the way for the Agency Workers Directive and, from October 2011, entitlement to a qualified parity with other workers after 12 weeks in any job. Rights to parental leave were introduced in 1999, while subsequent years saw the introduction of paid paternity leave, extended periods of maternity leave and rights to emergency leave. Finally, responding to pressure for an improved work-life balance, the government introduced in 2003 the right to request flexible working for parents, and extended it to carers for adults in 2007. In this typically British compromise, employers have a duty to seriously consider such requests, but not to concede them.

The key institutional changes have been the restoration of some organising rights for trade unions via the Employment Relations Act 1999, which may have helped to stem the decline in trade union representation (see Bryson and Forth, Chapter 17) and the reorganisation of the skill formation institutions of Britain. As is often lamented, the vocational training and education system is frequently changed, and the decade has seen both the creation and the demise of the Learning and Skills Council (LSC). However, of potentially lasting importance for job quality has been the setting up in 2002 of the system of Sector Skills Councils (SSCs), which aimed to facilitate and persuade employers to make the market for training in their own spheres. From 2008 a new overarching body, the UK Commission for Employment and Skills (UKCES), gained responsibility for providing central advice to government on the development of the skills system, for overseeing the SSCs, and for the 'Investors in People' badge. The UKCES's origins stemmed from the Leitch review in 2006, which advanced the opinion that the skills system needed to be more 'demand-led'; and though the national targets Leitch set for Britain's workers to become very much more skilled by 2020 were essentially supply-side targets, the UKCES's perspective has taken the demand-side deficiencies or the UK economy very seriously.

What has been the overall outcome of these various forces for change during the last decade? In the rest of this chapter I review what we know in four key areas: pay, working hours and work-life balance, skills, autonomy and work intensification.

Key aspects of job quality

Pay

Pay is arguably the most important aspect of job quality: it both determines how far jobs can satisfy material needs, and affects workers' sense of self-worth and respect. It is sometimes taken for granted that pay will increase in real terms in a growing economy. However, pay can stagnate if limited growth is accompanied by shifting income shares away from labour towards capital. Moreover, pay can rise at very different rates for different sections of the population. For example, in large sections of the US workforce, pay was unchanged or fell between the 1970s and the late 1990s.

The period between 1997 and 2009 has seen a real increase in pay at all levels of the spectrum (see Figure 8.1), and everyone's job quality has improved in this respect. At £11.03 in 2009, median pay had risen by 15% in real terms since 1997. At the bottom end of the spectrum, pay rose at the 10th percentile by 20%, which appears to be testimony to the impact of the NMW in narrowing the gap between the low-paid and those immediately above them. At the top end of the spectrum, real wages rose by 18%, also faster than at the median. Thus, over the period there has been little change in overall pay inequality, with some reductions at one end, some stretching at the other.

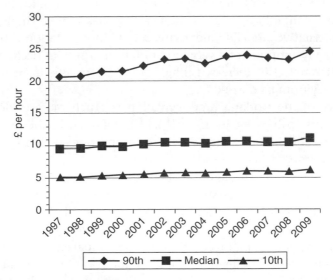

Figure 8.1: Real wages, 1997–2009

Notes: Hourly pay of all employees, indexed to 2009 prices: 10th, 50th and 90th percentiles.
Source: ASHE.

115

Not revealed in Figure 8.1, however, are the much more rapid changes that have taken place at the 95th percentile of the pay distribution and above. At these heights pay is often in highly valued stocks or other forms. An indication of the changes at the very top can be seen through examination of changes in the median pay of CEOs: according to one recent estimate, their pay rose by 161% between 1988 and 2005 (Mishel et al., 2008: 222). Thus business leaders have experienced enormous rises in this aspect of their job quality. The change in their rewards is easily the most dramatic pay story of the last two decades.

Work–life balance

Consider next another positive story. There have been some distinct improvements to work–life balance, providing some relief from the pressures which work places on family and other areas of life. One basic indicator is the proportion of employees working long hours. As can be seen in Figure 8.2, the percentage of males putting in more than 45 hours a week fell from 38% in 1997 to 28% by 2009—a substantial change. This decline has been linked to the European Directive on Working Time, which limits workers to a maximum of 48 hours a week averaged over 17 weeks. However, even though the legislation is thought to have a real effect in certain high profile cases (such as junior doctors), this causal link is not established in general. Working hours peaked in 1995–6, well before the legislation took effect; and the ability of workers to voluntarily opt out of the Directive has limited the legislation's bite. An alternative, arguably more satisfactory, interpretation is that falling hours were a resumption of a very long-run, if intermittent decline since the 19th century, reflecting increased affluence and a consequent greater demand for time away from paid work.

The force of the working time regulation is much more evident in the improvements to be seen in annual paid holiday entitlements, shown in Figures 8.3(a) and 8.3(b). As can be seen, the proportions with no paid holiday entitlement dropped very considerably after 1999 when the full force of the regulation took effect. Through the 2000s the average length of entitlement also rose. It could expect to be stimulated further from the end of the decade as the regulation entitlement expanded from 20 days to 24 days in 2007 and 28 days in 2009 (or part-time equivalents) in order to encompass public holidays. Unsurprisingly, not all employees take their full annual entitlement: in 2006 a quarter did not, and for one in four of these the reason was pressure of work (Hooker et al., 2007: 33–4). Nevertheless non-take-up of leave because of work pressure was less than in 2003. As far as holidays are concerned, then, the changes have been unambiguously positive. The most distinct beneficiaries

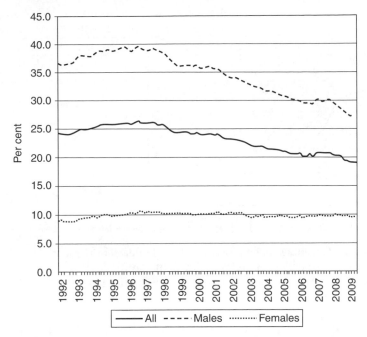

Figure 8.2: Percentage of employed people working more than 45 hours per week
Source: LFS.

have been those working in low-paid service industries, predominantly female workers.

Other improvements may be even more important. From the end of the 1990s there appears to have been a step change in the norms that describe and determine work–life balance. The proportions of workplaces that permitted flexi-time working, switching to part-time work, nine-day fortnights or four-and-a-half day weeks, job-sharing and homeworking all increased between 1998 and 2004 (see Figure 8.4). Between 2003 and 2006 we know also that the proportion of employees offered no flexible working time arrangement fell from 15% to 10% (ibid. 61–2). Thus the large majority of workers are now able in some way to work flexibly, though in 2006 only 56% took advantage. These rises in provision have been accompanied by a change in employer attitudes, with fewer believing that work–life balance was solely the individual's responsibility (Kersley et al., 2006: 273). In the two Work–Life Balance surveys of employers conducted in 2003 and 2006, the employers were found to generally favour work–life-balance policies, and (especially the larger ones) to believe that the benefits in terms of performance outweighed their costs. Even among those employers who reported that the 2003

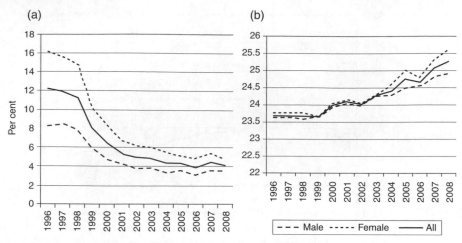

Figure 8.3(a): Percentage of employees with no holiday entitlement
(b): Employees' annual paid holiday entitlement (days)

Notes: All employees reporting any holidays; excludes Public Holidays.
Source: QLFS.

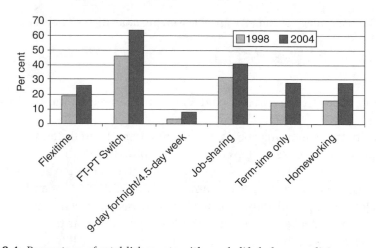

Figure 8.4: Percentage of establishments with work–life balance policies

Notes: Applies to continuing establishments, with at least 25 employees.
Source: WERS, 1998 and 2004 (Kersley et al., 2006: 254).

flexible working requirements had raised their costs, only a third believed that costs had risen more than the benefits.

To some extent, the government's legislation on flexibility, and on leave rights, has been swimming with the tide of opinion, rather than initiating change. But a case can also be advanced that the legislation helped to embed attitudinal changes, and enabled some doors to be opened. The 'right to request' legislation illustrates this latter point: although the 2002 Employment Act imposed no obligation on employers to grant flexible hours arrangements, some 17% of employees made requests in the two years leading up to February–March 2006, and of these 78% were fully or partially accepted by their bosses (Hooker et al., 2007: 54–8). It is hard, however, to establish scientifically what would have happened in the absence of legislation, and this has not been done.

Skills

So far I have dwelt on extrinsic aspects of job quality. I now focus on important intrinsic features of work in Britain. For these the story is less positive.

A high level of skill is desirable both for productivity and for job quality, and there is little doubt that the level of skills being used in UK jobs has been increasing steadily. Figure 8.5 shows four indicators of this trend. Between 1997 and 2006 there were distinct rises in the proportions of jobs requiring graduate skills, and high levels of literacy skills, influence skills (persuading, instructing and so on) and computing skills. Use of these skills

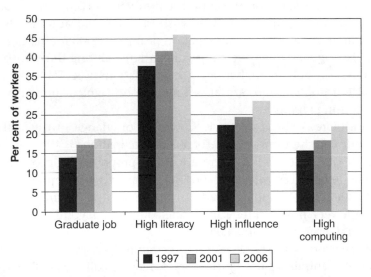

Figure 8.5: High skills requirements in British jobs, 1997–2006

Notes: Graduate job: degree or better needed to get job. High literacy: reading and writing activities average between 'very important' and 'essential'. High influence: influence/communication activities average between 'very important' and 'essential'. High computing: computer use at complex or advanced levels. For details see Felstead et al. (2007).

Source: The 1997, 2001 and 2006 Skills Surveys.

rose within each occupation, and also resulted from an evolutionary structural change towards higher skilled occupations. The rise since 1997 is part of a longer trend, can be projected to continue and indicates a positive outlook for job quality. Similarly, there have been substantial rises in the qualification levels of the UK workforce, and these are also predicted to continue rising for the foreseeable future. For example, in 2007, 31% of working age people were qualified to Level 4 or above. According to forecasts derived from demographic trends, this proportion will rise to 41% by 2020 (UKCES, 2009: 59).

Yet two prominent signs that skill transformation of workers and jobs is too slow in Britain may be noted. First, looking at the supply side, the rate of change can be gauged by comparing the qualifications of the 45 to 54-year-old and 25 to 34-year-old cohorts: a large difference implies greater change in the stock of qualifications as cohorts grow older. Yet the differences are rather small in Britain. For example, the younger cohort's secondary level proportion is roughly 10 percentage points higher in the UK, but in France the difference is 22 points. So after 20 years, the education level of the older French workforce will have improved substantially more than that of the older British workforce. This example is repeated for other countries, and as a result the UK is projected to move down the rankings of the OECD as measured by the qualifications of its workforce. There has also been no serious transformation in employees' participation in skill formation within companies that might have served to make up for the relative shortfalls in education levels. Work-related education or training participation peaked in 2000 for males, 2006 for females (see Figure 8.6) and remains concentrated among those with greater prior education and in higher-ranking occupations (see Table 8.1). While informal learning is important also, there are no signs at present that this activity is rising rapidly.

Second, there is also a relatively slow pace of change in the skills being demanded. The rise in prevalence of skilled occupations is the third slowest among all OECD countries. There are rising proportions of 'overqualified' employees (employees with education levels above what employers ask for) (UKCES, 2009: 113–22). In comparison with most other countries in Europe, fewer employers in Britain tend to require education beyond the compulsory stage from their recruits (Green, 2009).

For these reasons it is predicted that the 'ambition' set out by the government's Leitch enquiry to become a 'world leader' in skills by 2020, will not on current trends be achieved (UKCES, 2009: 54–61). To do so, there would need to be both a rise in the rate of acquisition of educational achievements, especially at intermediate levels, and a step change in employers' strategies which would lead to increased utilisation of skills in the workplace.

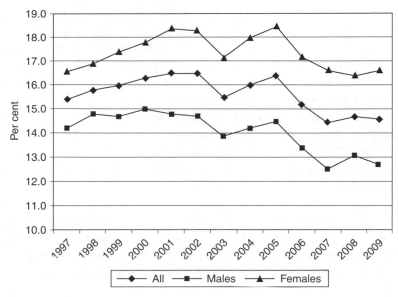

Figure 8.6: Percentage receiving work-related education or training, 1997–2009

Notes: UK employees, over a four-week reference period: men aged 16–64 and women aged 16–59; 2nd quarter, not seasonally adjusted.

Source: LFS.

Table 8.1: Training of employees by education level and by occupation class: participation in work-related education or training over four weeks, April–June 2009

Highest education level	%	Occupational class	%
Level 4 (equiv. to degree) and above	19.5	Higher managerial and professional	17.0
Level 3 (equiv. to A-level)	15.6	Lower managerial and professional	17.0
Trade apprenticeships	8.5	Intermediate occupations	12.4
Level 2 (equiv. to GCSE)	13.7	Lower supervisory and technical	12.0
Below Level 2	11.2	Semi-routine occupations	11.3
Other qualifications	8.9	Routine occupations	6.1
No qualifications	3.7		

Source: LSF.

Autonomy

For the employer, autonomy in the workplace is a two-faced affair. No employer can, or should even aspire to, control everything that an employee does. Apart from the fact that this is not feasible, and that therefore work contracts are always open-ended, the employee's initiatives and close knowledge of the workplace frontier are key resources to be harnessed for the organisation's purposes. This value from the worker's discretion over job tasks applies equally in the public and private sectors. It is likely to be greater where tasks are more complex, and hence more skilled, but even in the simplest occupations there remains a utility from giving employees their head. On the other hand, few employers will want to give their employees complete auton- omy to do what they want. Workers' tasks have to be managed, and their performance monitored, to meet organisational objectives. And so there is a balance to be struck, as to how much leeway employees are afforded. There is quite some variation in the way that managers strike this balance, depending on their cultural approaches, the loyalty and commitment of employees, the skills of the job and so on (Green, 2008).

This balance is very important, since it goes to the heart of the intrinsic quality of jobs in many occupations: for work to be meaningful the worker has to be able to approach it in a human way as its subject, not as an object following precise orders or rules all the time, as if waiting to be replaced by a computing machine. Work scientists have also established this connection empirically: workplace autonomy is strongly and robustly associated with health and well-being, and its beneficial effect is found to be especially strong in jobs that require hard and intensive work. So what has been happening to workplace autonomy in Britain?

We can measure workplace autonomy, using representative surveys of people's jobs across Britain. Figure 8.7 presents the 'Task Discretion Index', which sums up the extent to which employees can affect their daily tasks— what they do, how they do them, how fast they do them and to what standard. More skilled occupations tend to have higher autonomy, with managers unsurprisingly having the highest level on average, and elementary occupations the least. Yet, despite rising skills, there has been a substantial decline in the level of autonomy, between 1992 and 2006, signalling an unfortunate drop in this aspect of job quality. The decline began to level off at the end of the 1990s, especially in the private sector. The latter period then saw a convergence between the sectors. The declines have taken place across all occupations, but have been relatively high at either end of the spectrum; among elementary occupations but also among professionals.

We do not know for certain what the underlying causes of this decline in workplace autonomy in Britain are, since the decline does not appear to be related to any measurable factors associated with changing technology or organisational characteristics. Studies suggest that, in some instances, the decline may be associated with increased subcontracting (contractors may be compensating for the arm's-length nature of the market contract by specifying and closely monitoring the products and services provided); and in the public sector it has been conjectured that the decline is associated with the promi- nence of the use of targets (Gallie et al., 2004). In Britain, with its emphasis on

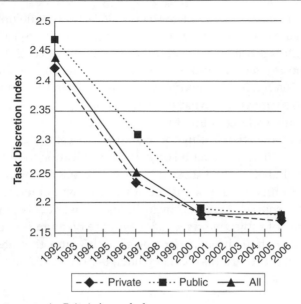

Figure 8.7: Autonomy in Britain's workplaces
Source: Employment in Britain, 1992; UK Skills Surveys 1997, 2001 and 2006 (Felstead et al., 2007).

liberal market principles, the development of the management of labour has been largely independent of government; except that, in its own backyard, the state's public sector managers have travelled along the same road, and in the faster lane. The decline is likely to be associated with changes in management culture which, as noted above, is an important factor that determines the amount of leeway for and trust in employees. However, management culture is one of those important variables that are hard to measure, and we do not have any reliable and representative indicators over time. One reason for attributing the decline to something as nebulous as management culture is that it is likely to vary across countries with differing histories and institutions, unlike technological factors which are broadly similar in advanced economies. Workplace autonomy has been changing in different directions across Europe, with increases being cited in Finland and Norway, for example, declines in Spain as well as the UK, and broad stability across the European Union as a whole.

Work effort

Declining autonomy is a worrying development, because it takes away something that is very important for people, to find some fulfilment in their working lives. Of course, this is only an average tendency, and there remain

123

many who succeed in this way. However, reduced personal control also has another consequence—especially if it is linked in with high work effort—namely stress. It is possible also to trace changes in work effort by comparing consistent reports over time using representative data. Here, I am referring to the intensity devoted to each hour of work, rather than the number of hours worked discussed above. So, what has been happening to the intensity with which people are working in Britain?

The short answer is that during the period of the Labour government very little has changed. The main period of work intensification in Britain occurred during the 1990s, before the Labour government came to power. Several data sources attest to this pattern of change, a fact that gives more confidence to these subjective sources. One can track changes in work effort by comparing consistent series of subjective responses over time on a range of effort-related indicators (rather than through retrospective estimates that are potentially biased). None of the indicators changed much between 1997 and 2006 (Green and Whitfield, 2009).

One reason for the earlier period of work intensification was changing technology and the growth of 'flexible' work organisation. Another may have been the changing balance of power in the workplace, with the declining influence of the trade unions. A third reason may have been the needs of consumers to work hard to maintain their pay at sufficient levels, though it has been hard to substantiate this argument (Green, 2006). These factors will have had varying force across different countries, but generally worked in the same direction; and indeed the workers in almost all European countries experienced work intensification at some stage between 1990 and 2005. However, there are limits to the amount of work intensification that can take place, especially given the human frame with a finite physical and mental capacity. These limits appear to have prevented any further intensification in Britain in the current decade; though the change of government nevertheless did not bring about any relaxation in the pace of work.

Did the pattern since the early 1990s—of increasing, then stable work effort and declining, then stable autonomy—have predictable consequences in terms of stress? It is recognised that stress is never an easy phenomenon to measure. Even though there are biometric indicators that can be used in workplace studies, we do not have objective indicators as to how stress has changed over time. But self-reported ill-health entailing stress and related conditions doubled, according to consistent estimates from the Health and Safety Executive, from 820 cases per 100,000 employees in 1990 to 1650 cases in 1998/9. After that, the 2000s saw a small improvement, and the decade ended with 1410 cases per 100,000. This pattern of change is consistent with the dynamics of change in effort and autonomy. Compared with other aspects of workplace health, the experience with stress-related illness rising contrasts with the ongoing decline in workplace injuries that took place in most years under both the Labour government and its predecessors (see <http://www. hse.gov.uk/statistics/history>).

Conclusions

There have been genuine improvements in some aspects of job quality during the period of the Labour Government since 1997: reduction in working hours, more paid holiday entitlements, gains in work-life balance possibilities and some increases in skills levels. Rises in wages at all points of the spectrum should also be included in this account.

It is often hard to attribute precise sources for change, and indeed many of the gains are part of a consumer society that has continued its long-term rise in affluence. By no means are all of the rises in work prosperity attributable to the government's own policies. Yet, the introduction of the NMW, and the imposition of mandatory holiday entitlements, are examples where government has made a distinct impact on job quality; while the growth of flexible working practices has arguably been helped along by a favourable legislative climate.

While government therefore can make a difference even in this apparently private domain of job quality, there remain some major areas to address. The most important contemporary concern is with employment insecurity, primarily the focus for good macroeconomic policy. At the end of the recession, it will also be important to confront the problems that arise from diminished autonomy and trust in the workplace, and from stubbornly high stress levels. At the same time, both the imperatives of competition and the objective of raising the level of jobs to give people more fulfilling work lives will mean that there is an ongoing need to improve skill levels—both of the workforce and of the jobs that they are doing. The UKCES's characterization of Britain's skills deficit as one that lies on both the demand and the supply side represents a significant change in understanding that could prove crucial in informing future skills policies.

This chapter has largely built its case on scientifically based representative surveys that aim to give representative and reliable accounts of what actually happens in Britain's workplaces. Yet even good quality surveys are imperfect instruments for viewing real labour markets. There is a small minority of workers who are not adequately represented: these are often the 'vulnerable' workers who are not reached for the same reasons—lack of empowerment, capacity and support—that their job quality is poor. Thus it is possible, for example, that the recorded residue of 4% of employees who lack paid holiday rights might understate the true proportion, because those missing operate in an informal economy, with a large imbalance of power between boss and worker. At this small but significant margin of work society, problems include inadequate awareness of rights, minimal enforcement from a state that relies largely on employer goodwill, and insufficient support from unions (TUC Commission on Vulnerable Employment, 2008). In some documented cases that reach Citizens Advice Bureaux, working conditions have been found to be quite shocking. After 13 years of Labour government, the labour market regulatory environment has been transformed, with replacement of the voluntarist system by a raft of entitlements and minimum standards (Dickens and Hall, 2009). Now, another key item of unfinished business is to square the preference for 'light-touch' monitoring and regulatory practice with the need to minimise super-exploitation of workers in contravention of the law.

References

Bryson, A. and Forth, J. (2011) Trade unions. In: Gregg, P. and Wadsworth, J. (eds.) *The Labour Market in Winter: The State of Working Britain*. Oxford: Oxford University Press.

Dickens, L. and Hall, M. (2009) Legal regulation and the changing workplace. In: Brown, W., Bryson, A., Forth, J. and Whitfield, K. (eds.) *The Evolution of the Modern Workplace*. Cambridge: Cambridge University Press.

Felstead, A., Gallie, D., Green, F. and Zhou, Y. (2007) *Skills at Work, 1986 to 2006*. Oxford: SKOPE.

Gallie, D., Felstead, A. and Green, F. (2004) Changing patterns of task discretion in Britain. *Work Employment and Society*, 18(2), 243–66.

Green, F. (2006) *Demanding Work: The Paradox of Job Quality in the Affluent Economy*. Woodstock: Princeton University Press.

—— (2008) Leeway for the loyal: a model of employee discretion. *British Journal of Industrial Relations*, 46(1), 1–32.

—— (2009) Job quality in Britain. *Praxis* No. 1. UK Commission for Employment and Skills, South Yorkshire and London.

—— and Whitfield, K. (2009) Employees' experience of work. In: Brown, W., Bryson, A., Forth, J. and Whitfield, K. (eds.) *The Evolution of the Modern Workplace*. Cambridge: Cambridge University Press.

Hooker, H., Neathey, F., Casebourne, H. and Munro, M. (2007) *The Third Work–Life Balance Employee Survey: Main Findings*. London: DTI.

Kersley, B., Alpin, C., Forth, J., Bryson, A., Bewley, H., Dix, G. and Oxenbridge, S. (2006) *Inside the Workplace: Findings from the 2004 Workplace Employment Relations Survey*. London: Routledge.

Machin, S. (2011) Changes in UK wage inequality over the last 40 years. In: Gregg, P. and Wadsworth, J. (eds.) *The Labour Market in Winter: The State of Working Britain*. Oxford: Oxford University Press.

Mishel, L., Bernstein, J. and Shierholz, H. (2008) *The State of Working America 2006–07*. Washington: Economic Policy Institute.

TUC Commission on Vulnerable Employment (2008) *Hard Work, Hidden Lives: The Short Report of the Commission on Vulnerable Employment*. London: TUC.

UKCES (2009) *Ambition 2020: World Class Skills and Jobs for the UK*. London: UK Commission for Employment and Skills.

9

Worker Well-Being in Booms and Busts[1]

Andrew E. Clark

Key findings

- The mental well-being of workers is pro-cyclical: their well-being is significantly higher in booms than in busts.
- More specific job domain well-being measures tell a more mixed story: pay satisfaction and job security satisfaction are also pro-cyclical, being higher in booms.
- However, satisfaction with the work itself is counter-cyclical, being higher in busts. The same is true of overall job satisfaction.
- The self-employed are systematically more satisfied with their jobs than are employees. There is no compelling evidence that this gap is affected by the economic cycle.

Introduction

Economists have over the past 15 years become more receptive to the use of measures of subjective well-being to summarise labour-market health. There are at least two reasons why subjective measures of well-being are of interest in the context of the labour market. First, in a purely descriptive way, policy should arguably be concerned with the distribution of well-being across the economy. Along these lines, if we want to know which groups are doing better or worse in the labour market, the simplest method is surely to interrogate the

[1] Data from the British Household Panel Survey (BHPS) was supplied by the ESRC Data Archive. Neither the original collectors of the data nor the Archive bear any responsibility for the analysis or interpretations presented here. I am very grateful to CEPREMAP for financial support, to Simona Baldi for excellent research assistance, and to Jonathan Wadsworth for perceptive comments.

individuals themselves and ask them what they think. It can be argued that individuals' responses to questions regarding their job and life satisfaction provide this kind of information. Second, the analysis of the level of well-being or utility associated with different jobs can help us to understand labour market behaviour. If, as seems likely, individuals are more likely to leave low satisfaction for higher satisfaction positions (see Clark et al., 1998; Clark, 2001 and Lévy-Garboua et al., 2007, amongst others), then the well-being scores in the labour market may well provide us with useful new knowledge about turnover in the labour market, the decision to go to work in the first place, and retirement.

This subjective approach to worker well-being has a number of advantages. Specifically, it can be seen as a complement to the extremely difficult task of measuring job quality, or the quality of working life, as some kind of weighted sum of individual job attributes. While it is difficult to argue with the general principle of the latter, its empirical application would seem to be very problematic indeed. There are at least three major stumbling blocks. The first is that we do not know what job aspects we should be adding up (pay, hours, job security and the intrinsic interest of the job would seem key, but what else would we need to add?). Second, even if we are able to identify all of the different salient aspects of a job, can we obtain sufficiently accurate objective measurement of them? While this seems reasonably direct in terms of pay and hours, there is far less agreement about objective measures of job insecurity,[2] and a fully objective measure of the intrinsic interest of the job is not easy to conceive. Last, were we to have objective measures of all relevant job domains, which weights should we use to add them up: is pay twice as important as hours, or just as important? Equally, how do we know if these weights are the same for different individuals?

The approach taken here is to avoid all of these tricky questions by essentially letting survey respondents do all of the hard work for us. In response to questions about job satisfaction (or some other form of well-being), individuals presumably weigh up all of the salient aspects, calculate some net total and then give us the appropriate satisfaction figure.

The work presented here is resolutely in this tradition of subjective indicators. While there has been a great deal of work that considers the value of work relative to unemployment (see Clark and Oswald, 1994, and Gregg and Wadsworth, Chapter 2 in this volume), we here want to say something about job quality. Specifically, we use British data from the early 1990s onward to investigate movements in various measures of worker well-being. The analysis allows us to describe well-being both *between* individuals (i.e. determining

---

[2] See Clark and Postel-Vinay (2009), Dickerson and Green (2009) and Green, Chapter 8 in this volume.

which groups of workers are doing better than others at any particular point in time, as in Warr, 2007), and any changes over time (have there been systematic movements in worker satisfaction since the early 1990s?).

There has been a fair amount of work on the former, so we will concentrate on the latter, and particularly ask whether any changes over time are related to the state of the macro economy: are jobs systematically less satisfying in recessions?

We have four main findings. First, different kinds of job satisfaction are indeed correlated with booms and busts. In particular, satisfaction with the work itself rises during recessions, whereas pay satisfaction and job security satisfaction both fall. Perhaps surprisingly, overall job satisfaction is counter-cyclical, falling in booms and rising in busts. However, job satisfaction is not the only thing that matters for individual welfare. The analysis of an overall well-being measure (the GHQ-12) shows that the general well-being of British employees falls in recessions and increases in booms (despite the contrary behaviour of overall job satisfaction). Third, there is some suggestive evidence that what workers find important in their jobs (their work values) changes over the economic cycle: good times are associated with increased importance of pay, but less importance assigned to job security. Last, we find, as is usual, that the self-employed are systematically more satisfied than are the employed. However, while the self-employment satisfaction 'premium' moves around substantially from year to year, there is no evidence that this movement is correlated with the unemployment rate.

Job satisfaction over the cycle

The data that we analyse here come from the British Household Panel Survey (BHPS). This general survey initially covered a random sample of approximately 10,000 individuals in 5500 British households per year, rising to figures of around 15,000 individuals in 9000 households in later waves. Seventeen waves of data are currently available. This data set includes a wide range of information about individual and household demographics, health, labour-force status, employment and values. There is both entry into and exit from the panel, leading to unbalanced data. The BHPS is a household panel: all adults in the same household are interviewed separately. The wave one data were collected in late 1991–early 1992, the wave two data were collected in late 1992–early 1993, and so on.[3]

The analysis here will cover employees only. The BHPS data include information on around 5000 employees per year initially, rising to 8000 per year in later waves. The survey includes a number of self-reported job satisfaction

---

[3] More details are available at <http://www.iser.essex.ac.uk/survey/bhps/>.

measures. Five job satisfaction questions were asked of those in employment over all 17 waves: satisfaction with pay, hours, work itself and job security, followed by a question regarding overall job satisfaction. These were all answered on a one to seven scale, where one refers to 'not satisfied at all' and seven to 'completely satisfied'.

There was unfortunately a change in the way the job satisfaction question was posed between the first and subsequent waves. In the first wave only the endpoints and the midpoint (i.e. the value of four) of the one to seven scale were given verbal labels; in subsequent waves all values were labelled.[4] To be sure that we are comparing like with like, information from the first wave was dropped when looking at job satisfaction. The distribution of job satisfaction amongst British employees over the 1992–2007 period is summarised in Table 9.1. This table shows that most employees are fairly satisfied with their jobs: over 50% report satisfaction of six or seven on this one to seven scale, with the exception of pay satisfaction, where the figure is 44%. The modal satisfaction response is six for all measures.

We are most interested here in the time profile of the different types of job satisfaction. As a first simple step, the unbroken line in Figure 9.1 shows average overall job satisfaction, which trended downwards up until the end of the 1990s, since when it has slowly drifted upwards again. In the same figure, the dashed line depicts the UK unemployment rate over the same period, which reached a peak of over 10% in 1993 before falling continuously up until 2001; from 2004 onwards the unemployment rate has been rising again. Are these two series correlated? Visual inspection suggests that there is indeed some kind of correlation; the correlation coefficient between the two is 0.6 (significant at around the 1% level).

Table 9.1: The distribution of the job satisfaction of employees in the BHPS, 1992–2007

	Percentage of Employees				
	Overall	Pay	Job security	Work itself	Hours worked
Completely dissatisfied	1.49	3.69	3.26	1.51	1.94
Mostly dissatisfied	2.73	5.22	3.09	2.48	3.03
Somewhat dissatisfied	6.81	14.27	7.48	6.2	10.82
Neither satisfied nor dissatisfied	7.55	8.23	9.01	7.74	10.29
Somewhat satisfied	22.53	24.9	18.66	20.78	21.94
Mostly satisfied	45.84	34.54	36.89	43.07	36.36
Completely satisfied	13.04	9.15	21.62	18.22	15.6

Note: Weighted data.

[4] This is discussed in detail in Rose (2005), note 6.

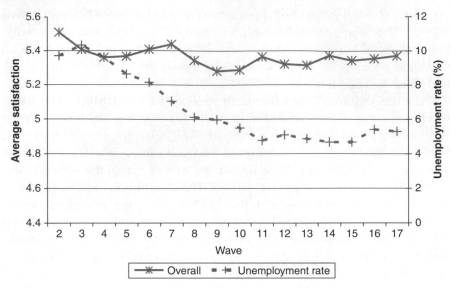

Figure 9.1: Overall job satisfaction and the unemployment rate, 1992–2007
Note: Weighted data.

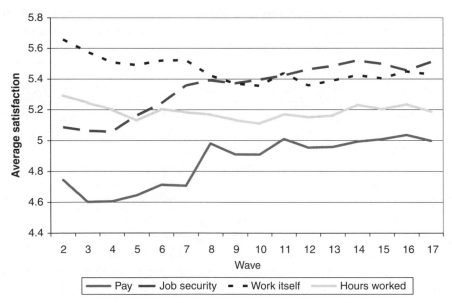

Figure 9.2: Domains of job satisfaction, 1992–2007
Note: Weighted data.

Figure 9.2 depicts the same time series for the four domain satisfaction measures which are consistently available in the BHPS data. These actually behave in notably different ways. While those for satisfaction with work itself and hours worked are similar to that for overall satisfaction in Figure 9.1, both pay and job security satisfaction have risen almost secularly over the 1992–2007 period (although they are fairly flat in the latter years). Consequently, we imagine that the correlation coefficients with the unemployment rate will not be the same, and this indeed turns out to be the case. The correlation coefficient for work itself (with respect to unemployment) are positive and significant at the 1% level, while that for hours worked is also positive, but not significantly so. The correlation coefficients for pay and job security are negative and significant at better than the 1% level.

This analysis of time profiles thus suggests that there is a relationship between the economic cycle and worker satisfaction. However, this relationship is far from being uniform. Recessions (in the sense of higher unemployment rates) are associated with lower levels of satisfaction with pay and job security, but are also associated with higher levels of satisfaction with both the work itself and hours worked. The correlation with overall job satisfaction is positive: on the face of it, then, recessions are associated with higher levels of job satisfaction amongst British workers.

There are a number of ways of interpreting this perhaps surprising finding. One is that those who remain in employment during hard economic times may indeed be happy to still have work, and thus mark up their satisfaction scores because they are comparing their own outcomes to the lot of some of their less fortunate former colleagues.

Another reading is that there is a kind of selection process. If those who lose their jobs during recessions were those who had less good jobs (and thus who were low job satisfaction workers), then the average satisfaction amongst those who remain in employment will be higher. This is not because recessions increase the job satisfaction of anyone: it is rather that some of the least satisfied workers have lost their jobs, so the average satisfaction amongst those who remain in work rises mechanically.

One way of choosing between these two rival interpretations is to carry out a regression analysis, whereby we essentially calculate how the satisfaction of an individual with given sex, age and education, in a certain occupation and industry, changes as the unemployment rate changes. By holding a host of worker and job characteristics constant, we can avoid the mechanical selection interpretation.

For space reasons, the output of this regression analysis is not presented here. However, Table 9.2 summarises the sign of the relationship between various measures of job satisfaction and the unemployment rate, holding worker and job characteristics constant. Broadly, the results are remarkably similar to those from Figures 9.1 and 9.2. Greater unemployment is associated

Table 9.2: Job satisfaction and the unemployment rate: regression analysis

	Overall	Pay	Job security	Work itself	Hours worked
Correlation with the unemployment rate	+	−	−	+	0

with lower levels of pay satisfaction and satisfaction with job security. This latter relationship might be thought to be unsurprising: unemployment reduces (satisfaction with) job security, and workers in OECD countries consistently rank job security as one of the two most important aspects of the job (see Clark, 2010). This was previously noted in a regression analysis of European data in Clark and Postel-Vinay (2009). The fact that pay satisfaction falls as the unemployment rate rises is very likely linked to the negative effect of unemployment on wages, as described notably in Blanchflower and Oswald (1994).

On the other hand, satisfaction with the work itself is positively correlated with the unemployment rate: workers feel better about the work they do in times of recession. Again, this could be due to comparison with their less fortunate peers, or simply because work pressure goes down during recessions.[5] In the regression analysis, there is no relationship between unemployment and satisfaction with hours worked.

There are likely many other facets of job satisfaction (unmeasured in this survey) which are correlated with unemployment. The total effect, as revealed by the first column correlation with overall job satisfaction, is positive: workers report higher levels of job satisfaction in recession years.

One restriction of the above analysis is that it concerns employees only, and only one aspect of their lives (their work). We may also be interested in how employees are doing overall in terms of their subjective well-being (and not only with respect to their job): this is the topic of the next section.

Overall measures of worker well-being

We here move away from the specific domain of the job to a general measure of individual well-being. In the BHPS, this latter is supplied by a score calculated from the General Health Questionnaire (GHQ). This latter is widely used by psychologists, epidemiologists and medical researchers as an indicator of mental functioning. The BHPS contains the 12-item version of the GHQ,

---

[5] Which is one of the channels proposed by Ruhm (2000) to explain the fact that causes of death rise during booms and fall during recessions.

based on 12 questions (administered via a self-completion questionnaire) covering feelings of strain, depression, inability to cope, anxiety-based insomnia and lack of confidence, amongst others (see the Appendix). Responses are made on a four-point scale of frequency of a feeling in relation to a person's usual state: 'not at all', 'no more than usual', 'rather more than usual' and 'much more than usual'. We here use the Caseness GHQ score, which counts the number of these questions for which the response is in one of the two 'low well-being' categories. This count is then reversed so that higher scores indicate higher levels of well-being, running from zero (all twelve responses indicating poor psychological health) to 12 (no responses indicating poor psychological health).

Figure 9.3(a) shows the average level of psychological well-being in the BHPS data by labour-force status. On the left-hand side of this graph, the self-employed and the employed report roughly similar levels of overall well-being. However, on the right hand side, much lower scores are reported by those who are not active in the labour force and (especially) by the unemployed. The fact that the unemployed do so much worse in well-being terms than other groups on the face of it contradicts the idea that unemployment is chosen by the unemployed.[6]

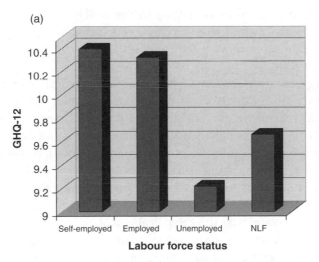

(a)

Figure 9.3(a): Psychological well-being (GHQ) and labour force status

Note: NLF = Not in the Labour Force.

---

[6] It can be countered that it is the unhappy who are more likely to become unemployed. This point can be addressed using panel data (where the same individual is followed over time). Even 'within subject', as psychologists say, unemployment is strongly negatively associated with well-being: those who lose their jobs and move into unemployment experience sharp drops in well-being.

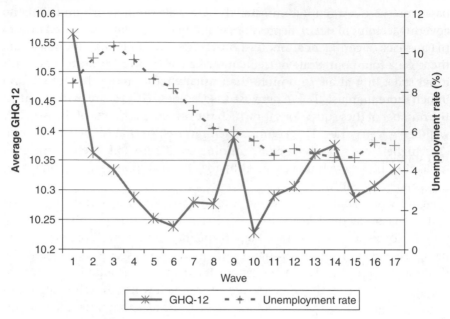

Figure 9.3(b): Psychological well-being (GHQ) over time, 1991–2007

We now turn to changes over time in the well-being of employees. The average GHQ score of employees over time is depicted in Figure 9.3(b): overall well-being amongst employees fell from 1991 to 1996, rose up to 1999 and then again to 2004.

We can then carry out the same type of regression analysis as described above for job satisfaction: holding sex, age, education, occupation and so on constant, does the GHQ measure of psychological functioning change as the unemployment rate changes? This analysis is again carried out for employees only.

The response is unequivocal: greater unemployment is associated with lower mental well-being scores than for those in employment.[7] While this might sound uncontroversial, it is worth remembering that the correlation with overall job satisfaction above was in fact positive. So despite this positive domain satisfaction effect, the overall effect of unemployment on worker well-being is negative: the GHQ score is pro-cyclical. This is likely due to lower incomes, a greater overall feeling of insecurity, or more generally to feelings of empathy: we feel sorry for those who have lost their jobs, especially if they are colleagues, acquaintances or family members.

This finding for employees is consistent with other analyses using different data sets which have explored the 'Macroeconomics of Happiness'. These

---

[7] Unemployment reduces the well-being of those who lose their jobs, as suggested by Figure 9.3(a). However, it also seems to be associated with lower well-being amongst those who remain in work.

papers (see e.g. Blanchflower, 2007 and Di Tella et al., 2001) find that the aggregate unemployment rate enters individual well-being equations nega- tively in multivariate analysis (as indeed does the inflation rate).[8] Overall then, it seems clear that worse economic conditions are associated with lower levels of well-being, both for the population in general and for workers in particular.

Job values

The BHPS also contains information on job values, with questions being asked in waves one, nine and 14. The question here is not absolute, but rather relative: respondents choose the first most important job aspect out of eight choices on a showcard. The job aspects concerned here are: Promotion pro- spects; Total pay; Good relations with manager; Job security; Using initiative; Actual work; Hours worked; and Something else.

The weighted raw numbers are presented in Table 9.3. These numbers refer to the responses given by full-time or part-time employees only. The asterisks between the columns indicate whether the changes from one wave to another are statistically significant. The changes over time in job values are depicted in Figure 9.4.

Table 9.3: Job values (percentage saying characteristic is the most important)

	Women			Men		
	1991	1999	2004	1991	1999	2004
Promotion prospects	2.08	2.39	2.01	3.57	3.33 *	2.32
Total pay	13.62 **	19.14	18.55	19.06 **	25.71 *	28.55
Good relations with manager	10.76	11.31	11.56	4.76	5.1	5.43
Job security	23.95 **	17.86	16.42	35.56 **	31.11 **	26.78
Using initiative	7.53 **	9.94	8.86	9.27	10.14	8.46
Actual work	34.43 *	31.4	33.26	24.07	21.87 *	24.77
Hours worked	5.99	6.32	7.61	1.19	1.2	1.75
Something else	1.63	1.64	1.73	2.53 *	1.55	1.94

Notes: Weighted data; **(*) = significant difference by year at the 1(5)% level.
Source: BHPS 1991, 1999, 2004.

[8] Which does not mean that everyone is hurt by higher unemployment rates. There is some evidence that the unemployed actually report higher levels of well-being on average in higher- unemployment regions: see Clark (2003).

137

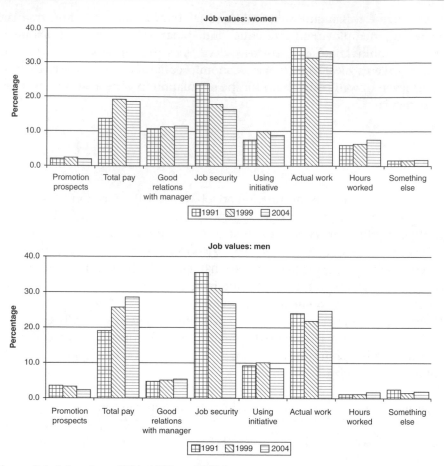

Figure 9.4: Job values: 1991, 1999 and 2004

There are a number of points that stand out from Table 9.3. The first is that men and women to a certain extent agree on what is important in a job (although women put more weight on the actual work itself and good relations with the manager, and less weight on pay and job security). The second is that, overall, the most important aspects of a job as identified by workers themselves are the actual work itself, job security and pay.

The third point is that these job values are not always fixed. The importance of different job aspects changes over time. Two particularly notable evolutions are that job security has been declining in importance for both sexes, while pay has on the contrary been gaining in importance, especially for men. There is also some evidence that having an interesting job has become more salient, although the changes here over time are only small in magnitude.

It is of interest to ask whether these movements in job values are systematically related to the economic cycle. Any conclusions here will have to be tentative, as we are looking for relationships based on only three data points (1991, 1999 and 2004). As unemployment fell secularly across these three years (see Figure 9.1), any job value which has systematically increased or decreased over this time period can be argued to be correlated with the economic cycle. As such, booms would seem to be associated with systematic changes in what workers value in their jobs: good times seem to be a synonym for increased importance of pay (especially for men), but less concern for job security. To this extent, booms shift workers' attention from the future to the present.

Job satisfaction, employment and self-employment

The results to date have concerned British employees. This last topic emphasises the specific relationship between self-employment and job satisfaction. As discussed in Blanchflower and Oswald (1998) and Clark (2010), the self-employed pose something of a puzzle. Despite having job outcomes that are often worse than those of employees (regarding pay, hours of work and job security, for example), they most often report higher levels of job satisfaction (at least in developed countries).

This phenomenon is illustrated using BHPS data from 1992 through 2007 in Figure 9.5. This figure illustrates the results of regression analysis of job satisfaction data. As opposed to the analysis described in the section on job satisfaction above, the satisfaction scores here come from both the employed

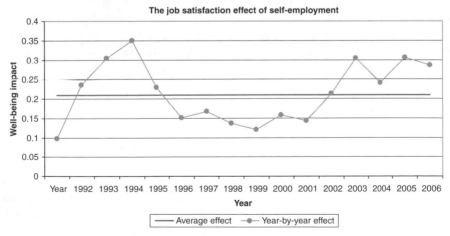

Figure 9.5: Job satisfaction and self-employment in booms and busts

and the self-employed. In addition to the standard control variables in this regression, a self-employment dummy variable is also introduced. The estimated coefficient on the latter will reveal whether, all other things equal, the self-employed are more or less satisfied with their jobs than are the employed.

The flat line in Figure 9.5 shows the value of the estimated coefficient on self-employment in this overall job satisfaction regression. This is positive, and very significant (the t-statistic is almost 20). As is very often found then, the self-employed in the UK labour market are more satisfied with their jobs than are employees.

The second line in Figure 9.5 shows what happens when we let this self-employment coefficient vary from year to year (instead of saying that the effect of self-employment is the same every year). The results here then show whether the positive relationship between self-employment and well-being at work has changed between 1992 and 2007. The self-employment advantage over employment grew from 1992 up to 1995, then fell back until 2002, since when it has been rising again.[9]

As above, one question that can be asked here is whether this year-on-year pattern is related to the economic cycle. One way of thinking about self-employment is that it is a solution to which individuals turn when the labour market sours. Along these lines, self-employment might be thought to be more satisfying for those who freely choose it, rather than for those who are to an extent forced into it by the lack of other employment opportunities. We might then expect the self-employment satisfaction premium to be pro-cyclical, increasing in booms but dropping in busts.

While the first few years in Figure 9.5 seem consistent with this hypothesis (the gap rising as the unemployment rate fell), the following years do not fit well. Overall, there is very little correlation between the unemployment rate and the job satisfaction gap between the self-employed and the employed. While the latter does seem to move around considerably from year to year, there is no evidence that this movement is driven by the economic cycle.

Conclusions

This chapter asked whether worker well-being is correlated with the economic cycle. We know that recessions increase unemployment and therefore job insecurity, and are associated with lower wages. Is it not then obvious that they should be negatively associated with workers' subjective evaluations too?

---

[9] This picture is consistent with the analysis of 15 OECD countries in Clark (2010), in which the satisfaction advantage of self-employment over employment increased between 1997 and 2005.

This prior hypothesis is only partly borne out by empirical analysis. We here consider data from the first 17 waves of the British Household Panel Survey, which includes a number of different measures of worker subjective well-being and work values.

It is indeed true that worker well-being in general (which will pick up work-related outcomes, but also those in all other domains which the individual finds important) is pro-cyclical: well-being is significantly higher in booms than in busts. However, once we move to more specific domain well-being measures, this simple story becomes more muddied. Considering various job satisfaction scores, both pay satisfaction and job security satisfaction are also pro-cyclical, being higher in booms. However, satisfaction with the work itself is counter-cyclical, being higher in busts. In addition, overall job satisfaction is also counter-cyclical. This opposition between the overall job satisfaction and the mental health of British workers in terms of movements over the economic cycle would seem to be of great interest and worthy of further study.

Last, the present chapter has considered well-being data from the UK only, in line with the aim of the current book. It would undoubtedly be worthwhile to replicate this work in other countries. In particular, institutions may well be key in moderating the correlation between aggregate unemployment and worker well-being. While this has been shown to be negative in the UK data analysed here, we may also suspect that (for example) employment protection legislation, unemployment benefit generosity and trade unions all play a role in this relationship. Comparative analysis across countries will help to establish whether this is indeed the case.

APPENDIX

The 12 questions used to create the GHQ-12 measure appear in the BHPS questionnaire as follows:

1. Here are some questions regarding the way you have been feeling over the last few weeks. For each question please ring the number next to the answer that best suits the way you have felt.

Have you recently:

a) Been able to concentrate on whatever you're doing?

Better than usual   1
Same as usual   2
Less than usual   3
Much less than usual 4

Then:

b) Lost much sleep over worry?
e) Felt constantly under strain?
f) Felt you couldn't overcome your difficulties?
i) Been feeling unhappy or depressed?
j) Been losing confidence in yourself?
k) Been thinking of yourself as a worthless person?

With the responses:

Not at all	1
No more than usual	2
Rather more than usual	3
Much more than usual	4

Then:

c) Felt that you were playing a useful part in things?
d) Felt capable of making decisions about things?
g) Been able to enjoy your normal day-to-day activities?
h) Been able to face up to problems?
l) Been feeling reasonably happy, all things considered?

With the responses:

More so than usual	1
About same as usual	2
Less so than usual	3
Much less than usual	4

References

Blanchflower, D. (2007) Is unemployment more costly than inflation? NBER, Working Paper No. 13505.

—— and Oswald, A. J. (1994) *The Wage Curve*. Cambridge, Mass.: MIT Press.

—— —— (1998) What makes an entrepreneur? *Journal of Labor Economics*, 16: 26–60.

Clark, A. E. (2001) What really matters in a job? Hedonic measurement using quit data. *Labour Economics,* 8: 223–42.

—— (2003) Unemployment as a social norm: psychological evidence from panel data. *Journal of Labor Economics*, 21: 323–51.

—— (2010) Work, jobs and well-being across the millennium. In: Diener, E., Helliwell, J. and Kahneman, D. (eds.) *International Differences in Well-being*. Oxford: Oxford University Press.

—— Georgellis, Y. and Sanfey, P. (1998) Job satisfaction, wage changes and quits: evidence from Germany. *Research in Labor Economics*, 17: 95–121.

—— and Oswald, A. J. (1994) Unhappiness and unemployment. *Economic Journal*, 104: 648–59.

—— and Postel-Vinay, F. (2009) Job security and job protection. *Oxford Economic Papers*, 61: 207–39.

Dickerson, A. and Green, F. (2009) Fears and realisations of employment insecurity. University of Sheffield, mimeo.

Di Tella, R., MacCulloch, R. J., and Oswald, A. J. (2001) Preferences over inflation and unemployment: evidence from surveys of happiness. *American Economic Review*, 91: 335–41.

Green, F. (2011) Job quality in Britain under the labour government. In: Gregg, P. and Wadsworth, J. (eds.) *The Labour Market in Winter: The State of Working Britain*. Oxford: Oxford University Press.

Gregg, P. and Wadsworth, J. (2011) Unemployment and inactivity. In: Gregg, P. and Wadsworth, J. (eds.) *The Labour Market in Winter: The State of Working Britain*. Oxford: Oxford University Press.

Lévy-Garboua, L., Montmarquette, C. and Simonnet, V. (2007) Job satisfaction and quits: theory and evidence from the German socioeconomic panel. *Labour Economics*, 14: 251–68.

Rose, M. (2005) Job satisfaction in Britain: coping with complexity. *British Journal of Industrial Relations*, 43: 455–67.

Ruhm, C. J. (2000) Are recessions good for your health? *Quarterly Journal of Economics*, 115: 617–50.

Warr, P. (2007) *Work, Happiness and Unhappiness*. Mahwah, NJ: Lawrence Erlbaum Associates.

10

Family-Friendly Policies

Jane Waldfogel

Key findings

The past decade has seen a sea change in the supports available for working parents. Most notably:

- Paid maternity leave has been doubled.
- Paid paternity leave has been introduced.
- Preschool is now universal for 3 and 4 year olds.
- Support for child care has been greatly expanded.
- Parents now have the right to request part-time or flexible hours.

Together, these policies have transformed the situation of working parents in Britain, although more remains to be done.

Reforms to leave policies

One of the most important family-friendly policies for working parents with young children is the right to take paid leave to take care of essential family responsibilities, such as the care of a newborn or an ill child. Parents who do not have adequate leave rights may not be able to take the leave they need or may have to cut their leave short, or they may end up leaving their jobs altogether in order to take care of their family responsibilities.

One of the earliest initiatives in this area was the introduction of parental leave in 1999, providing 3 months of job-protected parental leave, which mothers or fathers could use to meet childcare responsibilities or to address a family emergency. Although the programme was limited in that the leave was unpaid and could only be used once in the life of a child, it nevertheless was a welcome source of flexibility for working families.

The Employment Act of 2002 more significantly expanded leave rights for working parents with young children. The first policy it addressed was maternity leave. Although, in common with most other advanced industrialised nations, Britain already had a system of paid maternity leave, the leave it provided was short by European standards. In 2001, at a time when European countries provided an average of 10 months of paid maternity leave, Britain provided only about 4 months (18 weeks).

Comparative studies, taking advantage of natural experiments created by policy variation across countries and over time, indicated that when countries had longer periods of paid leave, infant mortality rates were lower. Research also showed that when mothers took longer periods of leave, their mental health was better, and children were more likely to receive recommended preventive health care such as regular visits to the doctor and immunisations (see review in Waldfogel, 2006). In the Employment Act of 2002, the government increased the period of statutory maternity leave to 6 months of paid leave followed by up to 6 months of unpaid leave. This was extended again in 2004 as part of the 10-year childcare strategy, as discussed below.

In addition to introducing these maternity leave expansions, the Employment Act of 2002 established 2 weeks of paid paternity leave, in recognition of the growing consensus that it was important for newborns to have their father home as well as their mother and that even the most important employees could be spared for a week or two of leave (as evidenced by the fact that both Prime Minister Blair and Chancellor Brown took paternity leave while in office).

Leave rights for families with infants were further extended in December 2004, in conjunction with the 10-year childcare strategy, discussed below. The 2002 reforms had instituted 6 months of paid maternity leave followed by up to 6 months of unpaid leave. However, the unpaid leave time was predominantly being used by higher-income women, since lower-income families could not afford unpaid time off work. For this reason, as part of the 10-year childcare strategy, the government announced in December 2004 that it would extend the period of paid maternity leave to 9 months, effective April 2007, with a commitment to eventually extend paid maternity leave to 12 months and with a promise of future legislation to allow mothers to transfer a portion of their paid leave time to fathers.

Although the goal of extending paid maternity leave to 12 months has proved elusive, the government has followed through on its commitment to provide more leave time for fathers. In January 2010, the government announced a plan to allow fathers to take up to 3 months of paid leave (if the mother was willing to transfer the last 3 months of her 9 months of paid leave), followed by up to 3 months of unpaid leave. This would effectively provide couples with 12 months of leave (9 months of paid leave for the mother, with up to 3 months transferable to the father, followed by 3 months of unpaid leave for the father).

145

Assessment

It is too soon to tell what the impact of these leave expansions has been on parental employment and leave-taking, and on child health and development. But the evidence from prior reforms suggests that the effects are likely to be important. For example, Gregg and co-authors found that earlier maternity leave expansions increased the likelihood that women returned to their jobs after childbirth rather than quitting work, thus leading to higher rates of employment among mothers of young children (Gregg et al., 2007). The fact that job tenure is rising among women with young children (see Faggio et al., Chapter 7 in this volume) suggests that this shift is likely occurring under the current reforms as well. There is also ample evidence that women offered longer periods of paid leave in fact take up that leave and remain home for longer (we have less evidence on men) (see review in Gregg and Waldfogel, 2005). As discussed earlier, prior research has also found that longer periods of paid leave have benefits to child health and development (see e.g. Berger et al., 2005).

Expanded supports for child care

Child care is clearly a key area for working parents. Particularly when children are preschool-age, the lack of available, affordable, and quality child care can pose a major barrier to parents working. Even when children are school-age, child care for the out-of-school hours—before school, after school, and during school holidays—can still be an important factor in enabling parents to work.

National childcare strategy

In May 1997, shortly after coming into office, the Labour government announced Britain's first national childcare strategy. The signature element of the strategy was a commitment to provide universal—and free—preschool for all 4 year olds by September 1998, a commitment which was later extended to 3 year olds, in April 2004. This new entitlement, which was enthusiastically taken up by parents, moved Britain from having one of the lowest preschool enrolment rates in Europe to being on a par with its European peers, most of whom had universal or near universal participation in publicly provided preschool in the year or two prior to school entry (Waldfogel, 2006).

The universal preschool entitlement was particularly consequential for lower-income families, who prior to the policy were the least likely to have their children enrolled in preschool. In 1997, 82% of low-income 3 and 4 year olds were enrolled in care, as compared to 93% of higher-income children of that age (Waldfogel, 2010).

The first national childcare strategy also included some attention to increasing the quality of child care. The Early Excellence Centres initiative, begun in 1997, supported the development and dissemination of model preschool programmes. The Neighborhood Nurseries Initiative of 2001 provided funding to support the establishment of preschools in low-income areas.

Support for child care was further extended in December 2004, with the release of the 10-year childcare strategy. Called 'Choice for Parents, the Best Start for Children', the 10-year childcare strategy emphasised supporting parental choice *and* improving child care.

For children under age 3, pilot programmes were introduced extending free publicly funded preschool to some disadvantaged 2 year olds (the goal was to have sufficient provision to reach the 15% most disadvantaged 2 year olds by September 2009), and funding for childcare subsidies was expanded, through increases in the childcare element of the Working Tax Credit (discussed further below). For older preschoolers, there were measures to increase availability and affordability—including extending the hours of free provision for 3 and 4 year olds from the existing 12.5 hours per week, 33 weeks per year, to 15 hours per week, 38 weeks per year.

In addition, recognising the still generally low quality of care in the early years sector, the 10-year childcare strategy introduced a host of measures to improve childcare quality. These included steps to further reform and integrate childcare regulation and inspections, building on the recent change (under the Children Act 2004) which gave responsibility for inspecting childcare and other children's programmes to the Office for Standards in Education (Ofsted), the respected agency that inspected schools. The strategy also included steps to raise the quality of the childcare workforce.

The aim of the 10-year childcare strategy was 'to make early years and childcare provision a permanent mainstream part of the welfare state' (Hodge, 2005: 1). To that end, the 10-year childcare strategy was followed by the Childcare Act of 2006, which placed a new duty on local authorities to provide adequate child care for all working parents who wanted it. And certainly, childcare provision expanded, with local authorities spending about £4 billion on provision for children under age 5 in 2007–8, as compared to around £1 billion in 1997 (Waldfogel, 2010). The government also strengthened its childcare infrastructure, introducing Children's Centres to coordinate childcare services in each local area. These Children Centres built on the earlier Sure Start programmes, which provided family support, home visiting and childcare services to families with young children in the most disadvantaged areas, but differed from Sure Start in that they were to be provided in all areas and with a much sharper focus on child care.

Childcare subsidies

An important element of the childcare reforms was a dramatic increase in the generosity of childcare subsidies for low-income working families. As described above, all 4 year olds have been entitled to a free, part-time early education place since 1998, and from 2004 this entitlement was extended to all 3 year olds. The free entitlement is funded with government subsidies given directly to providers. Most parents are expected to pay in full or at least contribute to the cost of other types of care (e.g. care to 'wraparound' early years education, provision for children under 3, and out of school services). A range of childcare subsidies is available directly to parents, typically to enable them to enter or remain in work, with most of the funding targeted at low-income families.

The main childcare subsidy is provided through the Working Tax Credit (formerly with Working Families Tax Credit). Under the Working Families Tax Credit (WFTC), introduced in October 1999, families with childcare costs could receive 70% of costs up to a limit of £70 per week for one child and £105 per week for two or more children. These were sizeable increases relative to the previous limit of £60 per week per family which could be disregarded from income under Family Credit. In April 2003, when WFTC was replaced by the more generous Working Tax Credit (WTC), childcare reimbursement remained at 70%, but the maximum allowable costs that could be claimed rose to £135 per week for one child and £200 per week for two or more children. The programme has since been made more generous, with reimbursement allowed up to 80% of costs, and with higher ceilings for weekly costs (a maximum of £175 per week for one child and £300 for two or more children as of 2008). Recognizing the particularly high costs facing parents in London, special childcare affordability programmes in the London area provide reimbursement for higher amounts.

Take-up of childcare subsidies increased dramatically with the transition to WFTC and later WTC. Nearly 450,000 parents claimed the childcare element of WTC in April 2008 compared to around 27,000 claiming childcare help through Family Credit in 1999, before it was abolished (Waldfogel and Garnham, 2008). There has also been an increase in the share of parents participating in employer supported childcare schemes.

Out-of-school care

The childcare expansions also included increased provision of out-of-school care (care for school-age children before school, after school, and during school holidays). Prior to 1997, schools differed widely in how much programming they offered to cover the hours before school, after school, or during school holidays. Although many schools had some form of after-school care available, the programmes were of poor quality and tended to be used primarily by children of low-income working parents, who had little choice but to use the care, while middle-class children tended to participate in privately purchased activities outside of school (music lessons, sports and so on). In order to improve the availability and quality of out-of-school programmes, and to narrow gaps in access to such programmes, the government in 2002 began taking steps towards instituting what they called 'extended schools'— schools that would be open and provide a range of services before school, after school and during school vacations. That year, legislation was passed giving local authorities extra powers that would allow them to provide before- and after-school care, and 25 pathfinder local authorities were identified to pioneer extended schools.

In July 2005, the government announced its ambition to have all schools be extended schools by 2010 and to have half of schools attaining that target by 2008. A year after the 2005 announcement, the share of primary schools offering care before school had risen from 40 to 53%, while the share offering care during school vacations had risen from 26 to 43%. (The share of schools offering after school care, already high in 2005, had risen from 87 to 91%.)

Assessment

The expansions in childcare provision are clearly very substantial. Britain has moved from being a laggard in the childcare arena to having childcare provision that is much more in line with that provided by other advanced industrialised countries. Although it is too soon to assess the effects of the recent British expansions, there is an extensive evidence base linking preschool provision to improvements in child health and development (see review in Waldfogel, 2006). Childcare policies are also a crucial support for parental employment, particularly for lone parents who do not have another parent with whom to share child care. Over the past decade, lone parent employment has risen 12 percentage points, from 45% to 57%, and the policy reforms (including the childcare reforms, but also the expansions in tax credits and other measures) are probably responsible for at least half that increase (see Waldfogel, 2010).

Nevertheless, gaps in provision remain. In addition to shortfalls in the supply of out of school care, there are also continuing gaps in provision for preschool-age children. Some providers such as nursery classes and playgroups still only offer part-time services, and many working parents need to find other (often informal) carers who can provide 'wraparound' care. While most day nurseries are open for a full day and for most days of the year, they can be very inflexible and, for example, do not allow parents to vary the days or hours when child care is used or to use a combination of morning and afternoon sessions. There is also hardly any formal provision available outside standard hours (before 8am, after 6pm or at weekends), although a growing number of parents need child care at these times, often to cover atypical working hours. There are also gaps in provision for children with special educational needs and disabilities, as well as continuing shortages of care for children under age 2. In addition, there is considerable regional variation in supply.

Moreover, quality and affordability of child care remained important issues, and of course the two are linked, since efforts to raise quality will also raise costs. On the quality front, the government, inspired by research from Britain's Effective Provision of Pre-School Education (EPPE) study, showing that children learned the most in centres led by staff with a university degree, moved towards a requirement that every childcare programme have a graduate leader (with programmes in disadvantaged areas having at least two graduates) by 2015 and committed funding (£305 million in 2008) to help programmes achieve this goal. This would be a sharp change for this sector where, as of 2008, only 4% of the workforce had a university degree. On the affordability front, the government has continued to expand the generosity of childcare subsidies and explored ways to extend universal provision.

The 'right to request'

One of the most important benefits from the perspective of working parents is workplace flexibility. Opportunities to work part-time, or flexible work hours, are particularly valued as ways to help parents to balance their work and family responsibilities. Although the British labour market is characterised by relatively high rates of part-time employment, particularly among working mothers, many working parents nevertheless complain that they are not able to work the jobs they would like to on a part-time or flexible basis. Often, working part-time (or flexible hours) can mean shifting to a different job altogether, rather than simply reducing (or altering) work hours in an existing job.

To address this problem, the Employment Act of 2002 introduced the right to request part-time or flexible work hours for parents of children under the age of 6 (as well as parents of disabled children), to go into effect in April 2003. This policy brought Britain into compliance with a European Union directive requiring member countries to provide a right for parents of young children to have the opportunity to switch to part-time or flexible hours in their existing jobs. The British policy did not give parents the right to make such a switch, but did give them the right to request part-time or flexible hours from their employer and to have the request reasonably considered.

The right to request policy proved to be popular among both parents and employers. In the first year alone, a million parents came forward with requests, the vast majority of which were granted, suggesting both that there was a large pent-up demand for more flexible working hours and that firms did not have strong objections to granting those requests.

Although some questions remain as to whether all types of employees are able to avail themselves of the right to request and, if not, which types of employees might be missing out, the policy is widely regarded as successful. Following a review in 2008, it was extended to cover parents with older children (up to the age of 16) in April 2009.

Assessment

We do not yet know what impact the right to request has had on other employment outcomes, such as job continuity and job tenure. Some of those taking advantage of the policy might otherwise have continued to work on a full-time basis, but others would likely have either switched to another (presumably lower-quality) job to obtain their desired schedule or would have left employment altogether. We also do not yet know whether the policy has increased the number of good jobs available on a part-time or flexible basis. However, certainly the intent of the law was to enable parents to remain in their existing jobs on a part-time or flexible basis rather than having to switch to other (presumably lower-quality) jobs in order to obtain their desired schedule. If this is the case, the policy should be resulting in more parents remaining in employment and remaining in their current jobs.

A sea change in support for working parents

The change in support for working parents over the past decade is nothing short of remarkable. Universal preschool has been rolled out to all 3 and 4 year olds, and parents are now eligible for paid maternity and paternity leave, a period of unpaid parental leave, and the right to request part-time or flexible hours. Childcare subsidies have been made much more generous. Childcare facilities have come under the inspection of Ofsted, the same agency that inspects schools, and the government is working to raise teacher qualifications in the childcare sector.

This expansion in support has not come cheap. Government spending on early learning and child care quadrupled between 1997–8 and 2007–8, when it reached more than £5 billion per year. Government support for paid leave also expanded. But clearly these policies will also yield substantial benefits. In addition to promoting better child health and development, the policies also provide an important boost to parental employment and family incomes.

At the same time, much remains to be done. In the leave area, moving to 12 months of paid maternity leave has proved challenging. In addition, the challenge of providing more leave for fathers, and more flexibility for mothers and fathers to share leave, remains. In the childcare area, Britain still has a long way to go to address the challenge of providing child care that is available, affordable and good quality. While child care is now more widely available, with particularly notable success in providing universal preschool for 3 and 4 year olds, there are still gaps in provision, and problems remain in the areas of both cost and quality. With regard to the right to request, this policy is now being extended to all parents with children, but we still have more to learn about whether all groups are able to take advantage of this or whether some working parents are missing out.

Nevertheless, the government can rightly take pride in what it accomplished in terms of family-friendly policies. As the Cabinet Office pointed out in 2009, 'This Government has doubled maternity leave and pay, introduced parental leave for fathers and given parents with young children the right to ask for flexible working. Free early learning and childcare places have been provided for all three- and four-year olds and over 3,500 Sure Start Children's Centres will be up and running by 2010' (Cabinet Office, 2009, p. 6). These are certainly accomplishments to be proud of, and ones that have made a difference in the lives of working families.

References

Berger, L., Hill, J. and Waldfogel, J. (2005) Maternity leave, early maternal employment, and child outcomes in the US. *Economic Journal*, 115: F29–F47.

Cabinet Office (2009) *New Opportunities: Fair Chances for the Future*. London: Cabinet Office.

Faggio, G., Gregg, P. and Wadsworth, J. (2011) Job tenure and job turnover. In: Gregg, P. and Wadsworth, J. (eds.) *The Labour Market in Winter: The State of Working Britain*. Oxford: Oxford University Press.

Gregg, P., Gutierrez-Domenech, M. and Waldfogel, J. (2007) The employment of married mothers in Great Britain: 1974–2000. *Economica*, 74(296): 842–64.

—— and Waldfogel, J. (2005). Symposium on parental leave, early maternal employment and child outcomes: introduction. *Economic Journal*, 115: F1–F6.

Hodge, M. (2005) *Choice for Parents, the Best Start for Children: A Ten Year Strategy for Child Care—Transmittal Memo*. London: Department for Education and Skills.

Waldfogel, J. (2006) *What Children Need*. Cambridge, Mass.: Harvard University Press.

—— (2010) *Britain's War on Poverty*. New York: Russell Sage Foundation Press.

—— and Garnham, A. (2008) *Childcare and Child Poverty*. Report prepared for Joseph Rowntree Foundation Initiative on Eradicating Child Poverty: The Role of Key Policy Areas. Available from <http://www.jrf.org.uk/publications/childcare-and-child-poverty> (accessed 28 April 2009).

Part III
Inequality

11

Changes in UK Wage Inequality Over the Last Forty Years

Stephen Machin

Key findings

- Wage inequality has risen significantly in the UK since the late 1970s.
- The most rapid widening out of the gap between high and low paid workers occurred in the 1980s, where earnings gaps widened throughout the distribution.
- In the 1990s, changes were more muted, but wage gaps continued to rise. In the 2000s, a rather different picture emerged, with upper tail wage inequality continuing to rise, but lower tail wage inequality stagnating.
- The standard supply-demand model of the labour market is relatively successful in accounting for some, but not all, of these observed changes. In addition in the 2000s, the national minimum wage is likely to have contributed to the stagnancy of lower tail wage inequality.

Introduction

This chapter offers an up-to-date picture of what has happened to wage inequality in the UK over the past forty years. I first focus upon documenting the patterns of change and trends in wage structures, and then on explaining why these changes have occurred. The chapter highlights that there have been different episodes of changes in wage inequalities. In the 1970s, there were reduced inequalities but, in terms of what followed, these narrowings were small in magnitude. The 1980s saw very rapidly rising wage inequalities, with wage gaps widening out at all parts of the wage distribution. In the 1990s, changes were more muted but wage gaps continued to rise. In the 2000s, a rather different picture emerged, with upper tail inequality continuing to rise, but lower tail inequality stagnating. Throughout this time period skilled workers improved their position relative to less skilled workers and there is evidence that labour market polarization caused a hollowing out of middle paying jobs.

Turning to explanations, I argue that the standard supply-demand model of the labour market is successful in accounting for some, but not all, of these observed changes. A key long-run driver has been skill-biased technology change (SBTC), which has been developed further in work that links closely to the polarization phenomenon from the observation that many jobs that have been lost have been through technology substituting for jobs that mainly involve routine tasks (task-biased technical change, TBTC). In addition in the 2000s, the national minimum wage is likely to have contributed to the stagnancy of lower tail wage inequality.

The rest of the chapter is structured as follows. The next section spends time describing the basic facts in terms of what has happened to wage inequality over the last four decades. The following section considers explanations of the observed patterns of change. The chapter ends with some general observations and concluding remarks.

Changes in UK wage inequality, 1970–2009

Overall changes in wage inequality since 1970

Figure 11.1 displays the evolution of the 90–10 earnings differential for full-time men and women since 1970, based upon New Earnings Survey (NES) and Annual Survey of Hours and Earnings (ASHE) data.[1] The figure reveals what by now has become a well-known pattern. From the late 1970s onwards the 90–10 ratio significantly increased and inequality is now a lot higher than it used to be. This is the case for men and women, though the increase in the 90–10 for women tends to taper off from the late 1990s.

Figure 11.2 separately considers the upper and lower halves of the distribution. For men, upper tail wage inequality (measured by the 90–50 wage ratio) rises sharply from the late 1970s and consistently throughout the entire period up until 2009. Male lower tail wage inequality (measured by the 50–10 wage ratio) also shows a significant increase, but with most of its increase concentrated in the 1980s and early to mid-1990s. Following that, it flattens out. For women, the story is similar, but with some subtle differences. Most

---

[1] The NES data runs up to 1996 and the ASHE data from 1997 to 2009.

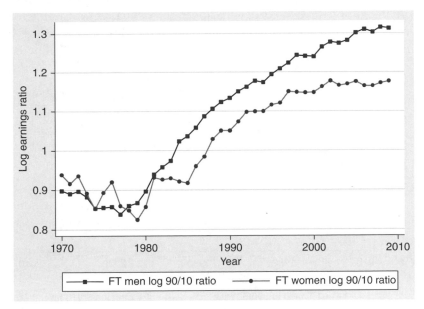

Figure 11.1: 90–10 Log weekly earnings ratios, full-time men and women, 1970–2009

Source: National Equality Panel Analysis; 1968–1996 New Earnings Survey (NES) and 1997–2009 ASHE.

notable is the halting of the increase in lower tail inequality from the mid-1990s.

Overall, however, what is very clear from Figures 11.1 and 11.2 is that wage inequality is significantly higher now than it was some thirty years ago. This is true for men and women, and is the case in both the upper and lower halves of the distribution.

Changes in educational wage differentials

Rising wage inequality has been accompanied by increasing gaps within and between different groups of workers. The wage premium received by graduates as compared to non-graduates is a between-group wage differential that has received considerable attention in the literature. Figure 11.3 shows the wage gap between graduates and non-graduates from 1980 to 2004. The premium rises sharply from 1.48 in 1980 to 1.60 by 1990 and continues to rise, albeit at a more modest pace, up until 2004. This is in line with the idea, recognised in various places in the literature, that education has become more highly valued in the labour market and that this is one of the key features of rising wage inequality.

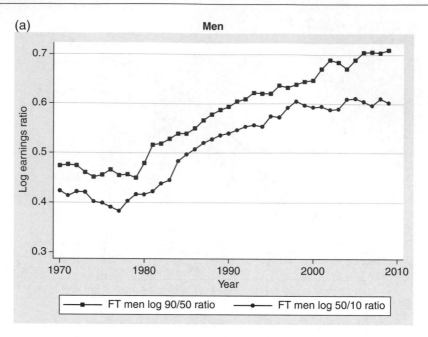

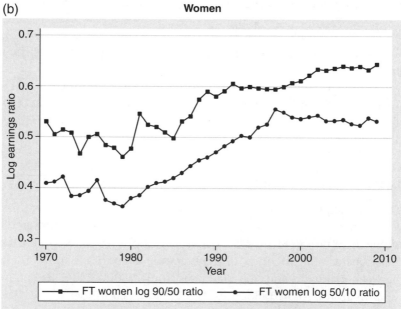

Figure 11.2: Upper tail (90–50 log earnings ratio) and lower tail (50–10 log earnings ratio) inequality, full-time men and women, 1970–2009 (a) Men (b) Women

Source: As for Figure 11.1.

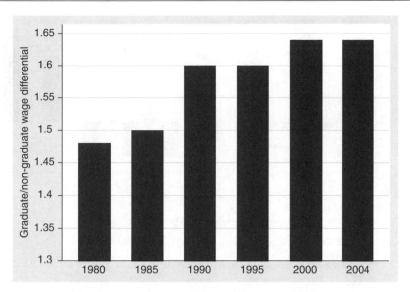

Figure 11.3: Graduate/non-graduate earnings differentials, 1980–2004

Notes: Wages are for full-time workers. The relative wage ratios are derived from coefficient estimates on a graduate dummy variable in semi-log earnings equations controlling for age, age squared and gender (they are the exponent of the coefficient on the graduate dummy).

Source: Graduate/non-graduate earnings differentials derived from General Household Survey (GHS) and Labour Force Survey (LFS) data. Updated from Machin and Vignoles (2005).

Labour market polarisation

In terms of employment, another key feature of rising labour market inequality has been the polarisation of jobs growth (Goos and Manning, 2007). Figure 11.4 (taken from Mieske, 2009) shows this very clearly, with there being very rapid growth over time in the top two deciles of job quality (as measured by median occupational wages from 1979). Employment actually fell from deciles 2 through 8, showing a hollowing out of the distribution, but there is positive growth for the bottom decile.

Decade by decade differences

The results presented to date make it very clear that wage inequalities are now significantly higher than they were forty years ago. However, looking at them more closely reveals different episodes of changes in wage inequalities. Table 11.1 looks at decade by decade changes in overall, upper and lower tail wage inequality. It reveals some different evolutions across the four decades covered by the analysis.

The table shows that the 1970s actually saw reduced inequalities (for women) but, in terms of what followed, these narrowings were relatively small in magnitude. The 1980s was very different. It saw very rapidly rising

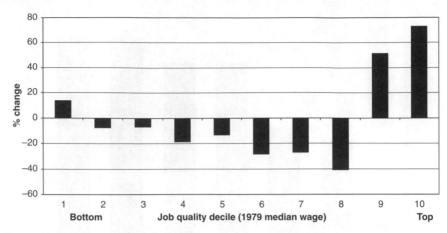

Figure 11.4: Polarisation of the UK labour market, 1979–2008

Notes: Taken from Mieske (2009). Percent changes are for the entire period.

Table 11.1: Trends in UK earnings inequality indices

	Trends in UK full-time weekly earnings inequality indices (annualised percentage points)			
	1970–1980	1980–1990	1990–2000	2000–2009
Men 90–10 Ratio	0.0	2.4	1.1	0.7
90–50 Ratio	0.1	1.2	0.6	0.6
50–10 Ratio	−0.1	1.2	0.5	0.1
25–10 Ratio	0.0	0.6	0.2	0.0
Women 90–10 Ratio	−0.8	1.9	1.0	0.3
90–50 Ratio	−0.5	1.0	0.3	0.3
50–10 Ratio	−0.3	0.9	0.7	0.0
25–10 Ratio	−0.1	0.3	0.4	−0.2

Source: National Equality Panel Analysis; 1968–1996 New Earnings Survey (NES) and 1997–2009 Annual Survey of Hours and Earnings (ASHE).

wage inequalities, with wage gaps widening out at all parts of the wage distribution, for both men and women.

In the 1990s, changes were more muted but wage gaps continued to rise, at approximately half the pace of the 1980s, and still being characterised by rising upper and lower tail inequality. In the 2000s, a rather different picture emerged, with upper tail inequality continuing to rise (albeit at a more modest rate, especially for women), but with lower tail inequality no longer increasing.

The stagnancy of the 50–10 differential in the 2000s based upon the ASHE data is an issue that requires comment as it has been stated in some places that lower tail inequality has fallen in the current decade. Other data sources do

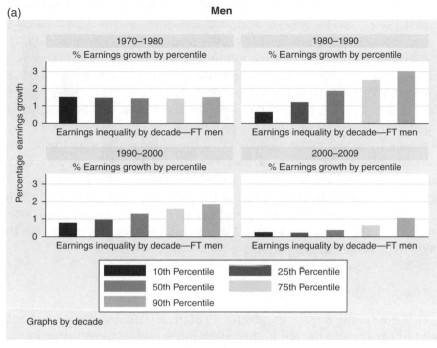

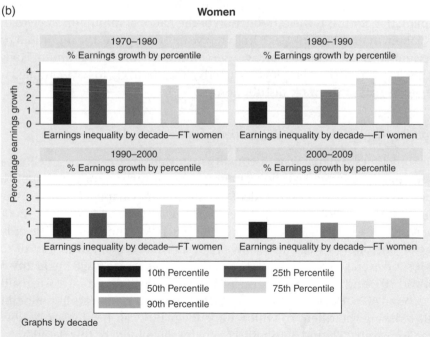

Figure 11.5: Real weekly earnings growth at different percentiles by decade (a) Men (b) Women

Source: ASHE.

suggest there may have been a modest reduction in the 50–10 ratio—in Brewer, Muriel and Wren-Lewis's (2009) analysis of FRS Survey data, the 50–10 differential is constant for full-time men and falls by 0.3 percentage points a year (up to 2008) for full-time women. In the ASHE data, the 25–10 differential for full-time women does fall slightly (by 0.2 percentage points a year). Probably the key thing to take from this is that lower tail inequality is no longer rising in the 2000s, and may be falling in its lower regions.

Overall, Table 11.1 makes it evident that the period where wage inequalities rose significantly and fastest was the 1980s. Considering different parts of the distribution in more detail makes this even clearer. Figure 11.5 shows real earnings growth at the 10th, 25th, 50th, 75th and 90th percentiles of the distribution by decade. The faster growth at the top that occurred in the 1980s is very clear. The 1990s looks rather like a toned down version of this, but the 2000s show a more mixed pattern.

The National Minimum Wage in the 2000s

A key feature of the 2000s is the stagnancy of the 50–10 wage ratio, which may well be characterised by falls in inequality further down the distribution (see the fall in the 25–10 ratio for women in Table 11.1). An obvious candidate explanation for this is the introduction of the national minimum wage to the UK labour market in April 1999. In its ten years of existence, the minimum has been raised at a faster rate than average earnings. While the minimum covers rather less than 10% of employees directly, it seems likely to have propped up the lower part of the wage distribution.

Mobility through the wage distribution

It is sometimes said that wage inequality in any given year can be ameliorated over time since individuals do not always stay at the top (or bottom) of the wage distribution (see also Blanden and Macmillan, Chapter 13, for a discussion of income mobility over generations). Dickens and McKnight (2008) analysed the extent to which earnings mobility over time reduces the cross-section snapshot of wage inequality. They concluded that at the start of the 1980s, on average, over four years, mobility reduced male wage inequality by around 30% and over ten years, on average, mobility reduced wage inequality by around 40%. However, throughout the 1980s and 1990s earnings mobility fell, reducing the extent to which wage inequality can be ameliorated over time (down to 25% and 30% respectively by the middle of this decade). Not only was the wage distribution getting wider, it was getting harder to move through the wage distribution over time. Since then mobility over time has started to rise a little again, but remains a long way below the mobility rates observed in periods when wage inequality was much lower.

International comparison

Many commentators have remarked upon the rapid wage inequality rise in the 1980s, arguing that, along with the US where wage inequality also rose very rapidly (and from higher starting levels), the UK labour market was pinpointed as one of the few places that then experienced rising wage inequality. Table 11.2 picks up on this by showing OECD data on male 90–10 wage ratios in 1970, 1980, 1990, 2000 and 2008 (or the closest year to that) for twelve countries.

Table 11.2 does confirm 1980s increases in the 90–10 for the UK and US, with relative stability elsewhere. However, when one moves to the 1990s and 2000s, the picture is not so clear. In the 1990s, wage inequality starts to rise in some countries like Australia, Germany, Korea, the Netherlands and Sweden. In the 2000s, rising wage inequality appears to be the norm, even in the Nordic countries where rises are small but there are increases, leaving only France having a relatively stable wage structure over time.

Explanations of changing wage structures

Changes in supply and demand

In recent times, there have been considerable adjustments in the skill structures of the workforces of many countries as the labour market has altered to

Table 11.2: Male 90–10 wage ratios across countries, 1970–2008

	1970	1980	1990	2000	2008
Australia	2.4[a]	2.7	2.7	3.1	3.5
Denmark		2.1	2.2	2.5	2.7[e]
Finland	—	2.5	2.5	2.4	2.6[e]
France	3.7	3.3	3.3	3.0	2.9[d]
Germany	—	2.5[b]	2.5	2.8	2.9[d]
Japan	2.6[a]	2.6	2.8	2.8	2.9
Korea	—	4.1[b]	3.2	3.7	4.7
Netherlands	—	2.3[b]	2.5	2.9	2.9[d]
New Zealand	—	2.2	2.5	2.7	3.1
Sweden	2.2[a]	2.1	2.1	2.4	2.4[c]
UK	2.7	2.7	3.3	3.4	3.7
US	3.4	3.6	4.4	4.8	5.0

Notes: Taken from OECD Stat Extracts web site (<http://stats.oecd.org/index.aspx>). Data are from different years from the column header for some countries as denoted by the following superscripts: a—1975; b—1984; c—2004; d—2005; e—2007.

cope with the new demands for work and with the new work systems that now operate. Employers have shifted their patterns of demand for labour towards workers who possess more education and skills. In many countries, these workers have not only increased their relative employment, but also their relative wages, thereby increasing labour market inequality.

Economic researchers have extensively studied changing wage gaps between workers at different points in the wage distribution in terms of the relative demand and supply of skills. This has been operationalised in empirical models that relate changes in the relative wages of groups of workers (e.g. more educated versus less educated) to changes in the relative demand and supply of these groups of workers. The logic goes that, if relative demand is growing faster over time than relative supply, then relative wages are likely to have risen, but if the opposite holds, they are likely to have fallen.

Table 11.3 presents UK estimates based on annual data from 1974 to 2007 relating the relative wage of graduates as compared to non-graduates to a demand index (proxied by a time trend) and the relative supply of graduates as compared to non-graduates.[2] The model seems to fit the data well. As expected, the estimated coefficient on the supply variable is negative and significant and in the range of −0.17 to −0.20. However, the positive coefficient on the trend variable shows that, despite the very sharp increase in the relative supply of graduates, there must have been an even faster growth in

Table 11.3: Estimates of the relative supply and demand model for the UK

	Relative Wages – Ln(Graduate/Non-Graduate Wage)		
	GHS, LFS earnings, GHS, LFS supply	GHS, LFS earnings, GHS supply	GHS, LFS earnings, LFS supply
Supply - Ln(Relative Graduate/Non-Graduate Employment)	−0.168 (0.032)	−0.174 (0.044)	−0.200 (0.079)
Demand - Time Trend	0.007 (0.001)	0.008 (0.002)	0.008 (0.003)
R-Squared	0.48	0.37	0.28
Sample Size	33	30	22

Notes: The earnings sources are General Household Survey (GHS) for 1974–91, Labour Force Survey (LFS) for 1993–2007; 1992 is omitted. The combined supply series are GHS for 1974–83 and 1986, LFS for 1984–5 and 1987–2007; the GHS supply series covers 1974–2006 (excluding 1997 and 1999) and the LFS series runs from 1984–2007 (excluding 1986). The preferred sample has 33 observations, and includes all years between 1974 and 2007 (inclusive), with the exception of 1992.

Source: Taken from Amior (2008).

[2] This type of model was first presented using US data in Katz and Murphy (1992) and more recently has been updated by Autor et al. (2008). The UK results discussed here are from Amior (2008).

relative demand for graduates. This shows that relative wages rose by the order of 0.7–0.8% per year over and above the increases in relative supply that occurred. Thus a key factor underpinning rising wage inequality has been a relative demand shift in favour of more skilled workers.

Skill-biased technical change

In the research on rising wage inequality and shifts in relative demand for skills, a strong focus has been placed upon asking what are the key drivers of these relative demand shifts. A lot of the literature has concluded that SBTC has been the key driver of such change.[3]

Stated in its simplest form, the SBTC hypothesis says that new technologies lead to higher productivity, but only some (more skilled) workers possess the necessary skills to operate them. Therefore in response to introducing these kinds of technologies into their workplace, employers raise demand and/or wages for highly skilled workers who are complements with the new technologies. Lower wages, or lay-offs, occur for less skilled workers who do not possess the skill to use the new technologies.

A typical empirical approach adopted to test this hypothesis asks the question as to whether plants, firms or industries that are more likely to have introduced new technologies are also those with faster increases in the relative demand for skilled workers. A large academic literature has considered this, using a range of data sources at different levels of aggregation, from different time periods and countries, and using different measures of skill demand and new technology. There is now an abundance of empirical research that suggests that SBTC is an important and international phenomenon. Table 11.4 reports results from some selected UK studies showing this, for a range of different technology indicators, time periods and data sources.[4]

It is worth noting that the studies reaching this conclusion for the UK (Machin, 1996, and Machin and Van Reenen, 1998) use data from the period where wage inequality rose fastest. A natural question to ask, given the decade differences in changing patterns of wage inequality noted above, is whether such effects still operate. A new analysis described in the first row of Table 11.4 confirms that they do. Even in the 2000s the industries experiencing faster increases in skill demand are those with higher R&D intensities.

---

[3] For straightforward descriptions of the SBTC hypothesis see Machin (2003). The assertion that SBTC is the key driver is by no means without controversy. See Card and DiNardo (2002) for a very sceptical position.

[4] Further international studies are surveyed in the more detailed table 2 in Machin (2008).

Table 11.4: Summary of UK evidence on changes in skill demand and technology

Study	Unit of analysis	Time period	Skill demand measure	Technology measure	Impact of technology measure	Controls
This chapter	17 manufacturing industries	2000–08[a]	Graduate wage bill share	R&D/value added (Y)	0.176 (0.081)	Capital stock, output
Machin and Van Reenen (1998)	15 UK manufacturing industries	1973–89	Non-production wage bill share	R&D/value added (Y)	0.026 (0.009)	Capital stock, output
Machin (1996)	16 UK manufacturing industries	1982–89[a]	Non-production wage bill share	R&D/sales (S)	0.065 (0.026)	Capital stock, output, industry
	16 UK manufacturing industries	1980–85[a]		Innovation count from 1970s	0.092 (0.053)	
	398 British workplaces	1984–90[a]	Managers, senior technical and professional employment share	Micro computers introduced	0.044 (0.022)	Employment decline, Industry

Notes: [a] denotes that models are long differenced (i.e. treated as a single cross-section in changes) and so no year dummies need to be included as controls.

Task-biased technical change

In an important recent paper, Autor, Levy and Murnane (2003) have recast the SBTC hypothesis, especially the impact of computerization, in a fresh light. They argue that the nature of jobs, and the tasks done by workers in their jobs, are key to thinking about the way in which technological changes impact on the wage distribution. They argue that computers raise the demand for jobs where non-routine tasks are required of more skilled and educated workers, but they substitute for jobs with routine tasks done by middle-educated workers (like manufacturing production, or secretarial jobs). Thus routine non-manual tasks may be replaced by computers, whilst some non-routine tasks done by manual workers (like cleaning) are largely unaffected by ICT.

Autor, Levy and Murnane present empirical evidence of non-monotone impacts of computers on the demand for jobs, with a strong complementarity between computerisation and the demand for non-routine jobs and a strong substitutability with the relative demand for jobs involving routine tasks. Autor and Dorn (2009) have also studied aspects of TBTC, arguing that the reason for increased demand for low wage service sector jobs highlighted in the labour market polarisation research occurred in places with high initial levels of routine tasks.

Empirical research has considered this by looking at data across areas over time to ask whether areas with higher shares of jobs involving routine tasks at the start of the analysis see faster increases in the share of non-graduate service sector jobs in the area over time. The key idea is that having more routine task jobs initially causes the hollowing out of middle of the distribution jobs and that this polarisation results in an increased demand for low wage service sector jobs.

Evidence for this idea based upon data on UK counties over time is reported in Table 11.5 (taken from Mieske, 2009). It shows faster cross-county growth in the non-graduate service share in places where there were initially more

Table 11.5: Some UK evidence on task-biased technical change

	Changes in non-graduate service sector employment share					
	1992 to 2008		1992 to 2000		2000 to 2008	
Initial routine	0.038	0.029	0.032	0.030	0.044	0.026
Employment share	(0.015)	(0.016)	(0.012)	(0.013)	(0.024)	(0.025)
Controls	No	Yes	No	Yes	No	Yes
R-squared	0.15	0.21	0.22	0.25	0.10	0.20
Sample size	392	392	196	196	196	196

Notes: Four-year differenced models based on 98 UK counties. The control variables included are (all in changes): graduate share, working student share, non-graduate migrant share, female employment share, elderly share, inactivity and unemployment.

Source: Taken from Mieske (2009).

routine tasks[5] that could be substituted by new technologies. Moreover, the finding remains robust both for the 1990s and 2000s, providing some evidence that TBTC matters for the changing nature of the UK labour market.

Conclusions

This chapter has studied changes in the structure of wages in the UK over the last four decades. Wage inequality is significantly higher now than it was in the past. This is the case for upper and lower tail wage inequality. There are decade to decade differences in the patterns of change and it seems clear that the 1980s was the period where wage inequalities seemed to open out at all parts of the distribution. After that, the picture has become more complex.

In terms of explanations, the evidence shows the wage distribution has been characterised by long-run growth in the relative demand for skills driven by technology change and that changes in skill supply and institutional changes (like the introduction of the UK minimum wage) have affected the timing of how skill-biased and task-biased technical change impact upon the wage structure.

References

Amior, M. (2008) The skill divide and the north-south graduate exodus: how have changes in the supply and demand for graduate workers affected Britain's regional labour markets? Unpublished MSc dissertation. University College London.

Autor, D. and Dorn, D. (2009) Inequality and specialization: the growth of low-skill service jobs in the United States. National Bureau of Economic Research Working Paper No. 15150.

—— Katz, L. and Kearney, M. (2008) Trends in US wage inequality: re-assessing the revisionists. *Review of Economics and Statistics*, 90: 300–23.

—— Levy, F. and Murnane, R. (2003) The skill content of recent technological change: an empirical investigation. *Quarterly Journal of Economics*, 118: 1279–333.

Blanden, J. and Macmillan, L. (2011) Recent developments in intergenerational mobility. In: Gregg, P. and Wadsworth, J. (eds.) *The Labour Market in Winter: The State of Working Britain*. Oxford: Oxford University Press.

---

[5] The definition of routineness is complex and described in detail in Mieske (2009). She mapped 1980 US Census occupation codes and corresponding task measures from the Dictionary of Occupational Titles (DOT) to their closest UK SOC2000 codes by hand. She then followed Autor et al. (2008) in ranking the routine task level of each occupation by the arithmetic average of DOT classifications 'Set Limits, Tolerances and Standards' and 'Finger Dexterity'.

Brewer, M., Muriel, A. and Wren-Lewis, L. (2009) Accounting for changes in inequality since 1968: decomposition analysis for Great Britain. London: Institute for Fiscal Studies Report for National Equality Panel.

Card, D. and DiNardo, J. (2002) Skill-biased technological change and rising wage inequality: some problems and puzzles. *Journal of Labor Economics*, 20: 733–83.

Dickens, R. and McKnight, A. (2008) Changes in earnings inequality and mobility in Great Britain 1978/9–2005/6. Centre for Economic Performance Occasional Paper No. 21, <http://cep.lse.ac.uk/pubs/download/occasional/op021.pdf>.

Goos, M. and Manning, A. (2007) Lousy and lovely jobs: the rising polarization of work in Britain, *Review of Economics and Statistics*, 89: 118–33.

Katz, L. and Murphy, K. (1992) Changes in relative wages, 1963–87: supply and demand factors. *Quarterly Journal of Economics*, 107: 35–78.

Machin, S. (1996) Changes in the relative demand for skills in the UK labour market. In: Booth, A. and Snower, D. (eds.) *Acquiring Skills: Market Failures, their Symptoms and Policy Responses*. Cambridge: Cambridge University Press.

—— (2003) Skill-biased technical change in the new economy. In: Jones, D. (ed.) *New Economy Handbook*. San Diego and London: Elsevier and Academic Press.

—— (2008) An appraisal of economic research on changes in wage inequality. *Labour*, 22: 7–26.

—— and Van Reenen, J. (1998) Technology and changes in skill structure: evidence from seven OECD countries. *Quarterly Journal of Economics*, 113: 1215–44.

—— and Vignoles, A. (eds.) (2005) *What's the Good of Education? The Economics of Education in the United Kingdom*. Princeton: Princeton University Press.

Mieske, K. (2009) Low-skill service jobs and technical change. Unpublished MSc dissertation. University College London.

12

Gender and the Labour Market

Joanna K. Swaffield

Key findings

- Headline figures published by the Office for National Statistics for the (median) gender wage gap between full-time employees suggest a continued movement towards reduced gender inequality in labour market outcomes. However, this average obscures the existence of more than one type of female labour market experience over the last decade.
- Evidence on both the full-time/part-time wage differential and the occupational downgrading associated with a move from full-time to part-time employment suggests that until 'better' jobs come in a part-time form, occupational downgrading coupled with a part-time pay penalty will continue as part of the female experience of part-time working.
- Summary labour market figures for 2008–9 suggest that the female experience of the recent UK recession is not any worse than that experienced by male workers. However, comparisons with previous recessions need to note that more women are likely to be *directly* affected by the recent recession due to greater numbers being formally engaged within the labour market.
- The main gender issue facing the British labour market over the next decade is whether the observed reduction in labour market gender gaps (e.g. wages and employment) over the last ten years will continue, but at a slower pace, or whether improvements to gender equality will in fact be stalled.

Introduction

In 2007 the Office of National Statistics heralded the gap of 12.5% between women's and men's full-time median hourly pay as being the lowest since records began. By April 2009 this figure had reduced again slightly to 12.2%. Such a historically low gender pay gap suggests a continued movement towards reduced gender inequality in labour market outcomes in Britain. However, just how true is this? Does the observed reduction in this raw gender wage gap really indicate a concerted movement towards gender pay parity, as well in other employment outcomes? Or rather does it suggest such a trend for certain groups of women in certain types of employment in the British labour market? These questions are the subject of this chapter on 'gender and the labour market'.

This chapter charts the changes in labour market outcomes for female workers in Britain, across a range of employment and wage measures from 1997 to 2009, a period of relative and increasing economic prosperity. The chapter then continues to chart changes in some of these measures across nine quarters of data from January 2008 through to September 2009, covering the period of the onset of the late noughties recession.

We begin by summarising the policy and legislation changes over recent decades which have impacted on female employment outcomes. The focus then moves onto employment changes and gender gains over the last decade, considering to what extent there is still an employment gap between male and female workers and the factors that contribute to this gap. The question of which is the *correct* or most informative gender wage gap to focus on is then considered, for example, which gender pay gap is the one that matters? Considering, with reference to potential differences in male and female characteristics, the extent to which these measurable differences can explain the gender wage differential. In particular, to what extent part-time employment and occupational segregation (along with downgrading) are contributing to the gender gaps in both wage and other employment outcomes.

A summary of the findings of a recent report from the Equality and Human Rights Commission (EHRC) on gender and discrimination issues in the financial services sector is then presented. This EHRC report is particularly interesting as it presents an illustration, within the financial services sector, of the various factors (and obstacles) encountered by many other women in their working environments in other sectors of the British economy. The final section of this chapter considers how the recent recession has impacted upon female employment and the degree to which it may have disproportionately hit female workers in the British labour market.

Policy and legislation

Historic labour market legislation to support gender equality in pay and employment outcomes includes the Equal Pay Act 1970 (ratified 1975) which prohibits the unequal treatment of workers in terms of pay and conditions of employment based on gender, as well as the Sex Discrimination Act 1975 aimed at protecting both men and women from discrimination on the grounds of gender. The impact of these two laws was fundamental in significantly reducing the gender wage gap in the British labour market. Further, the Maternity Rights Acts of 1978 and 1993 afforded women further rights within the labour market to the extent that job loss or demotion as a direct result of childbearing became illegal, and formal provision was given for leave.

More recently, family-friendly employment policies have helped strengthen the labour market attachment of women with young children. In April 2003 the Right to Request Flexible Working law gave parents of children under 6 the right to request an alternative, more flexible working arrangement, such as flexi-hours, home working, term-time working etc. This law has been very effective in encouraging employers to consider such flexible working arrangements, and the law has been recently extended (from April 2007) under the Work and Families Act 2006 to cover the care of adults—the other end of the care spectrum for many women. Although these laws have generally been relatively well received by employers, it should be remembered that the law only requires employers to *consider* changes to employees' hours/conditions of employment, in light of the individual's care obligations, rather than obliging them to necessarily agree to the requested family-friendly flexible working arrangement. Clearly the current legislation only affords the employee the right to ask, not the right to have.

Additional legislative changes over the last decade that have had the potential to positively impact upon the employment conditions and outcomes for women include the Part-time Workers Regulations introduced in 2000.[1] These regulations strengthened the employment rights of part-time workers, the majority of whom are female (and also low-paid), such that it is now unlawful to treat part-time less favourably than full-time workers in their working conditions, with the caveat of 'unless it is objectively justifiable' (Manning and Petrongolo, 2008: F45).

Other recent policy changes which have improved the relative position of women in the labour market include the UK's National Minimum Wage (NMW) introduced on 1 April 1999. The NMW adult rate was initially set at £3.60 and is currently after successive upratings set at £5.93 per hour (at October 2010). The NMW has effectively provided a wage floor to the UK labour market benefiting those at the bottom end of the wage distribution, a measure which has disproportionally affected women, and in particular part-time working women, due to the relatively low-paid status of such female

---

[1] SI 2000/1551 The Part-time Workers (Prevention of Less Favourable Treatment) Regulations 2000.

workers. By benefiting women at the lower end of the wage distribution, the NMW has undoubtedly contributed to the reduction in the (average) gender wage differential and particularly so within the lower deciles of the wage distribution. For example, the Low Pay Commission report in 2009 estimated that approximately two-thirds of minimum wage jobs are held by women, with the observed reduction in the gender pay gap since 1998 being evidence that the NMW is having a greater impact on female earnings than on males'. Further, it is argued that this gender parity effect has been achieved with little evidence of a negative impact on female employment.

However, the NMW should not be considered in terms of the key strategy to significantly reduce the persistently observed gender wage gap, as even large hikes (statutory increases) in the NMW would not be able to achieve this. Rather, in terms of gender wage issues, the NMW should be considered in terms of controlling the worst extremes of low pay in the labour market, providing an effective wage floor, which happens to benefit, disproportion-ally, female part-time employees.

Another notable change in policy over the last decade has been the replace-ment of Family Credit (FC) with the Working Families Tax Credits (WFTC) scheme. This change took place in October 1999 and was aimed at improving the incentives (and rewards) to work. Empirical evaluation of this policy change, which worked in tandem with the New Deal for Lone Parents (NDLP), suggests that the group whose labour market activity has been most affected has been lone mothers, whose participation rates have increased.

Although all the above policies and legislative changes have centred around encouraging women to work, through strengthening their labour market attachment by raising the returns to paid work, improving equality and rights within the workplace or increasing the possibility of flexible employment to fit around other caring responsibilities, there has been one notable policy change which has arguably been more stick than carrot. In November 2008 changes to the rules for lone parents to claim income support reduced the age of the youngest child for whom entitlement exists to 12 years of age. Further reductions in this age threshold mean by the end of October 2010 lone parents will only be able to claim income support until their youngest child reaches their seventh birthday (nine years earlier than the pre-November 2008 entitlement).

Employment changes and gender gains over the last decade

Table 12.1 provides the raw employment rates by gender from 1997 to 2009 in the British labour market. Overall the employment rate has increased slightly from 75% to 78% in 2008, though falling to 76% in 2009. However, this

Table 12.1: Employment rates by gender

Year	All	Females	Males	Gender gap in employment rates
1997	75.09	69.49	80.56	11.07
1998	75.65	69.99	81.17	11.18
2000	76.75	71.44	81.93	10.49
2002	77.08	72.17	81.92	9.75
2004	77.37	72.43	82.27	9.84
2006	77.64	73.16	82.04	8.88
2008	78.00	73.70	82.16	8.46
2009	76.18	72.63	79.57	6.94

Notes: Employment rates defined as percentage of working-age adults in work (employees, self-employed, government schemes and unpaid family work); excludes full-time students.
Source: LFS, Q2, April–June 1997–2009.

reasonably small increase is driven mainly by increases in the female employment rate. The female employment rate has increased from 69% in 1997 to almost 74% in 2008 (although again falling in 2009). Although a noticeable increase, it is much smaller than changes in the female employment rate observed over previous decades. In terms of the gender gap in employment rates, even against a small increase in male employment rates (up to 2008) the gender gap in employment rates has fallen slightly over the 1997–2009 period. The employment rate gender gap has fallen from 11 to 6.94 (in 2009) percentage points. As such, the period 1997–2009 shows a continuation of the trend in reduced gender gaps in employment rates observed from the mid-1970s until 1993, rather than the pause as was observed in the 1990s. However the 1997–2009 reduction in the gender employment rate gap is much less than for the mid-1970s to 1993 period, suggesting instead that the more recent period is exhibiting a flatter trend. Nevertheless, on some measures, convergence in employment by gender has almost been achieved. The LFS suggests that in the fourth quarter of 2009, for the population aged 16 to 59, the number of female employees was just 90,000 short of the 11,620,000 estimated number of male employees. Only the gender bias in favour of men in self-employment and differential statutory state pension age, now set in train to be equalised at 65 by 2020, sustains the gender gap in favour of men.

What causes the employment gap?

Although the percentages in Table 12.1 suggest a continued reduction in the employment rate gender gap, the average rates clearly cannot show the full picture or detailed employment experience for all women, across different ages and cohorts. Figure 12.1 shows this more detailed picture for female employment rates by age for 1988, 1998 and 2009. This figure clearly shows that there has been a noticeable upward shift in employment rates of women aged 22 to 35 between the years 1988 and 2009. Figure 12.1 also shows that there has been an upward shift in employment rates for women in their late forties and early fifties. Interestingly, the comparisons between the three time points show that the majority of this employment rate increase occurred between 1988 and 1998, with a much more modest upward shift between 1998 and 2009 for younger women.

Figure 12.2 compares the employment rates of male and female workers by age for 2009, showing that the male and female employment rates exhibit the greatest gender gap through the early twenties and late thirties. However, for the later periods of the working life (45+), there is a much more similar employment rate. Clearly the female mid-twenties–thirties reduced employment rates will be bound up with the peak child-rearing period, and the choices women are making regarding fertility, childcare provision and formal labour market activity. The importance of the presence of children (and specifically whether the youngest child is pre-school, less than 5 years of age) in explaining these gender differences in employment rates is shown in Table 12.2. Raw employment rates of females with their youngest child aged under 5 (age 0–1 and age 2–4) are roughly 55% and 57% compared to over 80% for women with their youngest child aged 16–18. Comparisons over 1997–2009 show the largest increase in employment rates to be for women with a youngest child aged 0–1, rising from less than half in 1997 to over 56%

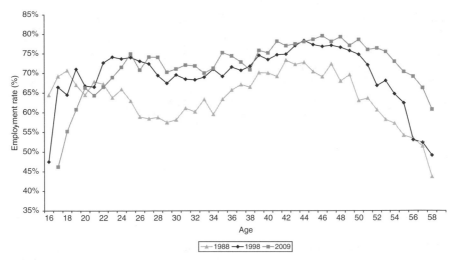

Figure 12.1: Female employment rates by age (1988, 1998 and 2009)

Notes: Employment rates defined as percentage of working-age adults in work (employees, self-employed, government schemes and unpaid family work); excludes full-time students.

Source: LFS, Q2, April–June 1988, 1998 and 2009.

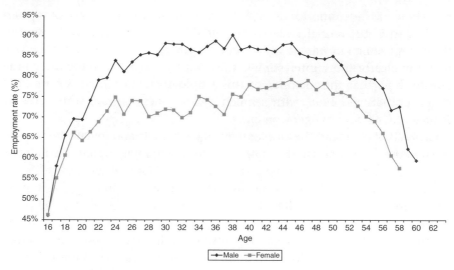

Figure 12.2: Male and female employment rates by age in 2009

Notes: Employment rates defined as percentage of working age adults in work (employees, self-employed, government schemes and unpaid family work), excludes full-time students.

Source: LFS, Q2, April–June 2009.

Table 12.2: Female employment rates by age of youngest child

Year	All females	Age of youngest child				
		Age 0–1	Age 2–4	Age 5–10	Age 11–15	Age 16–18
1997	69.49	48.25	54.35	66.89	74.76	77.59
1998	69.99	47.15	54.35	68.72	74.31	79.00
2000	71.44	52.35	57.15	70.21	75.48	79.17
2002	72.17	50.02	56.93	71.02	76.93	79.06
2004	72.43	51.92	55.95	71.83	77.12	77.92
2006	73.16	53.95	59.77	71.31	76.51	78.18
2008	73.70	56.25	57.90	71.49	77.32	81.09
2009	72.63	54.89	57.13	70.38	78.70	80.26

Notes: Employment rates defined as percentage of working-age adults in work (employees, self-employed, government schemes and unpaid family work); excludes full-time students.

Source: LFS, Q2, April–June 1997–2009.

in 2008 (though falling to approximately 55% in 2009). Although these percentages clearly show the impact of young children in explaining the formal engagement of a female with the labour market, they also show how the labour market attachment of women has been steadily increasing over time.

A further guide to labour market attachment by gender is through the changing nature of job tenures (see Gregg et al., Chapter 7, for further details). Traditionally, female job tenure (or length of time with employer) tended to be shorter, with females more likely to change jobs/employers than male employees. Although males do still, on average, have longer job tenure than women, this differential is decreasing, for females both with and without dependent children, providing support for the argument that women with children are continuing to increase their attachment to the labour market. Further support for this point and evidence of the increasing importance (and significance) of the female contribution within the labour market is noted by females' share of total household earnings. In 1999, 14.4% of two-person households with a working male and female were observed to have the female earning the dominant share of monthly earnings; in 2009 this is up to 21.3%.[2]

The gender wage gap: which is the one that matters?

The discussion so far has focused on gender difference in employment; however, this is only one dimension upon which the female experience of the British labour market might be distinct from that of a male worker. Table 12.3 presents various gender wage gaps from 2009 using the Annual Survey of Hours and Earnings (ASHE).

Table 12.3 illustrates various (employee) gender wage gaps across all, full-time and part-time employees, as well as across different percentiles of the wage

Table 12.3: Illustration of various (employee) gender wage gaps (April 2009)

	Male	Female	Gender wage gap (%)
Weekly pay (£)			
Median (all)	491.0	309.8	36.9
Average (all)	589.3	370.2	37.2
Median (full-time only)	531.1	426.4	19.7
Average (full-time only)	643.0	501.2	22.1
Hourly pay (£)			
Median (all)	12.42	9.68	22.1
Average (all)	15.84	12.64	20.2
Median (full-time only)	12.97	11.39	12.2
Average (full-time only)	16.07	13.43	16.4
10th percentile (full-time only)	7.14	6.60	7.6
90th percentile (full-time only)	28.35	18.10	36.2
Median: full-time males, part-time	12.97	7.86	39.4
females (Full-time females, part-time females)			(31.0)
Average: full-time males, part-time	16.07	10.40	35.3
Females (Full-time females, part-time females)			(22.6)

Notes:
1. Employees on adult rates whose pay for the survey pay-period was not affected by absence.
2. Weekly pay defined as gross. Hourly pay defined as excluding overtime.
Source: Published figures for ASHE, Office for National Statistics.

[2] Labour Force Survey, Q2 1999 and 2009.

distribution. The various wage measures and the gender gaps based on these measures highlight the sensitivity of the measured gender wage gap to the *type* of employees compared. Why this point is of interest is the following: the raw gender gap is often used to gauge the general level of gender wage inequality (and possibly also discrimination) within the labour market. As such, the consistent trend over the last 20–30 years of a falling gender wage gap is informative in suggesting there has been increasing gender equality in the labour market. However, if the standard groups over which the gender wage gap comparisons are constructed become less informative of the total female labour market experience, then the relevance of this declining gender wage gap, as part of an improving gender equality story, may decline also. The particular point here is the increasing distinction between full-time and part-time workers, and the disproportionate dominance of women in this latter group.[3]

The headline figure reported annually by the Office for National Statistics relates to the gender wage gap based on the differential between full-time male and full-time female median hourly wages. As can be seen from Table 12.3, this gender wage gap of 12.2% (row 7) is the smallest gender wage gap in the table. In comparison, the gender wage gap based on weekly wages (the upper panel of Table 12.3) shows a raw gender wage gap of 36.9% and 37.2% for median and average wages respectively; quite justifiably this large difference will be driven by the differences in compositions between part-time and full-time workers (see Table 12.6) and their length of working week. However, the difference between weekly earnings for full-time males and females (thus removing the part-time compositional difference) still shows a large gender wage gap, roughly 20%, which is likely to be at least in part the result of longer (contractual) full-time hours of male full-time workers than female workers and due to the possibility of overtime premiums which males are more likely to receive.

These points noted, it might suggest then that the control or removal of differences in hours of work per week and exclusion of overtime earnings would mitigate the (raw) gender wage gap; the evidence in the lower panel of the table shows some of these points to be the case. However, focusing on the hourly wage rate for *all* employees and excluding overtime results in a gender wage gap of roughly 20%, equivalent to the weekly difference for full-time employees. This is reduced further when the full-time only employees are focused upon (reducing to approximately 12–16%), suggesting some (potential) productivity differential between part-time and full-time workers (a point returned to below in relation to occupational downgrading).

---

[3] Though with increased female participation rates the concerns over selection effects (among women) and distortions that this can cause to wage comparisons are now much lower, in contrast the declining participation rates among males now raises this sample selection concern for males.

Although the comparison of part-time and full-time figures in Table 12.3 does suggest that comparing 'equivalent' workers with each other does reduce the observed gender wage gap, it also suggests that the magnitude of the gender wage gap is not constant across the wage distribution. Even within the full-time workers, the gender wage gap is seen to increase from 7.6% across the bottom decile, up to 12.2% at the median, up to over 36% in the top decile. These large mean gender wage gaps for the top end of the hourly wage distribution for full-time workers are matched by the average gender wage differentials between the full-time males and part-time females (39.4%), and also interestingly between the full-time females and part-time females (31%). This final point adds to the validity that there is some distinction within the female employed group (based on part-time vs. full-time working) which makes the standard median gender wage gap for full-time workers less informative as a barometer of the degree of gender parity (across all workers) in the British labour market.

A final point of interest, linking to the previous section on gender employment gaps, is that if female labour supply is rising (as evidenced in the previous section), this may well put downward pressure on the female wage, particularly if supply increases in the female-dominated sectors, and therefore on the gender wage gap (thus working against reductions in the wage gap). To the extent that this has not and does not appear to be happening, it suggests the possibility of offsetting factors.

Can the gender wage gap be explained?

Although gender wage gaps are interesting and comparisons across groups and even time are informative, the raw gender wage gap might not necessarily be of concern to us. The question, when considering the gender wage gap, is to what extent the observed difference is actually driven by differences in measured characteristics by gender (the explained), and how far it is due to differences in the returns to these characteristics (the unexplained). The second of these can arguably (although possibly debatably) be considered in terms of labour market gender discrimination. So what is likely to be driving the gender wage gaps shown in Table 12.3? A list of factors which are important to consider would include the occupational distribution of women, average education levels, female labour market attachment (or histories), employment in part-time jobs, and the importance of promotion or career advancement of women in the British labour market. Each of these factors is considered in turn below.

Figure 12.3(a) provides a simple illustration of the degree of gender-based occupational segregation in the British labour market. The histogram shows the proportion of total female employment engaged in each of the nine major

(a)

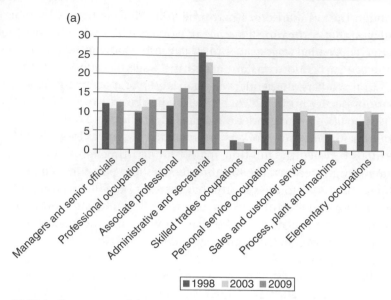

Figure 12.3(a): Percentage of female employment by occupation (1998, 2003 and 2009)

(b)

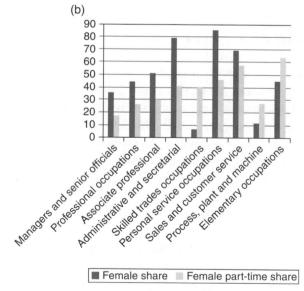

Figure 12.3(b): Within occupation female employee and part-time female shares (2009)

Source: LFS, Q2, April–June 1998, 2003 and 2009.

occupational groups for 1998, 2003 and 2009. The figure shows the large share of female employment within the administrative and secretarial occupations, and also the personal service and associate professional occupations (though the share in the first of these occupations has fallen over the decade considered). The relevance of occupational segregation to the observed gender wage gap is important if women are disproportionally located within the lower-paying occupations (or sectors) of the economy.

Figure 12.3(b) details the degree of occupational segregation of females in more detail for each of the nine major occupations in 2009. For each occupation the first darker vertical bar shows the share of employment in that occupation which is female, the second lighter bar shows the percentage (or share) of this female employment which is defined as part-time (female) workers. The first darker bars show the administrative and secretarial, personal service and the sales and customer service occupations to have large shares of women working in them, over 80% in the case of administrative and secretarial, for example. In comparison, the two occupations of skilled trades and process, plant and machine have (proportionally) very few females working in them. In terms of part-time female shares, the three occupations with a high share of female workers also have larger shares (in excess of 40%) of part-time workers.

If the occupational distribution of female employment is centred upon those occupations with lower wages, it is not surprising that the gender wage gap is sizeable. An obvious policy conclusion might then be to encourage an alternative occupation distribution producing a smaller wage gap; for example, encouraging women to consider non-traditional occupations (occupations which often replicate the traditional responsibilities within the home). However, a more fundamental approach might be to reconsider the level of remuneration within these female-dominated sectors.

Another factor potentially important in explaining the gender wage gap is level of education within the group of female workers. Historically, women were less likely to be as educated (on average) as male workers and therefore previously (or still for older cohorts) some of the gender wage gap may well have been due to differences in productivity levels resulting from stocks of educational investments. However, for younger or more recent cohorts of workers, the educational explanation of the gender wage gap is far from convincing as recent female labour market entrants are increasingly as educated (or even more so) than their male contemporaries. For example, in the UK the current female university graduation rate now outstrips that of males.[4]

One factor that is still relevant for explaining the gender wage gap (though as with education, much less so for more recent cohorts) is that of labour

---

[4] See 'Education at a Glance 2009' OECD Indicators, available at <http://www.oecd.org/document/62/0,3343,en_2649_39263238_43586328_1_1_1_37455,00.html>.

market histories (or the degree of labour market attachment). As women move in and out of the labour market over their life-cycle (as suggested by Figure 12.2), often due to caring (predominately childcare) responsibilities, with additional periods of part-time working, this can impact on their labour market wage. Formally, we can consider time out of the labour market and part-time working (which will accrue labour market experience at a slower rate than continuous full-time employment) as factors which need to be controlled for when comparing the wages of otherwise similar workers. Further, the importance of part-time employment in explaining the (hourly) gender wage gap has broader implications for female employment (and careers) which is discussed in more detail below. However, one female labour market characteristic that might tend to ameliorate the gender wage gap is that a relatively large share of female employment is in the public sector (as shown in Table 12.4). Employment in the public sector tends to be more transparent in terms of pay structures and also it is more likely that a union is recognised, both of which tend to reduce *unexplained* differences in wages between male and female workers (see Dolton and Makepeace, Chapter 18, for further details).

In Table 12.5 the explained proportion of the gender wage gap (that relating to the characteristics held) is presented for three samples (all employees, full-time only employees and full-time male vs. part-time female employees). In each panel and column, the proportion of the gender wage gap that can be explained by age and education levels has decreased between 1999 and 2009, for example, for the sample of all employees, from 18.8% to 2.7% across the ten years. In fact, the reduction in the explanatory power of these characteristics has decreased by so much that by 2009, for full-time employees only, females would have the wage advantage based purely on these characteristics (a finding which is consistent with both younger women being increasingly

Table 12.4: Private and public sector employment splits

	Private sector % of male employment	Private sector % of female employment	% Female within private sector	Public sector % of female employment	% Female within public sector
1997	83.50	66.94	40.30	33.06	62.80
1998	83.59	67.14	40.25	32.86	62.67
2000	83.62	66.82	40.47	33.18	63.28
2002	84.10	66.07	40.55	33.93	64.94
2004	83.32	64.42	40.26	35.58	65.02
2006	83.14	63.97	40.25	36.03	65.18
2008	83.71	64.47	40.09	35.53	65.47
2009	82.91	63.46	40.07	36.54	65.13

Notes: Employment rates defined as percentage of working-age adults in work (employees, self-employed, government schemes and unpaid family work), excludes full-time students.

Source: LFS, Q2, April–June 1997–2009.

Table 12.5: Decomposing the gender wage gap into the explained proportion (%) 1999 and 2009

	Age and education	Column (1) plus part-time and occupational controls	Column (2) plus public sector control	Column (3) plus control for presence of dependent child (aged under 19)
	(1)	(2)	(3)	(4)
All employees				
1999 gender wage gap 26.4%				
Explained	18.8	42.2	39.0	41.5
2009 gender wage gap 21.8%				
Explained	2.7	43.8	41.8	43.7
Full-time employees only				
1999 gender wage gap 18.5%				
Explained	9.3	−7.1	−11.5	−6.0
2009 gender wage gap 16.8%				
Explained	−14.7	4.4	2.7	8.2
Full-time male and part-time female employees				
1999 gender wage gap 39.3%				
Explained	20.6	36.2	34.2	28.0
2009 gender wage gap 33.8%				
Explained	13.7	50.4	50.0	41.6

Notes:
1. Sample of employees of working-age adults in work; excludes full-time students.
2. The proportion of the gender wage gap decomposed into the explained refers to the log gender wage gap ($\ln w_m - \ln w_f$).
Source: LFS, Q2, 1999 and 2009.

educated and possibly also older women being more attached to the labour market).

Also shown in Table 12.5 is the clear importance of the occupational controls (see column 2) which for all employees (panel 1) also includes a part-time working control. Including occupational controls shows the explained proportion of the gender wage gap to increase to over 40% for all employees and to over 50% for comparisons between full-time males and part-time females in 2009 (panel 3). In column 3, however, the inclusion of a control for public sector employment reduces the explained proportion for each year and for each of the three samples, although by only a reasonably small amount in each case. In the final column, the inclusion of controls for the presence of children increases the explained proportion for all employees and the full-time only employee samples (panels 1 and 2).

Although additional controls may well increase further the explained proportion of the gender wage differential, it is interesting to note that even with the basic sets of controls presented here, well over 50% of the gender wage gap remains unexplained (due to the different wage returns by gender to the same characteristics) and in 2009, in the case of full-time only employees, over 90% remains unexplained.

Although various explanations can be constructed to explain the existence (and persistence) of the gender wage gap, some unexplained features still do clearly remain. For example, the extent to which there are gender gaps in new hires and their starting wages, and that gender wage differentials are not uncommon even within grades and that women are often restrained in their career advancement by a glass-ceiling effect. As such, the gender wage gap is far from explained, with numerous studies finding that substantial, non-trivial unexplained portions of the gender wage gap remain even after formally controlling for many of the factors discussed above. So much so that the question of what is driving this gender pay gap has still not been conclusively answered. Indeed recent research has focused on the importance of the dual role that women often hold simultaneously both in the paid labour market and within the home, with the primary responsibility for home production contributing to the gender pay gap. However, other work has suggested that a sizeable gender wage gap remains even when one focuses on women with continuous full-time employment, who have had no children and express no desire for them, suggesting that there might not be an explanation for the wage gap routed in explainable productivity differences at all.

Part-time employment

Table 12.6 shows the shares of male and female employees working part-time from 1988–2009. The figures show clearly that part-time employment is a significant and important part of female labour supply within the British labour market. This high level of part-time employment is often cited as a way in which women retain attachment to the labour market during the peak child-rearing period, and also more generally for balancing labour market and home commitments and responsibilities. The importance of part-time employment during the period when women have younger children is clearly evidenced by the percentages engaged in part-time employment when children are particularly young (2–4). Though it should be noted that the (likely) reason that the part-time percentage figures are lower for women with children in the age 0–1 band than the age 2–4 band relates to sample selection (those women working when the child is 0–1 are more likely to be full-time workers). In comparison, the figures in the final column show the percentage working part-time is much lower (though still far from small) for those with no dependent children under 19. Table 12.6 also shows that although part-time employment is not a significant employment state for males, it is certainly something which has grown (roughly doubled) over the 20-year period, 1988–2009.

Table 12.6: Part-time employment rates by gender

Year	All employees	All males	All females	Females by age of youngest child					
				Age 0–1	Age 2–4	Age 5–10	Age 11–15	Age 16–18	No dependent children under 19
1988	19.52	3.19	41.16	61.86	70.48	70.40	59.62	52.73	32.76
1997	21.86	5.21	41.64	60.93	67.92	65.09	54.15	49.27	29.82
1998	21.77	5.20	41.52	61.54	66.73	64.07	53.51	47.78	30.31
2000	21.82	5.40	41.14	61.72	66.71	64.56	51.82	44.15	29.12
2002	22.16	5.81	40.98	64.06	69.94	63.15	52.31	44.29	28.81
2004	22.34	6.50	40.53	60.63	68.11	64.25	51.56	41.48	28.39
2006	21.72	6.54	39.07	60.49	66.89	62.30	49.00	39.57	26.58
2008	21.70	7.21	38.36	57.89	65.44	60.15	50.37	39.68	25.68
2009	22.47	8.35	38.64	54.56	64.96	58.52	51.12	43.38	25.78

Notes: Part-time employment is self-assessed. Percentages are of working-age adults in employment; excludes full-time students.
Source: LFS, Q2, April–June 1988, 1997–2009.

It is interesting to note though that the part-time figures in Table 12.6 will understate the full numbers of women who will have worked part-time at some point during their career. Such potentially flexible working which retains the female attachment to the labour market during periods of competing pressures of work and home commitments must be seen (to some extent at least) as a success of the flexible labour market. However, this is not the full picture. Although part-time employment has delivered for some women the desired flexibility on working hours, for many others it has not been so positive. Instead, resulting in a relatively high degree of occupational segregation, segregation into low-paying sectors, as well as, following movement into part-time from full-time employment, a marked degree of occupational downgrading.

Connolly and Gregory (2008) investigate the magnitude of the occupational downgrading as a result of women moving between full-time and part-time employment, finding approximately one-quarter of women experience occupational downgrading when making this move. Evidence is also presented that the risk of downgrading is even greater when the female employee changes employer at the same time as the full-time/part-time move. This effect has been described by the then Equal Opportunities Commission (now EHRC) as evidence of a brain drain, where women working in part-time employment are underutilised in terms of their employment and their skills.

In addition to this occupational downgrading, the extent to which (female) part-time employment is coupled with a pay penalty has been investigated by Manning and Petrongolo (2008). Findings suggest that a significant hourly pay differential exists of the order of about 25% and this has greatly increased over the last few decades. As with the gender pay differential discussed above, controlling for differences in the characteristics of full-time and part-time women explains a sizeable proportion of the differential; however, the inclusion of occupational controls all but removes the differential. This suggests that the part-time pay differential is driven by occupational segregation or the type of jobs on offer on a part-time basis, rather than the part-time status per se. Research evidence on both the full-time/part-time wage differential and the occupational downgrading suggests that until 'better' jobs come in a part-time form the downgrading (or brain drain), coupled with the part-time pay penalty, will continue. Suggesting, maybe not unsurprisingly, that the right to *ask* for flexible working is quite distinct from the employee's right to *have*.

Case study: sex discrimination in the financial services sector

In autumn 2009 the EHRC published a report on sex discrimination in the financial services sector. This was a detailed report looking at various aspects of female employment, pay and careers within the UK's financial services sector and illustrates many of the ways in which females are arguably disadvantaged within the British labour market.

The report found that gender wage gaps within the financial services sector are substantial; within a sample of full-time workers, the (average) gross annual pay gap was 55% and the gender pay gap was larger on total earnings than basic earnings, consistent with there being a gender bias in the distribution of bonuses and performance-related pay. It was also noted that when pay transparency was less, the greater was the observed gender gap, with pay transparency tending to be greater where there was a trade union or staff association recognised.

Pay is only one dimension along which gender inequalities might emerge and further areas identified included occupational segregation, recruitment, career progression and workplace culture. For example, of managerial and senior jobs, only a third were held by female employees, and only a quarter of professional jobs. Evidence in the report highlighted how recruitment methods might substantially discriminate against women in appointments, such as in terms of job stereotyping, informal recruitment (relying on personal referrals) and the asking of discriminatory (and unlawful) questions relating to family circumstances. Further anecdotal evidence was presented of female career progression appearing to be slower, with more women than men having experienced a peer being promoted above them, with requests for flexible or part-time working being met with occupational downgrading, and the impact of workplace culture adversely affecting female employment opportunities and outcomes in the industry.

Interestingly, though, the issues identified did not seem to be the result of a lack of gender equality policy. In fact the report identified the financial services sector as 'early and enthusiastic adopters of a range of equality initiatives' (EHRC, 2009: 13), the issue really was one of effective implementation of the policies, and even more importantly, the lack of recognition of the business case for gender equality.

A labour market gender summary of the UK recession (2008–9)

This chapter has summarised the main changes over the last 12 years in the British labour market (1997–2009) and covers the move into the late noughties recession at the end of the second quarter of 2008. However, to understand in greater detail how the recession has and arguably is still impacting on women, Table 12.7 is presented. Comparisons of the female experience within this recession with previous recessions must note that more women are more attached to the labour market than ever before. As such, the current recession has the potential to impact on women more fully, or at least more directly than during previous recessions. However, just because a greater number of women may well be more directly affected by the recession through their formal labour market activity now, than previously, does not necessarily mean that they will be disproportionally harder hit than men.

Table 12.7 provides summary statistics for female (male) employment and unemployment rates. These percentages suggest employment rates for females have fallen very slightly (by about 1 percentage point), with the unemployment (ILO) rate increasing slightly (by just over 1 percentage point), but that there is a much larger increase in the percentage of part-time workers who report themselves as working part-time because they could not get a full-time

Table 12.7: UK recession (2008–2009): a gender summary (2008 quarter 1–2009 quarter 3)

By female (males)	Employment rate	ILO unemployment rate	Share of part-time workers who could not find a full-time job
2008 quarter 1	73.69 (82.39)	3.36 (4.29)	8.32 (25.11)
2008 quarter 2	73.70 (82.16)	3.29 (4.36)	8.41 (24.03)
2008 quarter 3	73.17 (81.44)	3.72 (4.86)	7.90 (25.68)
2008 quarter 4	73.63 (81.53)	3.74 (5.47)	8.85 (29.57)
2009 quarter 1	73.17 (80.75)	4.39 (6.43)	9.72 (31.63)
2009 quarter 2	72.63 (79.57)	4.55 (6.88)	10.80 (33.92)
2009 quarter 3	72.52 (79.14)	4.64 (7.03)	11.04 (33.87)

Notes: Employment rates defined as percentage of working-age adults in work (employees, self-employed, government schemes and unpaid family work); excludes full-time students.
Source: LFS, Q1 2008–Q3 2009.

job (almost a 3 percentage point increase over the nine quarters). Comparisons with the male figures presented in Table 12.7 suggest a larger impact on the employment rates (decreasing) for males than females. As do the ILO unemployment rates, with the percentage of males unemployed rising by almost 3 percentage points over the period. Further, the percentage of part-time male workers who report themselves as working part-time due to being unable to find full-time work has also substantially increased (by almost 9 percentage points) and by far more than the equivalent female percentages.

Further research by Harkness and Evans (2010) suggests that unlike in the previous recessions of the 1980s and early 1990s, where evidence tended to show that when men lost their jobs their partner tended to follow, this time this does not seem to be the case. Rather, in the current recession, women whose partners have become unemployed are more likely to remain in work. This is arguably due to the significant changes in the taxation and benefit system since 1999, which within this recession has stopped a growth in workless (couple) households.

Indeed, female employment within the public sector (as shown in Table 12.4) may, although possibly only in the short run, provide a degree of insulation against the recession. However, against this, it should be noted that recessions tend to hit the relatively less skilled more than the skilled (particularly in terms of wages and employment) and women disproportionally make up this group too. On this point, then, there is clearly an important role for the NMW in protecting the wages of a large number of female workers within, and as, the economy moves out of recession. The LPC's recommendations for uprating of the NMW and the government's implementation of the recommendations will have significant implications for the wages of many working women.

Conclusions

The headline figures on the British gender wage gap show a continuation of the improvement of the position of women in the labour market. However, this average belies the existence of more than one type of female labour market experience and outcome. Significant groups of women are not benefiting from the perceived improvement in female labour market outcomes over the last decade or so, and even those arguably relatively better placed within the labour market still appear to face significant barriers to advancement compared to 'equivalent' male workers, whether it be in the form of glass ceilings, distinctly lower wage growth or reduced promotion possibilities. Even so, the last decade can be characterised by a policy agenda which has (at least publicly) supported family-friendly employment and the balancing of work–life responsibilities.

The question for the next decade is the extent to which the gender equality trend observed over the last ten to twelve years, which, although clearly slowing in terms of the gender gap in wages and employment rate, will further continue. As the EHRC's 'Sex and Power: Who runs Britain 2008?' publication clearly notes,[5] the trend that is emerging (at least in terms of the index of women in positions of authority and influence in Britain) is one of stalled if not reversed progress—an observation that may well have begun to be mirrored in the general gender pay gap and employment picture at the end of the first decade of the 21st century.

References

Connolly, S. and Gregory, M. (2008) Moving down: women's part-time work and occupational change in Britain 1991–2001. *Economic Journal*, 118(526): F52–F76.

Dolton, P. and Makepeace, G. (2011) Public and private sector labour markets. In: Gregg, P. and Wadsworth, J. (eds.) *The Labour Market in Winter: The State of Working Britain*. Oxford: Oxford University Press.

Equality and Human Rights Commission (2009) Financial Services Inquiry: Sex discrimination and gender pay gap. Report of the Equality and Human Rights Commission.

Faggio, G., Gregg, P. and Wadsworth, J. (2011) Job tenure and job turnover. In: Gregg, P. and Wadsworth, J. (eds.) *The Labour Market in Winter: The State of Working Britain*. Oxford: Oxford University Press.

Harkness, S. and Evans, M. (2010) The effect of recession in the UK on family employment: welfare reform, male unemployment and wives' (and partners') employment response. February, mimeo, University of Bath.

Manning, A. and Petrongolo, B. (2008) The part-time pay penalty for women in Britain, *Economic Journal*, 118(526): F28–F51.

---

[5] Available at <http://www.equalityhumanrights.com/uploaded_files/sex_and_power_ 2008_pdf.pdf>.

13

Recent Developments in Intergenerational Mobility

Jo Blanden and Lindsey Macmillan

Key findings

- Comparing children born in 1958 and 1970, those who enter the top professions in the second cohort were more likely to be from richer backgrounds; in contrast they had ability levels closer to the average. Such findings have contributed to a policy focus on 'fair access to the professions'.
- There is no evidence to suggest that intergenerational mobility in the UK will continue to decline for cohorts born after 1970.
- The impact of family background on educational attainment provides a guide to final mobility for children not yet old enough to be in work. There is evidence that family background inequalities are starting to narrow for children at the end of secondary school.
- Findings on the relationship between family background and degree attainment are less favourable; this may because older age groups have not had time to benefit from important policy reforms.
- Investments in Early Years have not had a dramatic effect on reducing the connection between early achievements and family background so far, but again, it may be too early to tell.

Introduction

In the early 2000s results from Blanden et al. (2004) showed that the association between parental income and children's adult earnings had increased for those born in 1970 compared to those born in 1958. This contributed to the sense that mobility in Britain at the turn of the century was too low and led to a consensus from all political parties that improving 'social mobility' was an important goal for public policy.

This chapter seeks to update our knowledge of social (or more correctly, intergenerational) mobility in a number of ways. First, we will examine what is meant when politicians pledge to improve mobility across generations. Given the huge policy focus on this area, clarity in these matters is essential, and it has only started to emerge quite recently.

A clearer idea of what mobility means enables us to take a more precise approach to evaluating the likely effects of recent government policy. The Social Mobility White Paper (HM Government, 2009) proposed a number of routes towards improved mobility. We shall outline the logic of these policies, focusing particularly on some of the findings from the Milburn Commission into Fair Access to the Professions; a body that was set up as a result of the White Paper.

In order to evaluate recent policies directly, we must attempt to understand the unfolding mobility paths of those who are not yet in the labour market. In the final part of this chapter, we review evidence on the changing relationships between family income and various measures of educational achievement for children born from 1958 to 2000; under certain assumptions, this will provide some tentative conclusions on recent mobility trends. Throughout the section on prospects for mobility, we comment on the role of government policy in generating the changes we observe.

Context: immobility and inequality

Economists tend to measure intergenerational income mobility by estimating a regression of children's income in adulthood on their parental income. The coefficient obtained is known as the intergenerational elasticity—a result of 0.3 would say that on average 30% of any income difference between two sets of parents would be passed on as the percentage income difference between their children. A higher correlation therefore represents lower mobility; an elasticity of 1 would indicate complete immobility as the income of parents would completely determine the future income of their children. In the UK, this correlation is 0.29 for the British birth cohort born in 1970. This is high in terms of both trends across time and comparisons across countries. For an older birth cohort, born in 1958, the correlation was lower at 0.2 (hence mobility was higher).

Figure 13.1 plots comparable intergenerational coefficients for a number of nations against the Gini coefficients (a widely used measure of inequality) at the time when the samples used for estimation were growing up. In the

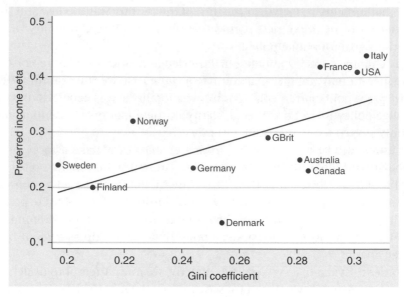

Figure 13.1: Associations between the income beta and Gini coefficient

Notes:
1. The preferred income beta is the beta regarded by the author as the most representative of the evidence for that country.
2. The Gini coefficient is obtained at the time the individuals in the data used to find the beta were teenagers, in the 1980s. They are taken from the Luxembourg Income Study.
3. The line shows the predicted relationship between intergenerational persistence and inequality, as revealed by a regression of the beta on the Gini coefficient.

Source: Blanden (2009).

context of developed nations, only the US fares worse, with a correlation of around 0.4. There appears to be a strong association between inequality and intergenerational persistence. An article in the *Guardian* in March 2010 ('Social mobility is dead', <http://www.guardian.co.uk/society/2010/mar/10/is-social-mobility-dead/print>), discussed how government should reduce their focus on social mobility because of the difficulty in measuring it, and focus instead on cross-sectional inequality. This evidence suggests that a focus on social mobility may require policy makers to reduce cross-sectional inequality.

The regression approach to measuring income mobility used by economists is based on an entirely relative concept of mobility; the amount of upward and downward mobility balance. An alternative conception of doing better is captured by sociologists in the idea of social class. Social class is determined by your occupation, but sociologists believe it captures much more than this. It is related to permanent income levels, job security and job autonomy and tends to be strongly related to health outcomes, civic engagement and the outcomes of the next generation. Absolute mobility in social class is concerned with how many people improve on their father's social class. The idea of 'each generation doing better than the last' has been frequently referred to in political speeches on social mobility; it seems that improving absolute mobility has been part of the New Labour government's focus.

Politically, absolute mobility is an easier 'sell' than improving relative mobility; everyone is doing better. Increased relative mobility means that some families must be moving down to allow others to move up. In the recent White Paper, the government were explicit about their policy focus on both absolute and relative mobility: 'These two elements, better jobs and fairer chances, will together produce a more upwardly mobile society'. It seems that the aim of policy has now been defined as promoting absolute social class mobility, as well as improving equality of opportunity as measured by relative income mobility.

An explicit policy focus

The Social Mobility White Paper contained a mix of policies, addressed to promoting both 'better jobs' and 'fairer chances'. On the better jobs side, promoting economic growth was the key, and to be achieved by investment in high-tech environmental industries, including tailored support for the low carbon technology industry, as well as by promoting skill acquisition across the board. In terms of fairer chances, there is a particular focus on helping disadvantaged groups in the Early Years through Family Nurse Partnerships and more free childcare places, improving the quality of teachers in more demanding schools, and providing support for young people without family experience of higher education, who want to apply. There is also a restatement of the government's commitment to eradicate child poverty by 2020.

One of the main proposals of the White Paper was the establishment of the Panel for Fair Access to the Professions led by Alan Milburn MP, now appointed social mobility czar by the coalition Government. This body was created to address an anxiety expressed in the White Paper that particular practices of the top professions, such as the need to complete unpaid work experience, might be preventing them from being viable career choices for talented individuals from modest backgrounds.

As a submission to the Panel for Fair Access to the Professions, Macmillan (2009) studied the trends in the average family incomes of those entering the top professions in 1991 and 2004. Using the 1958 and 1970 birth cohort studies, the occupation of the cohort members at ages 33/34 were identified to study the origins of those entering into the top professions across the

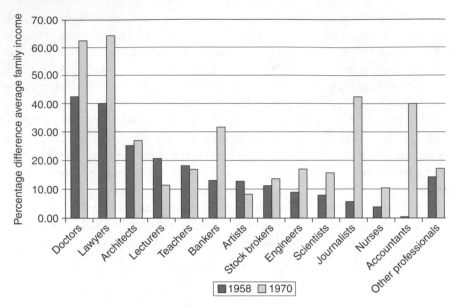

Figure 13.2: Percentage differences from the sample average monthly net family income at age 16 by destination occupation at age 33/34

Notes: Bankers and accountants significantly different across cohorts within a 1% confidence interval.
Lawyers and journalists significantly different across cohorts within a 5% confidence interval.
Doctors significantly different across cohorts within a 10% confidence interval.

Source: NCDS 1958, BCS 1970. CLS Cohort Studies.

cohorts. Whilst the average family incomes of those going on to become doctors and lawyers were higher than the average in both cohorts, in the NCDS they were much closer to the average in real terms than in the BCS,[1] as seen in Figure 13.2. When the test scores of these individuals were considered (Figure 13.3), the opposite was found. While the test scores were again above average for the top professions, they were closer to the average in the BCS than in the NCDS. Whilst those entering the top professions were looking less like the average in terms of family incomes in the later cohort, they looked closer to the average in terms of ability.

These findings were used as a central piece of evidence in the report to illustrate the necessity of action to break the barriers to entry to the top professions. The Panel set out a number of proposals to tackle this, including raising aspirations through the use of mentors and role models, and reforms to the 'Gifted and Talented' scheme in schools. There was also a focus on improving school quality in poor areas through giving parents a greater role.

---

[1] National Child Development Survey (NCDS); British Cohort Study (BCS).

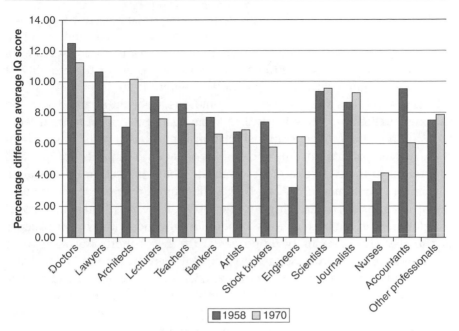

Figure 13.3: Percentage differences from the sample average IQ test score at age 10/11 by destination occupation at age 33/34

Notes: All professions significantly different from the sample average within a 5% confidence interval.
Accountants significantly different across cohorts within a 5% confidence interval.
Engineers significantly different across cohorts within a 10% confidence interval.

Source: NCDS 1958, BCS 1970. CLS Cohort Studies.

Transparency and fairness in internships was deemed to be essential to remove the nepotism which is often rife in setting up and allocating placements.

Future trends in intergenerational mobility

The picture of a closer attachment between family background and later life outcomes for the second birth cohort of 1970 is a worrying one. However, it says nothing about the likely mobility of individuals under the age of 40. Given the recent political interest in social mobility, there is an increased demand for new evidence on whether recent government interventions have helped to buck this trend. One of the main problems in attempting to go further with the research into intergenerational mobility is the data requirements placed upon the researcher. To investigate final mobility, researchers need information on incomes across two lifetimes; as a consequence, research into this topic in the UK has so far been restricted to the two longitudinal birth cohort studies which have information on both parents and children. These individuals are now aged 50 and 40, so estimates of intergenerational persistence to date can only tell us about the mobility of those who experienced all of their education before 1990.

New research has attempted to overcome this problem. In an advance on the previous literature, Blanden et al. (2007) used a new conceptual framework to decompose the intergenerational relationship into two parts: the relationship between parental income and childhood factors such as education, and the returns to these childhood factors in the labour market. In this research, educational attainment from age 16 was the major driver of the intergenerational relationship, accounting for over 50% of the total intergenerational correlation found in both cohorts. In addition, the increase in the persistence of the elasticity of mobility found across the two cohorts was seen to be working through an increased relationship between the parents' income and the education of the younger cohort member, or a widening in educational inequality. Given this finding, it is possible to think that the relationship between the income of the family in childhood and the child's educational attainment might tell us a lot about adult mobility.

This finding opens the door to research on younger generations. By measuring the relationship between family income and educational attainment and making some assumptions about the magnitude of the returns to education and other effects, we can get a handle on the likely magnitude of future mobility for current cohorts of youth. Recent research by Blanden and Machin (2008) and Gregg and Macmillan (2010) have used this framework, and we can put the findings of these papers together to make some tentative conclusions about future mobility trends.

In both cases, the research examines the relationship between the family incomes and educational attainment for younger generations of individuals, starting with the cohort studies of those born in 1958 and 1970 and going right through to children born in 2000. Educational attainment is thought of as both the achievement of qualifications, such as GCSEs, A-levels and bachelor's degrees, and as the ability of the individuals in terms of cognitive and non-cognitive test scores in early childhood. We find that these cognitive and non-cognitive test scores are a strong predictor of future educational attainment and can therefore be thought of as proxies for later educational attainment. The benefit of also measuring the relationship between test scores and family income is that younger cohorts who have not yet completed any formal education qualifications can be introduced into the analysis.

A wide range of new data sources are introduced to assess the relationship between family income and educational attainment. Each has its own strengths and limitations and must be used with particular caveats attached.

For educational attainment, a number of new cohorts can be introduced using the British Household Panel Survey (BHPS), a nationally representative panel of households collected annually from 1991 onwards. Each adult within the household is interviewed and as household members become eligible adults (16+), they enter the survey. The BHPS therefore provides a sample of individuals who were born from the mid-1970s and through the 1980s. This is a useful addition to the large gap in longitudinal studies for those born in the 1980s.

Both studies utilise this data to capture the income gradient, or the role of parental income, in degree attainment for quasi-birth cohorts born in the late 1970s and the early 1980s. Gregg and Macmillan (2009) also analyse the income gradient in GCSE attainment, staying-on decisions at 16 and 18, A-level attainment and early labour market attachment. Overall, the evidence suggests no change in the income gradient in post-16 education for these individuals from that observed in the BCS as seen in Table 13.1. The coefficients indicate that for a standard deviation increase in family income, the chances of obtaining a degree increase by around 10 percentage points. For this quasi-birth cohort therefore, there is a story of no change in income gradients in education. In addition, the relationship between family income and early labour market attachment has increased; family background is becoming a more important predictor of attachment to the labour market, consistent with the recent literature on NEETs (individuals not in education, employment or training) in the UK.

Still focusing on qualification attainment, the Longitudinal Survey of Young People in England (LSYPE) follows a school-year cohort of children born in 1989/1990. These individuals were first interviewed in 2004 as they

Table 13.1: Relationship between standardised family income and later educational attainment

Variable	NCDS 1958	BCS 1970	BHPS 1 1975–1980	LSYPE 1989–1990
Number of O-levels (A*–C)	0.72*	1.13*	1.06*	0.93*
Stay on post-16	0.10*	0.14*	0.11*	0.05*
Number of A-levels (if any)	0.16*	0.42*	0.47*	
Stay on post-18	0.06*	0.10*	0.07*	
Degree	0.06*	0.12*	0.09*	
Proportion time NEET	−0.01*	−0.02*	−0.07*	

Notes: Controls for parental age, parental age squared and gender.
* indicates significance at the 99% confidence level.
Family income is monthly net logged standardised family income. Income standardised to account for differential variation across cohorts.
Source: NCDS 1958, BCS 1970. CLS Cohort Studies. BHPS, ISER, University of Essex. LSYPE, ESDS.

entered school year 9 (at age 13) and have since been interviewed annually, with National Pupil Data (NPD) being matched in at Key Stage 4 to capture GCSE attainment. The benefit of the LSYPE data is that, in comparison to the BHPS, the sample sizes are very large and therefore more appropriate for drawing statistical inferences. As can be seen from Table 13.1, the measured income gradient in the number of GCSEs at grades A*–C obtained by the LSYPE is lower than the income gradient for the BCS cohort. The same is true for the income gradient in staying on post-16. The results indicate that for a standard deviation increase in income, or roughly a doubling of family income for the average family in the BCS, children are 14 percentage points more likely to stay on in education past age 16, whereas, in the LSYPE, this association has fallen to only 5 percentage points. The difference in coefficients between the BCS and LSYPE is statistically significant at the 1% level, implying that we can be 99% confident that there has been a real change in the population and that income is becoming a weaker predictor of educational attainment across time.

An additional way of examining the trend in inequality in achievements at age 16 is to use administrative data from the National Pupil Database (NPD). This data does not contain information on family income, but it does have information on whether the child is in receipt of free school meals (FSM). Table 13.2 illustrates that, consistent with the pattern seen in more recent cohorts of youth, there is faster growth in the proportion of children achieving 5 or more grade A*–C GCSEs from FSM families than there is from non-FSM families for children born in 1986 to 1992. Data from the Youth Cohort Studies (YCS) also illustrates a closing of the gap between the percentage of children from the top social class achieving level 2 qualifications compared to those from the bottom social class (Table 13.3). All of the evidence points towards a narrowing of the income gradient for age 16 attainments for the younger generation.

Table 13.2: Proportion of FSM and non-FSM individuals obtaining five or more GCSEs or equivalent at grades A*–C for those born 1986–1992

GCSE year	2002	2003	2004	2005	2006	2007	2008
Birth year	1986	1987	1988	1989	1990	1991	1992
Non-FSM	53.7	55.2	56.1	58.9	61	62.8	67.0
FSM	23.0	24.4	26.1	29.9	31	35.5	40.0
Difference	30.7	30.8	30.0	29.0	29.5	27.3	27.0
Ratio	2.33	2.26	2.15	1.97	1.95	1.77	1.68

Notes: Attainment and Post-16 Attainment by Pupil Characteristics, in England 2002–2008.

Source: www/dcsf/gov/uk—National Curriculum Assessment, GCSE and Equivalent.

Table 13.3: Proportion of individuals obtaining five or more GCSEs or equivalent at grades A*–C by parental occupation groupings for those born 1972–1990

GCSE year	'88	'90	'91	'93	'95	'97	'99	'01	'03	'06
Birth year	'72	'74	'75	'77	'79	'81	'83	'85	'87	'90
PARENTAL OCCUPATION (SEG)										
Managerial/Professional	52	58	60	66	68	69	70			
Other non-manual	42	49	51	58	58	60	59			
Skilled manual	21	27	29	36	36	40	45			
Semi-skilled manual	16	20	23	26	29	32	35			
Unskilled manual	12	15	16	16	24	20	30			
Top – Bottom	40	43	44	50	44	49	40			
Ratio of top/bottom	4.3	3.9	3.8	4.1	2.8	3.5	2.3			
PARENTAL OCCUPATION (NS-SEC)										
Higher professional								75	77	76	81
Lower professional								62	64	65	73
Intermediate								49	51	53	59
Lower supervisory								34	34	41	46
Routine								26	31	33	42
Top – Bottom								49	46	43	39
Ratio of top/bottom								2.9	2.5	2.3	1.9

Source: <http://www.dcsf.gov.uk/rsgateway/DB/SBU/b000795/Bulletin_tables_final.xls>, Sheet 4.1.1.

The mobility chances of the youngest generations can be modelled by associations between income and early cognitive and non-cognitive test scores. These are strong predictors of later educational attainment.

The upper panel of Table 13.4 considers test score data at ages 10/11. Again the LSYPE 1989/90 cohort is used, with test data from Key Stage 2 matched in from the NPD. The Avon Longitudinal Survey of Adults and Children (ALSPAC) can also be matched with Key Stage 2 data in the NPD. ALSPAC is a birth cohort of all children born in Avon in 1991/2. The ALSPAC data is not nationally representative as it only covers one area of the UK. Panel 1 of Table 13.4 illustrates that at age 10/11, the social gradients in test scores have declined from those seen in the BCS cohort for both the LSYPE and ALSPAC cohort members, consistent with the decline seen at age 16 for the LSYPE cohort. Once again, these differences are all statistically significant at the 1% level. Policies aimed at reversing trends in social mobility may be having an impact for school-age children, benefiting from the increased expenditure in schools, reduced class sizes and other policy interventions, such as literacy hour, aimed at school-age children.

Blanden and Machin (2008) use data from the children of the NCDS and BCS cohorts and the more recent Millennium Cohort Study (MCS) to analyse the income gradients in cognitive skills at around age 5/6 using reading and vocabulary test scores and non-cognitive skills using the Rutter scale. The children of the NCDS and BCS cohorts are all children born to a sub-sample of the original cohort members. As a consequence, this is not a nationally

Table 13.4: Relationship between standardised family income and earlier cognitive test scores

Test scores at age 10/11				
Data set and year of birth	NCDS 1958	BCS 1970	LSYPE 1989–90	ALSPAC 1991–2
Variable				
IQ	0.20*	0.28*		0.22*
Maths	0.20*	0.29*	0.18*	0.23*
Reading	0.19*	0.30*	0.17*	0.22*
Test scores at age 5/7				
Data set and year of birth	'Kids of NCDS' around 1985	'Kids of BCS' around 1999	MCS 2000–2001	
Variable				
Reading/vocabulary	0.17*	0.15*	0.22*	
Rutter behavioural	−0.21*	−0.14*	−0.18*	

Notes: Controls for parental age, parental age squared and gender.
* indicates significance at the 99% confidence level.
Family income is monthly net logged standardised family income. Income standardised to account for differential variation across cohorts.
Source: NCDS 1958, BCS 1970, 'Kids of NCDS', 'Kids of BCS', MCS. CLS Cohort Studies. LSYPE, ESDS. ALSPAC, University of Bristol.

representative sample of children. The sample design means that the oldest children will have the youngest parents; to avoid this problem we focus only on the youngest children. In the samples that we use, the children of the NCDS cohort were born, on average, around 1985, whilst the children of the BCS cohort were born, on average, around 1999. The MCS is a nationally representative birth cohort for children born in Britain in 2000. As can be seen in the second panel of Table 13.4,[2] there is no overall change in the correlation with family income across the children of the NCDS and BCS cohort members and the MCS cohort, suggesting that for all of the increased investment in Early Years, any return, in terms of reducing inequality in outcomes, is yet to be seen.[3]

The overall picture is therefore mixed. On the one hand, there has been an improvement in terms of the correlation between family income and attainment at 10/11 and 16, but on the other hand, these improvements have not been seen for post-16 attainments or for early test scores at 5/6. Drawing a conclusion on the likely social mobility of future cohorts is therefore not clear cut. More needs to be done to improve access to post-16 education and higher

[2] Results here are slightly different from the original paper; the test scores have been standardised to compare with results in the upper panel from Gregg and Macmillan (2009).
[3] Results from the National Evaluation of Sure Start (NESS) show some effects of Sure Start on behavioural variables, but no effects on language skills.

education, with no evidence so far of an increase in lower social class groups obtaining a degree. Evidence on AimHigher, a policy to encourage the Higher Education participation of the disadvantaged has not been very positive. The impact of the now abolished Education Maintenance Allowance (EMA) seems larger, but is yet to be seen in terms of actual realised attainment as the children are still too young. There are some positive notes to be drawn, however, as income gradients for children having experienced increased investments in schooling have reduced in terms of both cognitive test scores and realised attainment at 16. These could, other things held constant, be the signs of a turning point in social mobility in the UK. What is very clear is that social mobility in Britain seems unlikely to continue to decline for cohorts after 1970.

Conclusions

This chapter has sought to update our knowledge on intergenerational mobility in Britain. In the early 2000s the headline finding was that intergenerational income mobility in Britain had declined and therefore policy must be directed to raising intergenerational mobility. In recent years this picture has been refined, with more thought given by politicians, commentators and researchers to precisely what is meant by intergenerational mobility and therefore which policies can best address it. Recent policy commitments have been couched in terms of 'better jobs' and 'fairer chances'. While fairer chances are related to the relative measures of economic mobility measured by economists, better jobs are closer to the concept of absolute social class mobility used by sociologists. 'Better jobs' can be promoted by encouraging economic growth alongside improved working conditions, while fairer chances require policies which favour those from disadvantaged backgrounds.

In seeking to offer fairer chances, one of the most novel policy developments has been a new focus on fair access to the professions. Comparing the 1958 and 1970 cohorts, it can be shown that whilst those entering the top professions were looking less like the average in terms of family incomes, in the later cohort they looked more like the average in terms of ability. The average professional has become 'nicer' in terms of their family income, but 'dimmer' as measured by their performance on childhood tests.

Evidence on future patterns of mobility has been reviewed, and seems to reveal different pictures at different stages of the education system. Evidence on the achievements of children at the end of school show that this has become less strongly determined by family background; there is a suggestion that prospects for improved mobility are good. In contrast, there is less evidence that the impact of family income is having less of an effect on either degree attainment or performance in tests at very young ages. This may be because policies focusing on helping the disadvantaged at these points (e.g. the EMA at one end and Children's Centres at the other) occurred later than school reform policies and, as a consequence, their impacts cannot yet be observed.

References

Blanden, J. (2009) 'How much can we learn from international comparisons of intergenerational mobility?' Centre for the Economics of Education Discussion Paper No. 111.

—— Goodman, A., Gregg, P. and Machin, S. (2004) Changes in intergenerational mobility in Britain. In: Corak, M. (ed.) *Generational Income Mobility in North America and Europe*. Cambridge: Cambridge University Press.

—— Gregg, P. and Macmillan, L. (2007) Accounting for intergenerational income persistence: noncognitive skills, ability and education. *Economic Journal*, 117: C43–C60.

—— and Machin, S. (2008) Up and down the generational income ladder in Britain: past changes and future prospects. *National Institute Economic Review*, No. 205.

Cabinet Office (2009) Unleashing aspirations: The Final Report from the Panel for Fair Access to the Professions. <http://www.cabinetoffice.gov.uk/media/227102/fair-access.pdf>.

Gregg, P. and Macmillan, L. (2010) Family income and education in the next generation: exploring income gradients in education for current cohorts of youth. *Longitudinal and Life Course Studies*, 1(3), 259–80.

HM Government (2009) New Opportunities: Fair Chances for the Future <http://www.hmg.gov.uk/media/9102/NewOpportunities.pdf>.

Macmillan, L. (2009) Social mobility and the professions. CMPO report. <http://www.bris.ac.uk/cmpo/publications/other/socialmobility.pdf>.

14

Have Reforms to the School System Improved Educational Outcomes?

Sandra McNally

Key findings

- Evidence for cohorts born in 1958 and 1970 suggests that the move to the comprehensive education system increased average outcomes. The education system was not better in the old days.
- Over the last ten years, national data suggest that educational attainment has improved dramatically, but international data give a mixed picture. However, it seems to be that the pace of improvement has been greater in economically disadvantaged areas.
- Detailed analysis of the effects of increasing school expenditure gives evidence of positive effects. The magnitude is modest, though sufficient for likely benefits to outweigh costs.
- The 'marketisation' of the school system goes back about 30 years. This involves measures to improve parental choice, school accountability and competition between schools. Pupil-level analysis of the effects of choice and school competition does not suggest that they have led to improvements in educational attainment.
- The attempt to influence what is taught in schools through the National Strategies has led to improvements in educational attainment at a low cost. Clearly, it would be better to have a teaching profession that is fully equipped to make decisions on pedagogy that are appropriate for different contexts. US evidence on teacher quality suggests that this is important for influencing pupil outcomes. However, it is not a simple matter to improve teacher quality and recruiting more highly qualified teachers may be expensive given other lucrative options for graduates.

Introduction

It is well known (at least since the famous Coleman Report in 1966) that family background and early childhood experiences are the most important determinants of educational outcomes later on. Therefore government policy on areas that influence the home environment of students is important in thinking about how to improve educational outcomes. School policy also has an important role to play and much has been tried out in the last ten years. This chapter provides a brief overview of some important trends and the role of different policies in explaining (or not) what has changed. We start the chapter with a more historic question: was the move to the comprehensive education system a good thing at all? It can be difficult to change things fast in the education system and very often people look back to an era when there were grammar schools (typically from the minority of the population who were able to get into these schools!) So it is worth asking whether we are starting out from the right place before discussing trends in educational policy in the last ten years and the effectiveness of different types of educational reform. We focus on some of the most important reforms that we have been able to evaluate: the increase in school expenditure; choice, accountability and competition; and changing pedagogy. The evidence suggests that government policy can and does change things for the better, but it takes careful evaluation to reveal this. It cannot easily be inferred by looking at trends in educational performance. Another lesson is that evidence on the success (or otherwise) of market mechanisms in the education sector is fairly thin on the ground and it would be unwise to place too much hope in the efficacy of creating more choice and competition in the education system.

Did the move to the comprehensive system improve educational outcomes?

It is difficult to dramatically improve overall educational performance in a short period. However, many people give enormous credit to their school for their development. The apparent success of grammar schools in this respect often leads to debate on whether the decision to move towards a comprehensive model in the 1960s and 1970s was the right one. Before that time, pupils undertook tests at the age of 11 to determine whether they would attend schools with an academic orientation (i.e. grammar schools) or those with a vocational orientation (i.e. secondary modern schools). Nationally about 25% of pupils attended grammar schools. Like several other European countries, a decision was made to dismantle this system (which favoured those with the resources to invest in their child's human capital) in favour of one where children of all abilities would be taught together (closer to the US model). The effects of such reforms are always controversial because there are likely to be winners and losers. Such a reform is expected to have the following consequences: it increases the average ability of peers for those pupils who would not have attended grammar schools (in the old system); it decreases the average ability of peers for pupils who would have attended grammar school (who now go to school with those of low ability—as well as high ability). The net effect of changing the system depends on how these two (opposing) forces play out in practice. Furthermore, the 'grammar school' effect partly captures the positive effect of a more general, academically orientated education (in comparison with that which was available in secondary moderns). If the move to the comprehensive system led to a more generous distribution of this type of education across the population, then average outcomes may have increased.[1]

Maurin and McNally (2009) use two birth cohort studies (the National Child Development Survey, 1958 and the British Cohort Survey, 1970) to analyse whether or not the secondary school education available to the earlier cohort produced better educational outcomes than that available to the later cohort. They make use of the fact that the pace of change varied in different Local Education Authorities (LEAs) between these two periods. Figures 14.1 and 14.2 illustrate the main results of this analysis. In Figure 14.1, we plot the change in (standardised) age 16 test scores in Maths against the change in the probability of attending a comprehensive school within each Local Education Authority (i.e. comparing the 1958 birth cohort with the 1970 birth cohort).[2] This figure shows that the 'more comprehensive' the LEA became over this period, the larger the increase in average outcomes in the LEA. In Figure 14.2, we show a weaker association between the change in (standardised) age 11 scores and the extent to which the LEA became comprehensive (which is slightly negative). Therefore, one should not think of the relationship considered in Figure 14.1 as indicative of changes in pre-secondary school outcomes.

These results suggest that the move towards a comprehensive system was productivity enhancing: LEAs that transformed their system to a greater extent between these periods experienced a greater relative improvement in average test scores. Furthermore, regression analysis suggests that the benefits of this change were particularly evident for those from a low social class background, while being fairly neutral for those from a high social class.

---

[1] Average returns to academic qualifications are much larger than returns to vocational qualifications in the UK.

[2] Test scores are standardised such that they have mean equal to zero and standard deviation equal to one. The tests are comparable in the two data sets. However, we have done some sensitivity tests and considered examination outcomes (O-levels) and the results are robust.

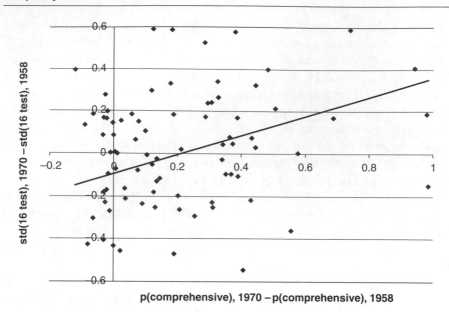

Figure 14.1: Change in age 16 test scores and the change in the probability of attending comprehensive school by Local Education Authority

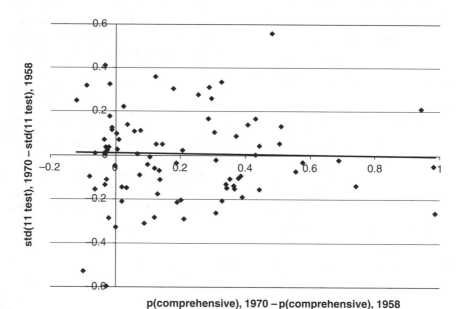

Figure 14.2: The change in age 11 test scores and the change in the probability of attending comprehensive school by Local Education Authority

Source: Maurin and McNally (2009).

Thus, it seems that the move to a comprehensive system helped to reduce socio-economic inequality in educational achievement. This analysis suggests that it is a mistake to think that educational quality was somehow higher for previous generations. The demise of grammar schools cannot be blamed for the increase of inequality in British society.

Trends in educational performance

The barometers used to measure educational performance in more recent times are how students (and schools) do in national tests at the end of primary and secondary school. These get published in 'league tables' and are publicly available in England (though not elsewhere in the UK). They are an important part of the accountability system, which will be discussed later.

The National Curriculum is divided into four 'Key Stages'. The end of primary school coincides with the end of Key Stage 2. In England, students undertake national tests at this stage of education, whereas teacher assessment is used in other parts of the UK. A key indicator is whether students get at least the level deemed appropriate for their age in tests of English, Maths and Science, as stipulated in the National Curriculum ('level 4 or above'). The period between age 11 and 14 is known as Key Stage 3. Before the end of compulsory education (i.e. at the end of Key Stage 4), pupils undertake the GCSE examination.[3] This is a high stakes examination for both schools and pupils. For example, it will influence what the student is able to do in further education. An indicator often used is whether the student achieves five or more grades at A*–C.

Figure 14.3 (and Table 14.1) shows the evolution of indicators at the end of Key Stage 2 in English and Maths (percentage of pupils attaining level 4 or above) and at the end of Key Stage 4 (percentage of students achieving five or

Table 14.1: Recent trends in educational attainment

	KS2 English % attaining level 4 or above	KS2 Maths % attaining level 4 or above	GCSE % with 5+ GCSEs or equivalent at grades A*–C
1996	57	54	44.5
2000	75	72	49.2
2004	78	74	53.7
2008	81	78	64.8

[3] There are also vocational equivalents. We use the term GCSE examination to include all variants. The examination is undertaken in England, Wales and Northern Ireland. Scotland has a different system.

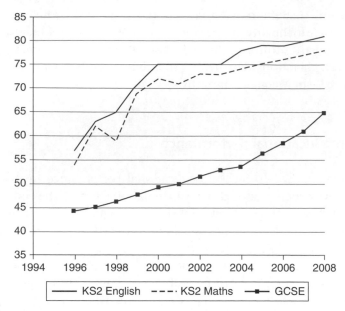

Figure 14.3: Recent trends in educational attainment

Notes: KS2 English: percentage attaining Level 4 or above. KS2 Maths: percentage attaining Level 4 or above. GCSE: percentage with five or more GCSEs at grades A*–C.

Source: DCSF. <http://www.dcsf.gov.uk/trends/>.

more A*–C grades at GCSE) between 1996 and 2008 in England. They all suggest great improvement over time. However, critics allege that grade inflation, 'teaching to the test' and attempts by schools to manipulate their performance (e.g. by encouraging students to take easier subjects) can account for a lot of this. A different criticism is that roughly a fifth of primary school children still do not achieve the required standard by the end of primary school, despite all the improvement.

All this prompts people to look at how the UK performs internationally. There are three international tests of relevance here: Progress in International Reading Literacy (PIRLS), conducted in 2001 and 2006 for pupils around 10 years old; the Programme for the International Student Assessment (PISA) conducted in 2000, 2003 and 2006 for 15-year-olds; and Trends in International Mathematics and Science Study (TIMSS) conducted in 1999, 2003 and 2007 for pupils of around age 10 and age 14 (i.e. years 5 and 9 in England). The UK's relative performance gives rather mixed results according to these studies. For example, in the TIMSS study, England's score was one of the highest in 2007 and has shown improvement over time. However, in PISA, the performance of the UK is much less remarkable, ranking 14th, 19th and 9th respectively in tests of reading, maths and science that were administered to students in 30 OECD countries. There is relatively little overlap between the countries covered in PISA and TIMSS and the tests focus on different things.[4] Particular problems with England's participation in the PISA survey have meant that it is difficult to infer much about change over time.[5] With regard to PIRLS, the most recent survey shows that England performed significantly above the international mean for the reading level of 10-year-olds. However, this was significantly below some major European countries, including Italy and Germany. The change over time suggests that English performance declined between 2001 and 2006, though it would seem that trends over time are sensitive to the methodology used for linking the tests.

Thus, different stories can be told about the evolution of the UK's educational performance, according to different data sets and how exactly they are used. One striking fact that has been ascertained using these international data sets is that family background is more strongly correlated with student test scores in the UK than in many other countries. This is another manifestation of inequality in the UK, which is evident on so many other dimensions and specifically an indication of the lack of intergenerational mobility (see Blanden and Macmillan, Chapter 13). In this context, it is of interest to look at how the relationship between schools' economic disadvantage and performance has changed over time. Figure 14.4 (and Table 14.2) shows the relationship between schools' ranking in the distribution of disadvantage (as measured by the percentage of students eligible to receive Free School Meals)

Table 14.2: Average performance of schools by decile of disadvantage

Decile	% of students with 5+ GCSEs or equivalent at grades A*–C		
	1997	2008	Change
1 (most advantaged 10% of schools)	76	88	12
2	59	76	17
3	53	70	18
4	47	68	21
5	43	65	21
6	39	61	22
7	36	58	22
8	30	58	28
9	25	55	30
10 (most disadvantaged 10 of schools)	20	54	34

[4] TIMSS is more curriculum-based, focusing on mathematical understanding, whereas PISA's mathematical literacy is about maths in everyday situations.

[5] In brief, England did not meet the OECD school response rate for PISA 2000. In 2003, participation rates at both school and pupil level did not meet OECD requirements and England was excluded from international comparisons.

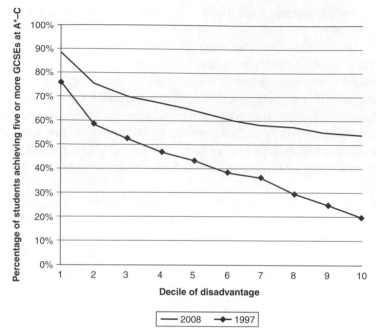

Figure 14.4: Average performance of schools by decile of disadvantage

Notes: Average performance measured by percentage of students achieving five or more GCSEs at grades A*–C. Schools divided into ten equal deciles, depending on their disadvantage in each period, as measured by the percentage of students eligible to receive Free School Meals.

Source: Derived from the Annual School Census and the School Performance Tables.

and their educational performance (as measured by the percentage of students achieving five or more grades at A*–C in GCSE). Schools are divided into deciles of disadvantage in 1997 and 2008 respectively, where decile 1 is the least disadvantaged and decile 10 is the most disadvantaged. In both periods, there is a strong negative relationship between schools with a high intake of pupils on Free School Meals and average GCSE performance. However, there has been a large narrowing of the gap in the last ten years, as more disadvantaged schools have improved at a much faster rate than relatively advantaged schools. The same is true (albeit less dramatically) for primary schools. It might be that improvement in the lower part of the distribution has to some extent been due to the development and inclusion of a wider range of vocational and functional qualifications. It might also be that the overall reduction in poverty has helped shift educational performance differentially for schools with disadvantaged pupils. However, education policy has also had a role to play and we now turn to consider several important reforms.

The role of education policy

Investing in schools

It may be difficult to measure educational outcomes, but there is no such difficulty with regard to the measure of cost. Figure 14.5 (and Table 14.3) shows the increase in per pupil school-based expenditure since 1997 in the case of secondary schools and 2001 in the case of primary schools. Expenditure on schools started rising in real terms in the year 2000 and increased by 45% between 1999 and 2007. As a percentage of GDP, expenditure and training rose from 4.9% (in 1997–8) to 5.9% in 2006. This is just above the OECD average of 5.7%. However, large as this rise is, it is small in relation to resources invested in the private sector. For example, OECD figures show that

Table 14.3: Recent trends in school expenditure (£ per pupil)

	Primary	Secondary
1996	—	£3,000
2000	£2,390	£3,110
2004	£2,970	£3,830
2008	£3,360	£4,320

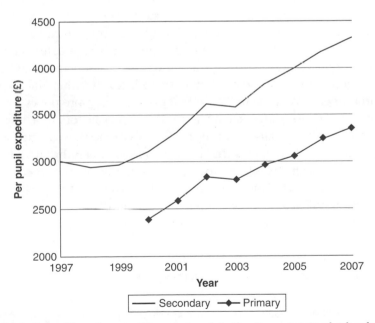

Figure 14.5: School-based expenditure in Local Authority maintained schools in real terms (2006–2007 prices)

Source: <http://www.dcsf.gov.uk/rsgateway/DB/TIM/m002001/index.shtml>.

average class size in primary schools is about 25 pupils in the UK, whereas it is 13 in private schools.

Evidence on the relationship between expenditure and educational outcomes is very controversial in the academic literature. Many studies fail to find evidence of a positive relationship between resources and educational achievement, although some high quality studies do. There have been a number of recent studies using English data to see whether there is such a relationship. All these studies found evidence of at least small positive effects of rising expenditure. The analysis based on most recent data is by Holmlund et al. (2010) who look at the issue for primary schools between 2002 and 2007. They analyse the relationship between expenditure on pupils and attainment in Key Stage 2 tests of English, Maths and Science, after taking account of pupil-level and school-level characteristics (including all effects that could be attributed to schools which do not vary over time). They find that expenditure has a positive and significant effect on all tests. The order of magnitude is modest (about 5% of a standard deviation for an increase in annual per pupil expenditure of £1000), but is sufficient for likely benefits to outweigh costs.[6]

Another way to examine the impact of rising expenditure on educational outcomes is to look at area-based initiatives. For example, in the late 1990s, the Excellence in Cities (EiC) programme was introduced as a key initiative to schools in disadvantaged urban areas. It quickly expanded in coverage and also to primary education (Excellence in Primary Schools). The resources were originally tied to particular initiatives but became more flexible over time. From an analytical viewpoint, such policies are easier to evaluate than policies that are introduced everywhere at the same time. Machin et al. (2007) make use of a 'difference-in-differences' analysis to assess whether the change in pupil attainment over time in EiC areas (i.e. post-policy–pre-policy) is greater than in non-EiC areas after taking account of other factors that might also have changed differentially over time for schools in these areas. Their analysis (for secondary schools) shows that extra resources offered by the EiC policy were effective in terms of improving Mathematics achievement and in increasing school attendance. The magnitude of the effect on test outcomes is again modest (around 2% of a standard deviation). However, the fact that the cost is also fairly low (an average of £120 per annum) suggests that the policy would pass a cost-benefit analysis under reasonable assumptions.

It is interesting to note that both Holmlund et al. (2010) and Machin et al. (2007) find evidence of differential effects by level of disadvantage. Holmlund

---

[6] Another outcome is that an increase of £1000 in average expenditure per pupil would increase the number of pupils attaining the expected standard (level 4) by 2.2 percentage points, 2.0 percentage points and 0.7 percentage points in English, Maths and Science. We make a back-of-envelope calculation of economic benefits by analysing the relationship between age 10 test scores and labour market earnings using the British Cohort Survey.

et al. (2010) show that increasing pupil expenditure has a larger positive impact on economically disadvantaged pupils (about 40% higher than other pupils). Machin et al. (2007) found the largest effects for pupils of high ability in the most disadvantaged schools. This is consistent with government expenditure having a larger effect in poorer schools and/or higher levels of expenditure being directed to disadvantaged schools.

The fact that resources are partly tied to disadvantage is one reason why it is important to control for detailed school and pupil-level controls when analysing the relationship between expenditure and educational attainment. However, although there is a link between disadvantage and funding, the extent of this link depends on the Local Authority (LA) in which a person lives. Funding to schools is provided by central government to LAs by a formula and then by LAs to schools using their individual formulae. LAs vary in the importance they place on disadvantage as a reason to allocate more resources to schools and it has been shown that many are less redistributive than central government (DfES/HM Treasury, 2005). Findings from the DfES/HM Treasury report (2005) include the following: 'there is a wide degree of variation between local authorities' strategies for assessing and funding the costs of deprivation, and there has often been no systematic approach to reviewing need'; 'schools facing the same scale of deprivation in different authorities often receive different amounts of funding from their authorities to deal with deprivation'. Holmlund et al. (2010) show that some of the most advantaged schools in the country have the same level of per pupil expenditure as some of the most disadvantaged schools. Thus, it would appear that more could be done to make the system fairer and research indicates that there might well be efficiency as well equity implications from further redistribution.

Choice, accountability and competition

Traditional resource-based policies are not the only ones that have been used extensively to try to improve the school system. Over the last 30 years, parental choice, school accountability and competition between schools have become increasingly part of the culture of UK education. They are all linked to each other: parents have choice about where to send their children to school; their choice is facilitated by the accountability system (i.e. publication of inspection reports and school 'league tables'); and where pupils go to school influences the resources obtained by schools (since pupil numbers are an important part of formula funding), which gives them an incentive to compete with one another. Different aspects of this 'marketisation' of the education system have been subject to academic analysis.

In the policy debate, parental choice is usually discussed as a good in itself rather than as a means to an end. Measures to increase parental choice (e.g. creating new schools) are often discussed, but not the barriers faced by many people in their ability to exercise choice. These come in two forms. First, even though parents have had the right to apply to any school of their choice since 1980, in practice, they cannot exercise this right if the school is over-subscribed and needs to apply selection criteria. Proximity to the school is usually among the most important of these criteria and this naturally discriminates against people of low income who cannot afford to live near to a popular school. A number of studies in the UK and elsewhere show that proximity to a 'good school' influences house prices. Using very recent data, Gibbons et al. (2009) show that school 'value added' and school composition are equally important for influencing house prices. Secondly, parents are not equally able to access and use available information. West and Pennell (1999) show that higher socio-economic groups have better information and understanding of school performance, for example via 'league tables'. When one remembers that many adults do not have high levels of literacy and that there is an important link between poverty and education, this is not surprising. However, this aspect of the barrier to making a choice is rarely discussed in the policy debate.

Parental choice, accountability and the funding structure should (if they are effective) give rise to competition between schools as they try to boost their pupil numbers and appeal to the parents of 'good' students. Allowing schools greater autonomy should give them the flexibility to respond in ways they see fit. On the other hand, the education system is not a proper market because there is no automatic mechanism to trigger the exit of failing schools. On the contrary, the closing down of underperforming schools can be slow, political and unpopular. This means that the government may end up simultaneously supporting expanding schools, new schools and failing schools. This can also generate greater inequality as the pupils who are left in the failing schools are probably the children of parents who could not afford to move nearer to 'good' schools. Evaluation of the Swedish reforms that expanded parental choice by allowing new independent schools to form shows evidence of only small positive effects (Bohlmark and Lindahl, 2008) and the authors speculate that one reason for this could be the fact that the entry of new private schools has not been followed by the closing down of public schools. The reality that governments will have to simultaneously support new schools and the older 'bad' ones and that the latter will not exit at an efficient rate needs to be factored into the expected cost-effectiveness of a 'school creation' policy.

There have been many studies on the effects of choice and competition in the US but the evidence is 'voluminous and mixed' (Gibbons et al., 2008). There is very little evidence on this for Britain (but this is also mixed in its results). The first pupil-level analysis on the subject pertains to primary schools in the south-east of England (Gibbons et al., 2008). The authors find that pupils who have a wider choice of schools at their place of residence perform no better than those with more limited choice. They find no evidence of a causal link between school competition and school performance. They conclude that choice and competition do not seem to be effective in raising standards.

However, the above arguments have not deterred all political parties from an intention to create more choice in the school system through the provision of new schools. The Academies programme is an example of this. It was originally conceived as a way of replacing failing maintained secondary schools located in socially disadvantaged urban areas, although now they have begun to take on several different forms with their coverage spreading geographically. Machin and Wilson (2009) consider some early evidence on their effects. They compare the growth in GCSE performance for schools that became academies with a comparison group of similar schools. While there was an improvement in the GCSE performance of schools that became academies, it was no different from the improvement for schools in the comparison group. However, they also say that it is still too early for the academies programme to be fully appraised on the basis of GCSE results. Other important issues (currently under investigation) are the effect of academies on the performance of schools in the same local areas and whether there are effects on urban regeneration.

Influencing pedagogy

In some areas of education policy, successive governments have tried to decentralise decision making so as to facilitate parental choice and schools' capacity to respond to increased pressures. In other areas, they have tried to increase their influence on what goes on in schools. Pedagogy is an obvious example of the latter. The National Strategies for the teaching of literacy and numeracy have been an important component of educational policies over the last decade and the introduction of synthetic phonics to early years' teaching in primary schools is a more recent example in the same spirit.

The National Literacy Strategy was preceded by an earlier initiative in a handful of Local Education Authorities known as the National Literacy Project (introduced by the Conservatives in 1996). Similarly the National Numeracy Strategy was preceded by the National Numeracy Project. The 'literacy hour' and 'numeracy hour' were key components of these Strategies and involved daily instruction with a very specific format. Both were supported by a framework for teaching, which sets out termly objectives for the 5–11 age range and provides a practical structure of time and class management. For example, with regard to the 'literacy hour', a range of texts were specified and teaching

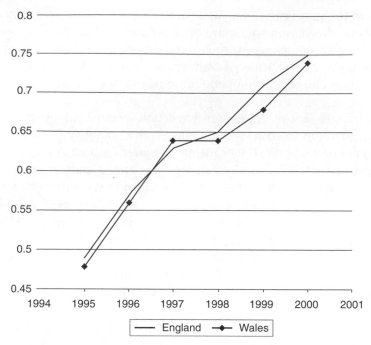

Figure 14.6: Proportion attaining level 4 or above in English

Note: Comparison between England and Wales (1995–2000). Literacy Hour introduced in England for exam year 1998.

Source: Machin and McNally (2010).

objectives set out at three levels (text, sentence and word) to match the text types studied. The daily literacy hour was divided between 10–15 minutes of whole-class reading or writing; a 10–15 minutes whole-class session on word work (phonics, spelling and vocabulary) and sentence work (grammar and punctuation); 25–30 minutes of directed group activities (on aspects of writing or reading) and a plenary session at the end for pupils to revisit the objectives of the lesson, reflect on what they have learnt and consider what they needed to do next.

The 'literacy hour' and 'numeracy hour' have been evaluated by Machin and McNally (2008, 2010) who show that they were successful in raising test scores in Maths and English at a very low per pupil cost. For example, the forerunner of the National Literacy Strategy (i.e. the National Literacy Project) increased reading scores by about 8% of a standard deviation at an annual cost of roughly £25 per pupil.[7] The strategies had lower effects than the

---

[7] Another outcome is that the National Literacy Project led to an increase in the number of pupils attaining the expected standard (level 4) in English by 3–3.5 percentage points.

smaller-scale 'projects' but were still cost-effective. It is particularly interesting to note that England overtook Wales at the point at which these strategies were applied in comparable tests (see e.g. Figure 14.6 in relation to the literacy hour). In Wales, Local Authorities were allowed to do their own thing and thus there was far more decentralisation than in England. This suggests that a centralised approach to pedagogy can be more effective in practice, even though intuitively one might expect teachers to be in a better position to discern what works best for their students. In the longer term, one would clearly want to attract and retain teachers who know different pedagogies and who can judge when and how to apply them. Rivkin et al. (2002) show that having a teacher at the higher end of the quality distribution is important for raising student achievement. However, the cost of recruiting, retaining and on-going training of teachers is an expensive policy. A consequence of the increase in graduate opportunities over recent decades (especially for women) is that it is more difficult to attract highly qualified people into teaching. In this context, attracting more highly qualified people into teaching in sufficient numbers is a difficult challenge.

Conclusions

The trend in national tests suggests that educational performance in England has improved over time. However, there is reason to be sceptical about the extent to which trends are informative and international data give a rather mixed picture. In any case, it is not possible to read off whether government policies have been successful, based on consideration of trends in raw data.

Careful evaluation of government policies has been possible in several important cases. We give a selective overview in this chapter. The results of this review are summarised in Table 14.4. We can use this to come to three main conclusions. First, the policy to increase school expenditure has had moderate success in improving educational outcomes both in general terms and in an important specific initiative (Excellence in Cities). It would appear that the investment has been cost-effective (based on simple back-of-envelope calculations). Secondly, efforts to influence pedagogy through the National Strategies have also improved educational outcomes and this has been achieved at a low cost. Thirdly, existing evidence does not suggest that measures to increase parental choice or school competition have been efficacious and thus it seems unlikely that further measures to increase parental choice will improve educational outcomes in the system as a whole.

217

Table 14.4: Evaluation of government policies

Policy	Sector	Project	Positive	Little or no effect	Additional comments
Choice and competition	Primary	Gibbons, Machin and Silva (2008).		√	Suggestion that small effect might be possible in schools with greater autonomy
Increasing overall school expenditure	Primary	Holmlund, McNally and Viarengo (2010)	√		Modest effects, but large enough to be cost-effective. Effects 20–40% higher for disadvantaged students
Literacy and numeracy strategies	Primary	Machin and McNally (2008, 2010)	√		Moderate effect at very low cost
Academies	Secondary	Machin and Wilson (2009)		√	Early days in the evaluation of this policy
Excellence in Cities	Secondary	Machin, McNally and Meghir (2007)	√		Modest effects, but large enough to be cost-effective. Effects are highest for the most able pupils in schools with highest rate of deprivation

Note: A summary of selected studies that have been conducted by the Centre for Economic Performance, LSE.

References

Blanden, J. and Macmillan, L. (2011) Recent developments in intergenerational mobility. In: Gregg, P. and Wadsworth, J. (eds.) *The Labour Market in Winter: The State of Working Britain*. Oxford: Oxford University Press.

Bohlmark, A. and Lindahl, M. (2008) Does school privatisation improve educational achievement? Evidence from Sweden's voucher reform. IZA, Discussion Paper No. 3691. Bonn: Institute for the Study of Labor. Available at <http://www.iza.org/>.

Department for Education and Skills/HM Treasury (2005) Child poverty: fair funding for schools. London: Department for Education and Skills/Treasury.

Gibbons, S., Machin, S. and Silva, O. (2008) Choice, competition and pupil achievement. *Journal of the European Economic Association*, 6(4): 912–47.

—— —— —— (2009) Valuing school quality using boundary regressions. Spatial Economics Research Centre (SERC) Discussion Paper No. 18. London: London School of Economics.

Holmlund, H., McNally, S. and Viarengo, M. (2010) Does money matter for schools? *Economics of Education Review*, 1–30. Available at <http://www.elsevier.com/wps/find/homepage.cws_home>.

Machin, S. and McNally, S. (2008) The literacy hour. *Journal of Public Economics*, 92: 1141–462.

—— —— (2010) The three Rs: The scope for literacy and numeracy policies to raise achievement. Centre for Economic Performance, LSE, Mimeo.

—— —— and Meghir, C. (2007) Resources and standards in urban schools. Centre for the Economics of Education (CEE) Discussion Paper No. 76, February. London: London School of Economics. Available at <http://cee.lse.ac.uk/cee%20dps/ceedp76.pdf>.

—— and Wilson, J. (2009) Academy school and pupil performance. *CentrePiece Magazine*, 14(1), spring. Centre for Economic Performance, London School of Economics and Political Science.

Maurin, E. and McNally, S. (2009) The consequences of ability tracking for future outcomes and social mobility. Report to the Sutton Trust.

Rivkin, S., Hanushek, E. and Kain, J. (2002) Teachers, schools and academic achievement, *Econometrica*, 73(2): 417–58.

West, A. and Pennell, H. (1999) School admissions: increasing equity, accountability and transparency. *British Journal of Education Studies*, 46: 188–200.

15

Ethnicity and Second Generation Immigrants

Christian Dustmann, Tommaso Frattini and Nikolaos Theodoropoulos

Key findings

- Ethnic minority individuals constitute a large and growing share of the UK population: they were 7% of the British working-age population in 2000, 10% in 2005 and 12% in 2009. Over one-third of ethnic minority individuals are UK born (36.5% in 2009), but ethnic minorities also constitute a sizeable share of recent immigrant inflows: 47.5% of immigrants who arrived since 2005, and are still in Britain in 2009, belong to an ethnic minority group.
- British-born white and ethnic minority individuals have a distinct regional distribution. Minorities are disproportionately more concentrated in London than white natives.
- All minorities experience a lower employment rate than white natives. They also tend to have lower wages, if we control for their regional distribution and education. However, there are considerable differences between ethnic groups.
- Second-generation ethnic minority immigrants tend to be better educated than their parents' generation, and better educated than their white native peers. The relative improvement in education between the parent and descendant generation is far larger for ethnic minorities than for white natives. Still, British-born ethnic minorities are less likely to have jobs and earn on average lower wages, even if they have the same characteristics as their white British-born peers.
- Minority children experience achievement disadvantages before starting school. These disadvantages are reduced considerably during compulsory schooling, and turn into substantial advantages for some ethnic groups at the end of compulsory schooling.

Introduction

According to the 2001 Census, the percentage of non-white individuals (which includes both ethnic minorities and individuals of mixed ethnicity) in the British population was 8.1% (or 4.6 million), up from 5.5% (or 3 million) in 1991. While a precise assessment of the current size of the minority population will be possible with the 2011 Census, the Labour Force Survey (LFS) shows that in the third quarter of 2009, about 11.7% of the working-age population (16–64 years for men, 16–59 years for women) was non-white.

British-born descendants of ethnic minority immigrants represent an increasing share of the ethnic minority population in the UK. According to the LFS, in 1991 25.2% of the individuals of working age who identified themselves as members of an ethnic minority group were born in the UK. This share has increased in 2001 to 35% and in 2009 to 36.6%.

How do Britain's ethnic minorities perform in the labour market? Do those who are born in Britain outperform their parents, and are the same relative disadvantages across groups that are visible in the parent generation transmitted to descendants who are born in Britain? How do British and foreign-born ethnic minorities perform compared to their British-born white peers? How does educational achievement at an early age develop in contrast with white majority individuals, and how does it translate into wages and employment? This chapter provides answers to these questions.

The chapter is an assessment of how the economic performance of ethnic minorities relative to the white native population has changed over the last decade. If not otherwise specified, the figures reported have been computed from the UK Labour Force Survey (LFS). We start with a description of the size and geographic distribution of the minority population in the UK. In the following section, we concentrate on the relative economic performance of minorities, and its evolution over time. We then focus on second-generation immigrants, presenting an intergenerational comparison of education, employment, and wages of different ethnic minority groups born in Britain compared with their parents' generation, and to equivalent groups of white native-born individuals. We next investigate the early stages of educational attainment of British-born minority children: analysing the evolution of the attainment gap between white British-born and ethnic minority pupils throughout compulsory schooling.

Ethnic minorities in Britain

Large-scale immigration of individuals of ethnic minority descent to Britain started after the Second World War. Today, the six largest ethnic minority groups in Britain (in descending population size) are Indian, Pakistani, Black Caribbean, Black African, Bangladeshi and Chinese. These groups differ in the timing of their arrival. While the majority of immigrants from the Caribbean arrived in the period between 1955 and 1964, the main time of arrival for Black African, Indian and Pakistani was between 1965 and 1974. The 2001 Census counted 565,876 Black Caribbean, or 1.0% of the total UK population and 12.2% of the ethnic minority population. Black African migration to Britain has increased since the immediate post-independence period of the 1960s, with a marked increase in the number of Africans travelling to Britain for higher education and technical training. Large-scale labour migration from India to Britain took place mainly in the 1950s and 1960s. Indians were—according to the 2001 UK Census—the largest ethnic minority group, making up about 22.7% of the minority ethnic population and 1.8% of the total UK population. Bangladeshi arrivals were later, and peaked in the period 1980–4. The Chinese form the smallest ethnic group. Since the 1980s, there has been a resurgence of immigration from mainland China, consisting mainly of students and scholars arriving in Britain, and staying on after completing their education. We summarise some of these trends in Figure 15.1, which reports (for the period 1979–2009) the evolution of the share of foreign-born individuals of all ethnicities in the working-age population, the share of white

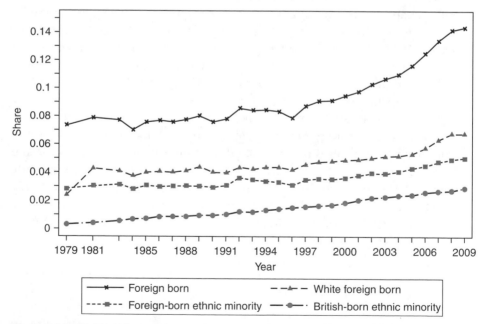

Figure 15.1: Share of foreign-born/ethnic minority in working-age population

foreign born, the share of ethnic minority foreign born (excluding individuals with mixed ethnicity), and the share of ethnic minority native born.

All the lines in the figure show a clear upward trend. The share of foreign born in the working-age population almost doubled between 1979 and 2009, increasing from 7.3% to 14.4%. Almost a third of this increase was due to the growth of ethnic minority foreign-born individuals, whose share in the working-age population increased from 2.8% to 5%. Most of the remaining change was due to the increase in the share of white foreign born (from 2.4% to 6.8%).[1] However, the graph also outlines the dramatic growth in the share of British-born ethnic minorities (self-defined) in the working-age population, which increased tenfold over the observation period. While in 1979, only 0.3% of the working-age population was composed of British-born ethnic minority individuals, this share is 1% in 1990, 1.8% in 2000, and 2.9% in 2009.

Figure 15.2 displays information on the evolution in the shares of working-age first-generation ethnic minority immigrants and ethnic minority individuals who are born in Britain for the six largest non-white minority populations (Black Caribbean, Black African, Indian, Pakistani, Bangladeshi and Chinese). Panel A of Figure 15.2 shows a significant downward trend in the share of first-generation Black Caribbean, due to return migration after retirement, onward migration to North America as well as to a fall in inflow rates over time. Black Caribbean have also the highest share of British-born descendants relative to all other ethnic groups until 1997, which is not surprising, given their earlier arrival in Britain. The remaining panels show that other ethnic minority groups have markedly different trends. First-generation Indian immigrants, the single most numerous ethnic group over the entire period, are a more or less constant share of the working-age population (Panel C). In contrast, first-generation immigrants of all other ethnic groups exhibit a clear upward trend, particularly so for Black Africans (Panel B), but also sizeable for those of Indian (Panel C) and Pakistani (Panel D) descent. Bangladeshis (Panel E) and Chinese (Panel F) form the smallest groups among both first- and second-generation immigrants, which is explained partly by their later arrival in Britain compared to the other ethnic minority groups. Overall, these figures suggest a considerable increase in the fraction of ethnic minorities, both foreign born and British born, in the British population over the last three decades.

Of interest is the geographic distribution of ethnic minorities, which differs quite dramatically from that of British-born whites. Further, their regional distribution is relatively stable over time. Table 15.1 reports the geographic

---

[1] The remaining change is explained by an increase in immigrants of mixed ethnicity.

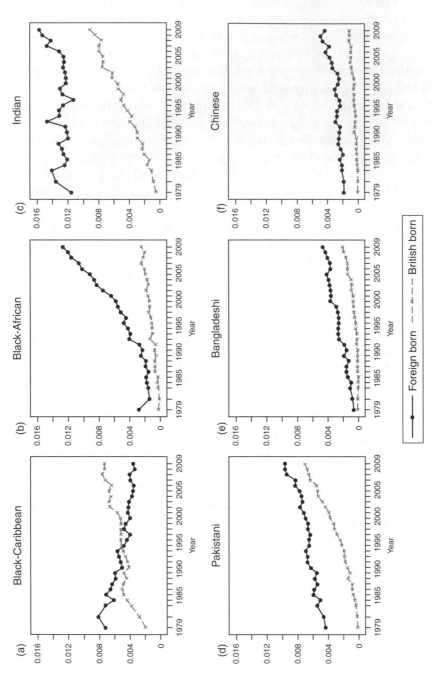

Figure 15.2: Share of foreign and British-born ethnic minorities in working-age population

Table 15.1: Regional distribution of white natives and ethnic minorities

Region	1979–1983		1989–1991		1999–2001		2007–2009	
	White natives	Ethnic minorities	White natives	Ethnic minorities	White natives	Ethnic minorities	White natives	Ethnic minorities
North	6.1	1.0	5.9	1.1	5.8	1.1	5.8	1.8
Yorkshire	9.3	8.6	9.2	7.4	9.0	7.1	9.3	7.5
East Midlands	7.1	3.9	7.4	6.7	7.6	5.8	7.8	6.5
East Anglia	3.5	1.9	3.7	1.5	3.9	1.0	4.1	1.3
London	10.6	43.0	9.8	45.4	9.2	47.6	8.2	42.5
South East	18.5	12.3	19.4	10.3	19.9	10.7	19.9	12.1
South West	8.0	2.6	8.5	2.7	8.8	1.7	9.3	2.2
West Midlands	9.5	17.4	9.4	14.0	9.1	14.9	8.8	14.1
North West	12.2	6.4	11.7	7.9	11.5	7.1	11.4	8.3
Wales	5.3	1.5	5.4	0.9	5.4	1.0	5.5	1.0
Scotland	10.0	1.4	9.8	2.1	9.7	2.0	9.8	2.6

Notes: The table reports the regional distribution of white natives and ethnic minorities (foreign and native-born) in 1979–83, 1989–91, 1999–2001, 2007–9.

Source: Labour Force Survey (LFS), several years.

distribution of white natives and ethnic minorities over nine English regions, Wales, and Scotland[2] in 1979–83, 1989–91, 1999–2001, 2007–9 (we had to pool several years to increase the sample size). In all years ethnic minorities are four to five times more concentrated in London than white natives. They also tend to cluster in the West Midlands more than white natives, although the difference is not as large as in London. The share of individuals from an ethnic minority group living in London has increased over time from 43% in 1979–83 to 47.6% in 1999–2001, and has slightly decreased again to 42.5% since 2007. Over the same period, the share of white natives living in London has steadily decreased from 10.6% to 8.2%.

Labour market performance of ethnic minorities

How do individuals belonging to a minority group perform in the labour market, relative to white natives, and has this relative performance changed over time? In this section we address this issue, comparing the probability of employment and the wages of minorities and of white natives.[3]

Table 15.2 reports the difference in the employment rate (defined as the ratio of employed individuals to the working-age population) for men and

Table 15.2: Difference in employment rate between white natives and ethnic minorities

	1993		2000		2009	
	Men	Women	Men	Women	Men	Women
Black Caribbean	−18.3*	−9.7*	−13.5*	−6.9*	−13.9*	−4.8*
Black African	−32.3*	−24.8*	−17.5*	−21.5*	−12.0*	−25.4*
Indian	−7.8*	−13.1*	−5.7*	−11.9*	−0.8	−10.5*
Pakistani	−24.1*	−49.4*	−18.1*	−45.1*	−10.2*	−43.5*
Bangladeshi	−27.3*	−51.3*	−26.5*	−53.2*	−6.9*	−44.4*
Chinese	−13.9*	−19.1*	−20.5*	−21.0*	−19.0*	−9.2*
Total difference (minority)	−17.2*	−23.0*	−13.8*	−22.4*	−8.2*	−22.0*
White natives' employment rate	76.2	66.4	80.4	71.1	77.0	72.0

Notes: The table reports the difference in employment rate between white natives and each ethnic minority group (or all minority groups), net of seasonality effects, in 1993, 2000, 2009. The last row reports the average employment rate of white natives.
*Indicates that the difference is statistically significant at 5%.
Source: Labour Force Survey (LFS), 1993, 2000, 2009.

---

[2] The regions are defined based on the variable URESMC in the LFS. Because of the small sample size in some regions, the following groupings have been made: 'Tyne & Wear' and 'Rest of Northern Region' into 'North'; 'South Yorkshire', 'West Yorkshire' and 'Rest of Yorkshire & Humberside' into 'Yorkshire'; 'Inner London' and 'Outer London' into 'London'; 'West Midlands (met county)' and 'Rest of West Midlands' into 'West Midlands'; 'Greater Manchester', 'Merseyside' and 'Rest of North West' into 'North West'; 'Strathclyde' and 'Rest of Scotland' into 'Scotland'.
[3] See also Wadsworth (2003) for an earlier assessment of this topic.

women, between white natives and each of the six minority groups, net of seasonal effects, in 1993, 2000 and 2009.[4] The last row reports the employment rate of white natives. The employment rate of ethnic minority men and women is generally lower than those of white natives. The only exception is for Indian men in 2009, whose employment rate is not significantly different from that of white natives. Even in earlier years, Indian men are the least disadvantaged group: their employment rate is 6 percentage points lower than white natives in 2000 and 8 percentage points lower in 1993. By contrast, Pakistani and Bangladeshi men are significantly disadvantaged relative to white native men in all years, although the gap is reducing over time. In 1993 Pakistani (Bangladeshi) men were 24 (27) percentage points less likely to be working than white natives, while in 2009 the difference reduces to 10 (7) percentage points. The employment rate among Pakistani and Bangladeshi women is between 43 and 53 percentage points lower than among white native women in all years, although the gap is slightly decreasing in the most recent year. Interestingly the employment differential with respect to white natives is in all years smaller for Black Caribbean women than for Black Caribbean men. We display in Table 15.3 the percentage difference in average hourly wages between white natives and ethnic minorities for the same years, and we again distinguish between men and women. In Panel A we only control for seasonality.[5] Again, the disadvantage of the Pakistani and Bangladeshi minorities is evident. In 2009, Pakistani men earn on average 26% less than white natives, while Bangladeshi men have 35% lower wages. However, while for the Bangladeshi minority wage differentials are closing over time (from −53% in 1993, to −50% in 2000 and −35% in 2009), for the Pakistani ethnic group wage differentials are rather stable. Among the other minorities, Black Caribbean men display a 27% wage disadvantage in 2009. Black Caribbean women do not have significant wage differentials in 2009, but exhibit 15% higher wages than white native women in earlier years. Indian men and women earn respectively 14% and 18% more than white natives in 2009. These results indicate wage disadvantages only for men of some ethnic groups, and even show wage advantages for other groups and for women.

However, we have shown in Table 15.1 that ethnic minorities are much more concentrated in London than white natives, where wages (and prices) are higher than the rest of Britain. It is therefore important to control for the

---

[4] To obtain the numbers in the table, we have run, for every year reported, regressions of a dummy variable for employment on quarter dummies, and ethnicity dummies (whose coefficients we report). The technically interested reader can find more details in Dustmann, Frattini, and Theodoropoulos (2010).

[5] We use regression analysis (as explained in Dustmann, Frattini and Theodoropoulos, 2010) to net the figures of seasonal effects (in Panel A), and additionally from regional and composition effects (in Panels B and C).

Table 15.3: Percentage difference in mean hourly wages between white natives and ethnic minorities

	1993		2000		2009	
	Men	Women	Men	Women	Men	Women
		Panel A				
Black Caribbean	−18.9*	15.0*	−12.1*	15.0*	−27.2*	6.8
Black African	−20.1*	24.9*	−10.0	11.1*	−9.0	3.3
Indian	4.2	1.7	−3.0	3.1	14.4*	17.6*
Pakistani	−29.1*	2.6	−25.4*	−6.4	−25.8*	−7.1
Bangladeshi	−53.0*	9.8	−49.6*	−21.9	−35.2*	−5.9
Chinese	−0.8	13.5	−6.4	7.9	−17.8	21.5*
All minorities	−11.6*	9.5*	−12.5*	6.1*	−7.7*	9.6*
		Panel B				
Black Caribbean	−27.1*	−4.4	−24.0*	−1.5	−38.6*	−10.0*
Black African	−31.8*	1.4	−29.2*	−12.6*	−25.0*	−12.4*
Indian	−2.5	−11.0*	−13.1*	−10.6*	6.6	7.7*
Pakistani	−30.7*	−2.0	−31.3*	−13.2*	−30.0*	−13.5*
Bangladeshi	−64.5*	−12.5	−63.6*	−31.9*	−43.4*	−18.8*
Chinese	−10.1	5.1	−18.0*	−4.1	−25.5*	7.4
All minorities	−18.6*	−6.1*	−23.8*	−9.0*	−16.5*	−2.5
		Panel C				
Black Caribbean	−23.3*	−7.0	−23.8*	−2.0	−33.5*	−8.3
Black African	−49.6*	−19.8*	−45.7*	−29.2*	−39.4*	−26.5*
Indian	−19.8*	−20.8*	−26.0*	−19.6*	−9.6*	−8.0*
Pakistani	−34.7*	−7.6	−37.5*	−15.0*	−35.2*	−15.2*
Bangladeshi	−71.2*	−20.1	−62.8*	−31.3	−45.4*	−13.6
Chinese	−39.2*	−18.9	−29.7*	−24.7*	−41.1*	−8.7
All minorities	−29.1*	−15.3*	−32.4*	−16.4*	−27.0*	−12.3*
White natives mean wages	9.35	6.82	10.53	7.95	12.22	9.79

Notes: The table reports the percentage mean hourly wage differences between white natives and each ethnic minority group (or all minority groups), net of seasonality effects, in 1993, 2000, 2009. Panel A controls for seasonality; panel B additionally controls for region of residence; panel C controls additionally for age and education. The last row reports the mean hourly wage for white natives. Wages are discounted using the 2005-based CPI.
*Indicates that the difference is statistically significant at 5%.
Source: Labour Force Survey (LFS), 1993, 2000, 2009.

regional distribution when computing average wage differentials. Panel B of Table 15.3 shows that, after controlling for the regional distribution, wage differentials become negative and significant for almost all ethnic groups and years. The exceptions are Chinese women, who do not display any significant wage difference with respect to white natives, and the Indian minority, which has a negative wage differential only in 2000 (and in 1993 for women only), and a positive differential for women in 2009. Finally, in Panel C we show wage differentials after accounting for the differences in age and education structure. In this case, almost all groups exhibit negative and sizeable wage differentials in every year, with Bangladeshi men having the highest wage disadvantage (−45%) in 2009. Thus, Britain's ethnic minority population, if it had the same age and education structure, and the same regional distribution as native whites, would experience large and significant wage disadvantages. This is particularly so for males.

Intergenerational comparisons

Performance (and integration) of immigrant populations is a long-term process that spans multiple generations. One key question is then whether, and to what extent, the children of immigrants improve *relative* to their native-born peers, and in comparison to the respective parent generations. In this section we compare the educational and labour market achievements of second-generation immigrants with those of their parents' generation, relative to white natives.

Data and sample construction

Although the LFS classifies people according to their country of birth as well as their ethnicity, it does not collect information on the parental country of birth. In this section, we provide an attempt to assess the intergenerational mobility of Britain's ethnic minority populations, following and extending work by Dustmann and Theodoropoulos (2010). We construct two samples: the first consists of first-generation ethnic minority immigrants of Black Caribbean, Black African, Indian, Pakistani, Bangladeshi and Chinese origin, born between 1933 and 1954, and whom we observe in the LFS between 1979 and 1988. The second sample is their likely descendants: British-born ethnic minorities, born between 1963 and 1975, and observed in the LFS in 1998–2009. The second group is in a similar age range as the first group 20 years earlier. For each of these samples we construct a white British-born comparison sample of individuals of the same birth cohort.[6]

Educational achievement

The LFS offers two measures of educational attainment, one based on the age at which an individual left continuous full-time education, and the other based on educational qualifications. However, since the variable coding for educational qualifications does not record foreign qualifications, we base our analysis on the number of years of study. To obtain a measure of years of continuous full-time education from the age at which individuals left full-time education, we adjust for the different ages at which individuals start full-time education in different countries. We also make adjustments for the individuals who started full-time education abroad or came to Britain before the starting age of primary school.

---

[6] See Dustmann and Theodoropoulos (2010) for more detail. Other than in their paper, we have increased the observation window for the two groups by five years.

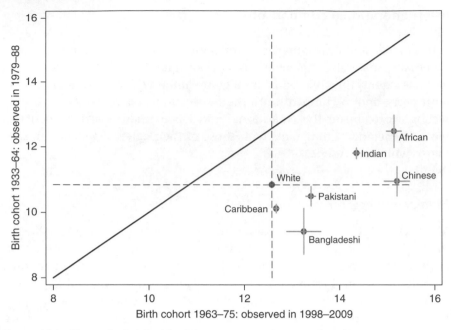

Figure 15.3: Years of schooling by ethnic group and status of generation

Figure 15.3 presents the mean educational achievements of first-generation immigrants and their descendants, measured as the age at which individuals leave school minus the school entry age,[7] and based on the cohorts constructed as described above. The corresponding numbers for white native-born reference groups are also included.

In the figure, entries on the diagonal line indicate that educational attainment of the parent generation is equal to that of their descendants. For all groups (including whites), entries are below the main diagonal, suggesting a higher educational attainment of the later cohort than of their parent generation. The vertical and horizontal lines that cross at the 'white' entry define different areas, which compare the relative educational improvement from the parent and offspring generations of white British born with the relative educational improvement of British-born minorities and their foreign-born parent generation. All minority groups with entries in the upper-right rectangle are groups where both the British born as well as their foreign-born parent generation have higher levels of education. The grey lines through the

---

[7] For foreign-born individuals we use the school entry age of their country of origin at the time they started full-time education. See Dustmann and Theodoropoulos (2010) for details.

entries are the confidence intervals, which indicate the precision of our measure.[8]

For the African and Indian groups, the parent generation has more years of full-time education than the white British-born reference group. The Chinese and Pakistani first-generation groups are similar to whites, and the Caribbean and Bangladeshi have slightly lower years of full-time education. More importantly, for all groups (except for the Caribbean), those who are born in Britain have more years of full-time education than their white British-born peers. Furthermore, for some groups, the difference between the parent generation and the generation of their descendants is quite dramatic, and far larger than for British-born whites.

Overall, the figure suggests that the descendants of British ethnic minority immigrants (born between 1963 and 1975 in Britain, and observed between 1998 and 2009) have higher levels of full-time education than their parents, and (except for the Caribbean) higher levels of full-time education than their British-born white peers.[9] Also, the difference between parent and child generations is larger for all minority groups than for whites, with the exception of the Black Caribbean. That is quite remarkable, and paints quite a positive picture of the educational attainments of Britain's ethnic minorities.

Employment

Do these educational advantages translate into employment and wage advantages? In Figure 15.4 we present a similar graph, but for employment differences between parent and descendant generations. The figure is constructed in the same way as before.[10] However, this time it suggests a marked disadvantage for ethnic minority individuals, with a large heterogeneity between the different ethnic groups. Most ethnic minority individuals of both first and second generations have markedly lower employment probabilities than their white native-born peers, with the largest differences for individuals from the

---

[8] Formally, the confidence interval denotes the range of values within which the educational achievement of the whole population of interest lies with 95% probability.

[9] It is also worth noting that among this recent cohort, 21% of the white natives have a university degree, versus 17% of the Black Caribbean, 47% of the Black African, 39% of the Indian, 27% of the Pakistani, 34% of the Bangladeshi and 54% of the Chinese.

[10] Our measure for the overall economic activity of individuals distinguishes between paid employment, self-employment, unemployment, economic inactivity as well as people on government schemes. We consider here only individuals in dependent employment, and exclude the self-employed (these are 7.2% of white natives and 6.1% of British-born ethnic minorities, respectively, in year 1998 and for the 1963–75 birth cohort) as well as those individuals on government schemes. The latter group is about 0.1%. We also drop all those individuals who were in full-time education at the time of the survey. We define an individual to be employed if he/she is in paid employment, as opposed to being economically inactive or unemployed.

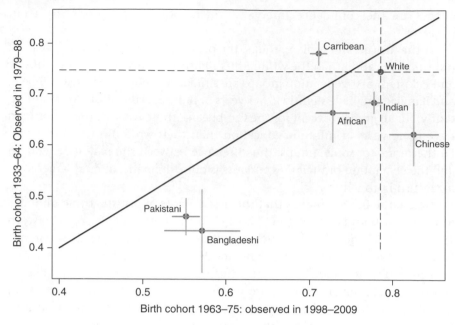

Figure 15.4: Employment rate by ethnic group and status of generation

Bangladeshi and Pakistani communities.[11] Individuals of the most recent generation from all communities (including whites) have higher employment rates than their parents' generation, which reflects the higher average employment rate in the most recent period (77.3% of the individuals in our sample are in dependent employment in the second period vs. 74.4% in the first period). The only exception is Black Caribbean. For this group, the employment rate was higher than for whites in the first generation, but it is markedly lower in the second generation. The opposite is true for the Chinese community, while second-generation Indians have an employment probability that is very similar to that of natives.

Thus, British-born ethnic minority individuals, despite having more schooling, have lower employment probabilities than their British-born white peers. Further, there is substantial heterogeneity in employment between the different minority groups.

[11] When we break these numbers down by gender, it turns out that these differences are mainly driven by females, who—in both the first and the second generation—have substantially lower employment probabilities than their male counterparts. See Dustmann and Theodoropoulos (2010) for details.

Wages

We now turn to wages, and we concentrate here on the above-defined cohorts of British-born ethnic minorities.[12] Table 15.4 presents percentage differences in wages between British-born ethnic minorities and white natives. We start by reporting (in Panel A) differences in mean wages, expressed in

Table 15.4: Percentage difference in mean hourly wages between white natives and second-generation ethnic minority immigrants

Ethnic groups	Birth cohort 1963–1975 observed in 1998–2009 (Minorities: all British born)		
	(1)	(2)	(3)
	Total	Men	Women
	Panel A		
Black Caribbean	1.1	−9.7*	13.1*
Black African	9.4*	−1.7	21.2*
Indian	8.6*	5.0*	12.7*
Pakistani	−0.8	−8.0*	6.4*
Bangladeshi	7.4	0.5	12.6
Chinese	17.1*	11.1	24.0*
All minorities	4.8*	−2.7	13.3*
	Panel B		
Black Caribbean	−0.2	−9.8*	10.2*
Black African	−8.1*	−20.4*	4.9
Indian	−4.2*	−8.4*	0.8
Pakistani	−11.9*	−20.9*	−1.4
Bangladeshi	−7.1	−9.8	−7.0
Chinese	−1.9	−4.7	1.7
All minorities	−3.7*	−11.6*	5.1*
	Panel C		
Black Caribbean	−7.0*	−15.8*	2.7
Black African	−17.6*	−28.5*	−5.7
Indian	−7.6*	−11.1*	−3.2
Pakistani	−12.2*	−20.3*	−2.8
Bangladeshi	−13.1	−14.7	−13.9
Chinese	−5.6	−9.3	−1.2
All minorities	−8.8*	−15.8*	−0.8
White natives mean wages	11.06	12.31	9.70

Notes: Panel A reports percentage differences in real hourly wages between British-born ethnic minorities and white natives from the same cohort (born in 1963–75) in years 1998–2009, net of year and seasonal effects. Panel B additionally accounts for differences in age and education, while Panel C controls also for the regional distribution. The last row reports the average hourly wages of white natives in that cohort over the period, discounted with the 2005-based CPI.
*Indicates that the difference is statistically significant at 5%.
Source: Labour Force Survey (LFS), 1998–2009.

[12] We compare only British-born ethnic minorities with white natives, as the LFS did not collect information on earnings prior to 1992.

2005-equivalent pounds, and net of time and seasonal effects.[13] The last row of Panel A suggests an overall wage advantage for British-born ethnic minorities of 4.8%. Breaking this down by gender shows that British-born ethnic minority males face a wage disadvantage of 2.7%, while British-born ethnic minority females face a wage advantage of 13.3%. These figures may be driven by the educational advantage of ethnic minorities as well as by different regional distributions. The female wage advantage may also be partly explained by higher selectivity in labour market participation among minority females (Dustmann and Theodoropoulos, 2010 provide evidence for more selective workforce participation among minority females). Thus, in Panel B we also control for the age and education structure. The last row of Panel B suggests that the wage advantage observed in Panel A turns into an overall wage disadvantage once we control for the age and education of the individual. Breaking down the results by gender, we see that for males, the wage disadvantage has increased by 8.9 percentage points, whereas the wage advantage of ethnic minority females has decreased by 8.2 percentage points. In Panel C we control—in addition—for differences in the geographic distribution. The overall wage disadvantage increases further for males, whereas for females, the wage advantage disappears. It is also interesting that—for males—there is now a wage disadvantage in each ethnic group.

Thus, these numbers suggest first that male and female British-born ethnic minorities differ in their wage position, in comparison with their white peers: while male ethnic minority individuals earn slightly lower wages than their white counterparts, females earn—on average—substantially more. However, once we keep educational attainment and regional allocation the same for the two groups, the female advantage disappears, and the male disadvantage increases substantially. Thus, male British-born ethnic minorities who have the same education and age structure, and the same regional distribution, as their British-born white peers, earn substantially lower wages.

Performance at school

In the previous sections, we provided an analysis of British-born ethnic minorities in the labour market, and reported their overall educational attainment. With respect to the latter, we reported British-born ethnic minorities' quite considerable educational advantages. In this section, we investigate the attainment gap at a very early stage: between the ages of 5 and 16, and through Key

---

[13] We use regression analysis for eliminating time, regional and compositional effects from average wages (reported in Panels B and C). See Dustmann, Frattini and Theodoropoulos (2010) for details.

Stage 1 to 4. We draw here on research by Dustmann, Machin and Schoenberg (2010). We analyse the evolution throughout compulsory school.

How does the achievement of white British children differ from that of children from ethnic minorities just before the start of school, at the age of 5? Table 15.5 (from Dustmann, Machin and Schoenberg, 2010) reports achievement gaps based on a Vocabulary Naming Assessment, a Picture Similarity Assessment, and a Pattern Construction Assessment, from the Millennium Cohort Survey (MCS).[14] The MCS is a longitudinal survey that follows a random sample of about 20,000 children born in the UK between September 2000 and August 2001. Ethnic minorities are over-sampled.[15]

According to all tests, white British pupils outperform ethnic minority pupils, which is in contrast with the overall educational advantage of ethnic minorities at working age shown in Figure 15.3. According to the Vocabulary Naming Assessment, scores of all ethnic minority children are at least 42% of a standard deviation lower than those of white British children; for non-Caribbean Black, Bangladeshi and Pakistani children, the gap is larger than one standard deviation. Achievement gaps are substantially smaller for the Picture Similarity and Pattern Construction Assessment. There is again substantial heterogeneity across ethnic groups: while the achievement gap is at least 30% of a standard deviation for Black Caribbean, other Black (Pattern Construction Assessment), Pakistani and Bangladeshi children (Pattern Construction and Picture Similarity Assessment), it is insignificant or even positive for Indians, Chinese and other ethnic minority children—although these groups fall behind in the Vocabulary Naming Assessment quite considerably.

Does the disadvantage of minority children remain constant throughout the school curriculum? Figure 15.5 plots the English (Panel A) and

Table 15.5: Ethnic test-score gaps at school entry

	Vocabulary	Pictures	Patterns
Black, Caribbean	−6.61*	1.84	−2.68*
Black, Other	−10.58*	−0.89	−4.95*
Bangladeshi	−15.14*	−3.66*	−5.39*
Pakistani	−15.51*	−2.84*	−4.87*
Indian	−6.18*	0.31	−0.99
Chinese	−6.44	5.21	4.33*
Other	−4.21*	0.62	−0.97

Notes: The table shows achievement gaps at age 5 (before the start of school) between ethnic minorities and the white British in three tests: vocabulary test, picture similarity test, and pattern construction test.
*Indicates that the difference is statistically significant at 5%.

Source: Millennium Cohort Survey (MCS), age 5.

[14] Test scores have been standardised to have mean 50 and standard deviation 10.
[15] See Dustmann, Machin and Schoenberg (2010) for more details.

Mathematics (Panel B) test-score gaps at the end of year 2 at the age of 6/7 (Key Stage 1), at the end of year 6 at the age of 10/11 (Key Stage 2), at the end of year 9 at the age of 13/14 (Key Stage 3) and at the end of compulsory schooling at the age of 15/16 (Key Stage 4). Information on test scores at each key stage comes from the National Pupil Database (NPD) for years 1998–2007, and has been matched with information from the Pupil Level Annual School Census (PLASC), which has information on pupils' background and ethnicity. Note that these gaps are not comparable to those at age 5, which we report in the previous table: they refer to a different cohort of children, born about ten years earlier than the children in the MCS, and the achievement outcomes are not directly comparable. However, a certain pattern is visible. Ethnic groups that performed poorly in the Pattern Construction Test at age 5 (i.e. Black Caribbean, Black other, Bangladeshi, and Pakistani) tend to perform poorly, while groups that performed well at age 5 (i.e. Indian, Chinese and other background) tend to perform somewhat better in the Key Stage 1 English and mathematics exams.

Do achievement gaps between white British and ethnic minority pupils widen or narrow throughout primary and secondary school? Figure 15.5 shows that through primary school, from Key Stage 1 to Key Stage 2, most ethnic minority groups catch up, or in the case of Chinese and Indian pupils, even overtake white British pupils, in both English and mathematics. The catch-up (or overtaking) is most striking for Bangladeshi and Chinese pupils, for whom the gain exceeds 20% of a standard deviation. The only group for which we do not observe a narrowing of the achievement gap in primary school, is Black Caribbean pupils. For this group, both the English and mathematics test-score gap widened by about 6% of a standard deviation over a four-year period. Does the catch-up (or, in the case of Black Caribbean pupils, the fall-back) of the achievement gap continue through secondary school? The widening of the achievement gap between white British and Black Caribbean pupils appears to have stopped, as the English and mathematics gap at the end of primary school at Key Stage 2 and at the beginning of secondary school at Key Stage 3 is roughly the same. All other groups continue to catch up or, in the case of Chinese pupils, pull away from white British pupils throughout compulsory schooling. All groups, including Black Caribbean pupils, experience particularly large gains between Key Stage 3 and Key Stage 4. At the end of compulsory schooling, Indian and Chinese pupils outperform white British pupils by more than 30% of a standard deviation in both English and mathematics. All other ethnic minorities perform slightly worse on average than white British pupils, where Black Caribbean pupils lag behind most.

Dustmann, Machin and Schoenberg (2010) investigate different reasons for the evolution of the achievement gap between the different minority groups, and white natives. They conclude that language spoken at home is the single

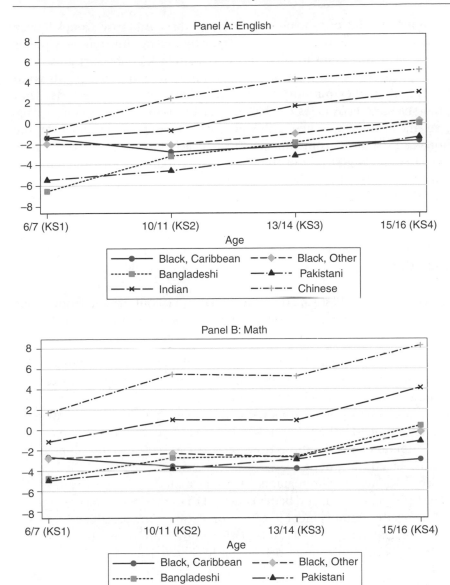

Figure 15.5: Ethnic test-score gaps throughout compulsory schooling

Notes: The figures show the evolution of the ethnic test-score gap throughout compulsory schooling, at age 6/7 (Key Stage 1), age 10/11 (Key Stage 2), age 13/14 (Key Stage 3), and age 15/16 (Key Stage 4). Test scores are standardised with mean 50 and standard deviation 10.

Source: National Pupil Database (NPD) and Pupil Level Annual School Census (PLASC), Key Stage 1 exams in 1998 and Key Stage 4 exams in 2007. N = 469 848.

most important factor to explain why most ethnic minority groups have a considerable disadvantage at school entry, why most ethnic minority pupils improve relative to white British pupils, and why Black Caribbean pupils make smaller progress than any other ethnic group. Ethnic minority pupils go to schools with higher minority shares than their white counterparts, with higher shares of classmates eligible for free meals, and with lower average achievements of classmates, although these differences decline over the school curriculum. Dustmann, Machin and Schoenberg (2010) also show that, while the largest part of the relative improvement of ethnic minority pupils takes place within schools, a substantial part of the improvement takes place at the transition from primary to secondary school, and between schools.

Conclusions

In this chapter we investigate the educational and labour market performance of Britain's ethnic minority individuals in comparison to their British-born white peers. The most important findings can be summarised as follows:

- British white born and ethnic minority individuals have a distinct regional distribution. In particular, minorities are disproportionately more concentrated in London than white natives.
- All minorities experience a lower employment rate than white natives. They also tend to have lower wages, if we control for their regional distribution and education. However, there are considerable differences between ethnic groups.
- Second-generation immigrants tend to be better educated than their parents' generation, and better educated than their white native peers. The relative improvement in education between the parent and descendant generations is far larger for ethnic minorities. Still, these British-born ethnic minorities are less likely to have jobs and earn on average lower wages, even if they had the same characteristics as their white British-born peers.
- Minority children experience achievement disadvantages before starting school. These disadvantages are reduced considerably during compulsory schooling, and turn into substantial advantages for some ethnic groups at the end of compulsory schooling.

Thus, British-born ethnic minorities, despite their initial disadvantage in the British education system, perform remarkably well in terms of their educational achievements, catching up continuously throughout the British compulsory school system, and achieving higher shares of college education than their British-born white peers. We should note, however, that there is a considerable heterogeneity between the different minority groups.

Despite their educational success, their employment probabilities are lower than those of whites, and for some groups dramatically so. Further, while for the same educational achievements, and the same regional allocation, wages for White and ethnic minority British-born females are about the same, ethnic minority males experience a wage disadvantage of about 16%. It should be interesting for future research to analyse the reasons for this disadvantage as well as for the heterogeneity between genders and ethnic groups.

References

Dustmann, C., Frattini, T. and Theodoropoulos, N. (2010) Ethnicity and second generation immigrants in Britain. CreAM Discussion Paper No. 04/10, February, London: University College London.

—— Machin, S. and Schoenberg, U. (2010) Ethnicity and educational achievement in compulsory schooling. *Economic Journal*, 120(546): F272–97.

—— and Theodoropoulos, N. (2010) Ethnic minority immigrants and their children in Britain. *Oxford Economic Papers*, 62(2), April: 209–33.

Wadsworth, J. (2003) The labour market performance of ethnic minorities. In: Dickens, R., Gregg, P. and Wadsworth, J. (eds.) *The Labour Market under New Labour: The State of Working Britain*. New York: Palgrave Macmillan.

16

Child Poverty in Britain: Did Work Work?

Richard Dickens

Key findings

- After a decade of the previous Labour government about half a million children were lifted out of relative poverty, reversing the previous record increases under the Conservatives.
- Real income growth has been high among the poor so that they are much better off than they were in 1997 as absolute child poverty rates have halved.
- Strong growth in median income has meant that relative poverty has not fallen as much as predicted and with child poverty increasing since 2004–2005 the government were a long way short of achieving their child poverty target.
- Labour's Welfare to Work reforms have increased employment among households with children, particularly among single parents whose employment rate has increased from 45% to 57% in ten years. However, work alone is not enough for most households to lift them out of poverty.
- By far the largest impact on child poverty has come about through the increased generosity of both in work and out of work benefits. Without these reforms there would be an extra 1 million children living in poverty in Britain today.

Introduction

> And because child poverty demeans Britain, we have committed our party to tackle and to end it.... And so today I announce my intention to introduce ground-breaking legislation to enshrine in law Labour's pledge to end child poverty.
>
> Gordon Brown, Speech to the Labour Party Conference, 2008

Shortly after Labour came to power in 1997 Gordon Brown, as Chancellor of the Exchequer, pledged to abolish child poverty over 20 years. He set about introducing a raft of reforms aimed at 'making work pay' for low income families with children. Child poverty fell over Labour's first two terms in office, albeit by not as much as predicted. However, the fall then stalled, with child poverty rates increasing again since 2004. Despite being a long way short of their own interim targets for child poverty, the Labour government reaffirmed its commitment to abolish child poverty. Gordon Brown, now as Prime Minister, introduced the Child Poverty Bill which enshrined in law the commitment to abolish child poverty as a legacy for all future governments.

The outgoing Conservative government in 1997 had presided, through their period in office, over a doubling of the number of children living in poverty. Many of these were living in households with nobody in work. Consequently, the strategy of the New Labour government was to focus on increasing employment among low income families through the introduction of a range of measures designed to increase the incentives for working. They introduced the Working Families Tax Credit (WFTC), which provided more generous in-work support, provided a wage floor for the low paid with the introduction of the National Minimum Wage and reformed the National Insurance system for the low waged. A range of 'New Deal' initiatives were established to ease the transition back into work. The package of reforms was supposed to make work more attractive to those on benefits.

Indeed the evidence suggests that the reforms did increase work among target families. See, for example, Brewer et al. (2006). Furthermore, there is growing evidence that the reforms introduced by the Labour government had a range of beneficial impacts beyond employment change. Gregg et al. (2006) show that the extra cash received in government benefits to poor households with children shifted expenditure patterns within the household towards child-related items and durable goods, while Gregg et al. (2009) show improvements in child and adult mental well-being linked to the reforms. Brewer et al. (2008) assert that fertility among couples increased due to the labour market reforms, while Anderberg et al. (2008) argue that the reforms have impacted upon partnership formation. However, there is little analysis of the impact of these reforms on child poverty.

In the last edition of this book, Dickens and Ellwood (2003, 2004) examined the impact of these policies on changes in child poverty in the short period up to 2000–1. The results suggested that increased work had contributed somewhat to falling child poverty at that point, but the largest impact was coming from changes in government benefits. These policies, and subsequent policies introduced to tackle child poverty, have now had a longer period in which to establish themselves. While work incentives can be changed fairly quickly by policy, this may take some time to feed into a household's behaviour. This chapter provides an analysis of child poverty in recent times, with a particular emphasis on the factors behind changes in child poverty over the ten years of the Labour government.

What has happened to child poverty?

Here we document the changes in child poverty that have occurred over the past few decades. Different people will have different views on what is meant by poverty. So before we look at the figures, let us first think about how to measure poverty.

Measuring child poverty

Child poverty in developed countries is usually measured in terms of the income of the household in which the individual lives. If their total household income falls below some threshold, they are deemed to be living in poverty and the poverty rate is then the proportion of children living below this threshold. The choice of the income threshold (or poverty line) is therefore crucial to how much measured poverty there is. The Labour government's commitment to abolishing child poverty was made with reference to a relative poverty threshold. Here, the poverty line is defined as 60% of contemporary median income. This means that the poverty line will change from year to year as median income rises or falls. Relative poverty captures the degree of inequality in incomes between poor children and the middle classes. Under a relative poverty measure, the real incomes of poor children can rise, but unless they increase faster than median income the poverty rate will not decline.

An alternative is to use some fixed real income threshold that doesn't change over time to calculate the extent of poverty. For example, one could measure poverty using 60% of median real income in 1997. What is important here is the absolute growth in real incomes of the poor (without reference to what is going on among the middle classes). The concept underlying this poverty measure is the ability to purchase a bundle of essential goods and services. The official US poverty line is set in this way, with reference to an absolute real income threshold that has been unchanged for 40 years. Both measures have their merits. It is important to understand whether the poor are better off now than they were ten years ago in real terms or whether they are closing the gap on the middle classes. The absolute measure is probably more useful over relatively short time periods. For example, it is probably more informative to ask if the poor are better off in real terms than they were in 1997, but not whether they are better off than the poor in 1870!

A criticism of these measures of poverty is that they both use a snapshot of income at a point in time. Of course, household incomes change from year to year and some children may be more prone to chronic poverty than others. In response to this the last government introduced in the Child Poverty Bill targets for both persistent poverty and a measure of material deprivation. Here persistent poverty is defined as being in relative poverty in three out of four years. The measure of material deprivation includes things like access to outside space, whether the child has a holiday, etc. These measures are designed to capture a deeper measure of deprivation and to force future governments to focus on this. Here we focus on the snapshot measures of income poverty since this is the measure on which the labour government initially set its child poverty targets.[1]

Changes in child poverty under the Conservatives and Labour

Figure 16.1 presents relative child poverty based on calculations from the Households Below Average Income (HBAI) data from 1979 to 2007/8.[2] The figure reports the percentage of children living in households where income is less than 60% of the contemporary median income. Figures are reported for incomes both before and after housing costs have been deducted. The idea here is that because housing is an essential we should treat it as a foregone cost, a bit like taxes, that the household has to bear. A counter-argument to this is that since households have at least some choice over their expenditure on housing, we should focus on the before housing costs measure. Indeed, the Labour government's targets were framed in terms of the before housing measure and we will focus on this measure throughout the chapter.

In 1979 some 14% of children were living in relative poverty. This increased rapidly through the 1980s so that child poverty had doubled by the early 1990s. By the time the Labour government came to power in 1997, there were an extra 1.7 million children in poverty than in 1979 and about a third of all children lived in poverty. As we have already discussed, the New Labour government pledged to reverse these increases in child poverty and introduced some tough poverty targets. So how did poor children fare under Labour? Child poverty fell pretty sharply in the first two terms of the Labour government. By 2004–5 there were somewhere between 600,000 and 700,000 fewer children in relative poverty, depending on the income definition used. However, since then child poverty rose slightly so that about 22.5% of

---

[1] The poverty measures enshrined in the new Child Poverty Act are a composite of relative and absolute income poverty, a measure of material deprivation and a measure of persistent poverty. For details see <http://www.opsi.gov.uk/acts/acts2010/ukpga_20100009_en_1>.

[2] Figures are from the Institute for Fiscal Studies. For details see <http://www.ifs.org.uk/fiscalFacts/povertyStats>.

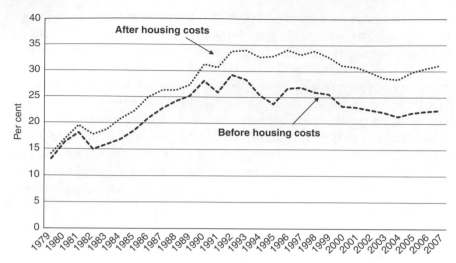

Figure 16.1: Official child poverty, 1979–2007/2008

children now live in poverty under the previous government's preferred before housing cost measure. After ten years the number of children in poverty was still some 500,000 below the level when they took office in 1997, but they look a long way short of achieving their original target of halving child poverty by 2010.

Given the huge investment made to tackle child poverty, why did the Labour government find it so hard to make significant inroads into reducing child poverty and meeting their child poverty targets? One reason is that it is an incredibly hard target to meet. In measuring poverty in relative terms, one benchmarks any income growth for the poor against the growth in median incomes, those of the middle classes. So as median income grows, the incomes of the poor have to grow even faster in order for them to catch up. Real income growth among the poor is not enough on its own to reduce relative poverty.

Figure 16.2 presents child poverty measured in relative terms but also in absolute terms. This is defined as the proportion below 60% of the 1996–7 median real net income. Also reported is the relative poverty threshold, 60% of contemporary median income, indexed to one in 1979. This shows the rate at which incomes of the poor have to grow for relative poverty to fall. Median income growth was strong in much of the 1980s, which is one reason that poverty rose so sharply then. Absolute child poverty actually fell for most of this period as the real incomes of the poor grew, albeit at a slower rate than that of the middle classes.

Median real income growth was flat for much of the early 1990s, which may go some way to explaining why child poverty stopped rising. But then from the mid-1990s median real incomes rose strongly so that the relative poverty

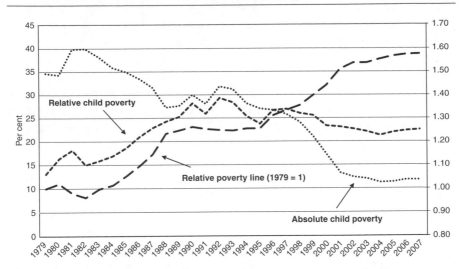

Figure 16.2: Child poverty and the relative poverty line, 1979–2007/2008

line increased sharply; by about 15% in the period 1997–2002. What is perhaps surprising is that relative child poverty fell significantly, with most of the gains Labour made occurring over this period. This is despite the fact that the incomes of the poor had to rise faster than these strong increases in median incomes. This is reflected in a sharp fall in absolute poverty over this period; from about 26% to 12%, as the real income of children in poor households increased substantially. So while the policies introduced by Labour led to substantial real income growth among the poor, the strong growth in median incomes watered down the decline in relative child poverty. We now turn to look at what factors contributed to falling poverty.

The factors explaining child poverty

The aim here is to understand why child poverty changed as it did, or indeed didn't fall as much as it might have. A natural starting point is to examine the changing components of income for each household. Whether a child is defined to be poor or not depends on the income of the household they live in. Household income is composed of income from a number of sources; income from employment, government benefits and other income from investments, pensions, etc. Employment income is made up of the hourly wage and the hours worked for each adult in the household. Net, or disposable, income is then calculated by subtracting direct taxes. We would like to know the extent to which child poverty has changed due to changes in employment and work hours, changes in wages rates, the benefit income that households receive and the taxes they pay. Child poverty rates can also change due to demographic changes. For example, if children are more likely to live in single parent households, which on average have lower incomes, then poverty may increase.

The difficulty in isolating the influence of each of these factors is that they have all changed significantly over the last decade or so. Real wages have risen over time and the National Minimum Wage is likely to have raised wages for the low paid. Employment rates have also risen, particularly among single parents. Benefit incomes have increased, especially for low income households with children, and there have been some changes to the tax system. Child poverty has changed between 1997 and 2007 because all of these components have changed. The approach taken here is to ask what would have happened to child poverty if say only work patterns had changed and all the other components had remained at their 1997 levels. This then tells us how much of the change in poverty is due to changing work. We can then ask what would have happened to child poverty if only wages had changed and all the other components had remained at their 1997 level. This then gives us the influence of wages. Taking each component in turn helps us to build up a picture of the role of each of these factors in changing child poverty over time.[3]

What has happened to demographics, work, wages, benefits and taxes?

Before turning to the results of this exercise let us just first review some of the key facts about changes in each of these factors. This provides some background to the changes over the past decade but is also informative in terms of the likely impacts upon child poverty.

Demographic changes

The proportion of children in single parent households has continued to increase since 1997–8 from 22% to 24% in 2007–8. This may contribute to increases in both relative and absolute poverty. In addition, education levels have continued to rise. Although education levels have risen among single parents, they are falling behind in relative terms compared to the whole population in work. This is likely to mean that demographic change may increase relative poverty as median incomes rise, but may help to reduce absolute poverty as the poor's education levels increase.

---

[3] See Dickens and Ellwood (2003) for a more detailed description of this methodology.

Wage changes

The past decade has been one of strong average real wage growth with average real earnings increasing by 18% between 1997–8 and 2007–8. This can raise individuals out of poverty, but is also likely to significantly increase the relative poverty threshold which will result in increases in poverty. In April 1999 the National Minimum Wage (NMW) was introduced. Since the late 1990s real hourly wages at the bottom of the distribution have been increasing faster than the median. Evidence suggests that this is a result of the introduction and subsequent increases in the NMW (see Machin, Chapter 11). This fall in inequality in the bottom part of the wage distribution is likely to lead to falls in both relative and absolute poverty.

Work changes

One of the key reasons for the rise in child poverty in the 1980s and 1990s was the poor work record among households with children. The employment rate among single parents was one of the lowest in Europe. Furthermore, a fifth of children lived in a household where nobody worked. Poverty rates among workless households were very high. The previous government's push to increase employment among low income families certainly paid off. Employment rates among single parents rose from around 45% in 1997 to 57% in 2007. While some of this increase was going on anyway, evidence suggests that part of this increase was due to policies such as the WFTC, New Deal for Lone Parents (NDLP), etc. In addition, the percentage of children in workless households fell modestly from about 19% to 16% (see Gregg and Wadsworth, Chapter 5 on Workless Households). Work also increased among couples with children, but not at the same rate. We would expect these changes in work patterns to help reduce both relative and absolute poverty, particularly among single parents.

Benefit changes

Since 1997 there have been a large number of reforms to the benefit system designed to help low income households into work and to raise their children out of poverty. There is a balance here between reducing poverty among poor workless households and maintaining work incentives. The Working Families Tax Credit (superseded by the Working Tax Credit) essentially increased the generosity of in-work benefits and reduced the rate at which they are withdrawn as incomes rise. This was coupled with some generous support for child care. But benefits were also increased for those households with children who are not in work. These changes are likely to play a significant role in reducing both relative and absolute child poverty.

Tax changes

Similarly, there have been some significant tax changes since 1997. The basic rate of income tax was cut in 1999 and again in 2007 and the lower rate was reduced to 10%, although this was later removed altogether. Furthermore, the starting rate of National Insurance contributions was cut. This may well increase the net incomes of the poor, but will also impact upon median incomes and hence the poverty threshold. Consequently, it is not clear what the overall impact of tax changes on child poverty will be.

Why did poverty fall between 1997–1998 and 2007–2008?

Table 16.1 presents the results of the decomposition of poverty change into each of the factors described above. To begin with, let's take the Labour government's preferred measure based upon relative poverty before housing costs. As we saw in Figure 16.1 above, this fell from 26.2% in 1997–8 to 21.3% in 2007–8.[4] However, the influence of demographic change was to increase child poverty by some 2.4% points over this period. This is likely to be driven by a combination of increases in the proportion of single parent households, but also rising education levels, which drive up median incomes and hence the relative poverty line. The impact of wage changes on poverty is likely to feed through two different mechanisms: changes in average wages and changes in the inequality of wages. Increases in median hourly wages over this period also pushed up relative poverty, resulting in a 2.6% point increase. Again, this is likely to be because strong average wage growth raises the relative poverty threshold, rather than having much of an impact on the incomes of the poor. However, changes in wage inequality have had a modest effect in reducing relative child poverty by 0.7% points. Similarly, despite all the efforts to get individuals from low income households into work, this only resulted in a modest reduction in poverty of 0.4% points. This suggests that the wages individuals receive when entering work are not enough on their own to push them over the poverty line. By far the biggest impact on poverty comes from changes in government benefits, which includes both in- and out-of-work benefits. The changes to the benefit system have resulted in a fall in relative child poverty of some 7.7% points. Finally, changes to the tax system have resulted in a further reduction of 1.1% points.

Without the tax and benefit reforms of the past decade, child poverty would have continued to increase significantly. Taken together, the changes to the tax and benefit system have resulted in approximately 1 million fewer

[4] Note these figures are slightly different from the official HBAI numbers. We focus on Great Britain for consistency over time, whereas the HBAI report poverty for the UK after 2002–3. In addition, we do not have information on Council Tax payments in calculating direct taxes.

Table 16.1: Factors affecting changes in relative and absolute net poverty, 1997/1998–2007/2008

	Before housing costs		After housing costs	
	Relative poverty (based on 60% of median income)	Absolute poverty (based on 60% of median income in 1997)	Relative poverty (based on 60% of median income)	Absolute poverty (based on 60% of median income in 1997)
ALL CHILDREN				
Poverty in 1997/8+	26.2%	26.2%	33.1%	33.1%
+ Demographics	+2.4%	−2.9%	+3.0%	−3.8%
+ Aggregate wage levels	+2.6%	−0.9%	+1.4%	−1.3%
+ Inequality of wages	−0.7%	+0.1%	−0.7%	+0.1%
+ Work patterns	−0.4%	−0.4%	−0.4%	−0.3%
+ Government benefits	−7.7%	−11.2%	−5.5%	−12.5%
+ Taxes	−1.1%	+0.8%	−0.5%	+1.2%
= Poverty in 2007/8	21.3%	11.8%	30.4%	16.5%

Source: Author's calculations using Family Resources Survey; note that government benefits include tax credits.

children in poverty than would have otherwise been the case.[5] The reason that poverty rates have not fallen by this much is that the relative poverty threshold has been increasing due to demographic and aggregate wages changes. The problem for the Labour government was that they were chasing a fast moving target. This can be seen in the impacts on absolute child poverty in the second column of Table 16.1.

Absolute child poverty is defined with reference to 60% of median 1997/8 household net income. So in 1997–8 the absolute child poverty rate was 26.2%, the same as the relative measure for that year. Because we are now comparing the incomes of the poor with a fixed income threshold, absolute poverty falls much faster than relative poverty. By 2007–8 just 11.8% of children were below the poverty threshold of 1997–8. We also see that the role of the different factors in explaining child poverty are somewhat different than when looking at relative poverty. Demographic change now leads to a reduction in child poverty of 2.9% points. Similarly, aggregate wage change now results in a small reduction in absolute poverty of 0.9% points, perhaps as wage growth raises the incomes of the poor without increasing the poverty threshold. Changes in wage inequality have no effect on child poverty and work again results in a very modest reduction of 0.4% points. Once again benefit reforms have played the biggest role in reducing child poverty by some 11.2% points. Had the relative poverty line not changed since 1997–8, then

---

[5] The Treasury's own estimates suggest that had the Labour government done nothing other than simply uprate the 1997 tax and benefit system, there might have been 1.7 million more children in poverty than there are today.

benefit reforms alone would have reduced child poverty down to 15%. This is much closer to the target of halving child poverty by 2010.

Table 16.1 also reports this same decomposition for relative and absolute net poverty after housing costs. The general picture is the same except the poverty falls are smaller than when using the before housing costs measure. Again the main driving force for poverty reduction has been benefit changes, rather than work changes alone.

Changes in child poverty among different household types

Table 16.2 presents these poverty decompositions separately for children living in couple households and for those living with single parents. Some important differences emerge in both the overall reductions in child poverty and the role of the different factors. Relative child poverty (before housing) among couple households fell from 19.7% to 16.0% between 1997–8 and 2007–8. The story here is essentially one of aggregate wage growth leading to an increase in child poverty among couples of 1.3% points as the relative income threshold increases. This is then more than offset by changes in

Table 16.2: Factors affecting changes in poverty by type of family, 1997/1998–2007/2008

	Before housing costs		After housing costs	
	Relative poverty (based on 60% of median income)	Absolute poverty (based on 60% of median income in 1997)	Relative poverty (based on 60% of median income)	Absolute poverty (based on 60% of median income in 1997)
Children living in couple households				
Poverty in 1997/8	19.7%	19.7%	23.9%	23.9%
+ Demographics	−0.0%	−3.7%	+1.1%	−4.6%
+ Aggregate wage levels	+1.3%	−0.8%	+0.5%	−1.2%
+ Inequality of wages	−0.3%	+0.1%	−0.3%	+0.2%
+ Work patterns	+0.3%	+0.0%	+0.5%	+0.1%
+ Government benefits	−4.5%	−6.2%	−3.4%	−6.8%
+ Taxes	−0.5%	+0.6%	−0.2%	+1.2%
= Poverty in 2007/8	16.0%	+9.6%	22.1%	12.7%
Children living in single parent households				
Poverty in 1997/8	47.3%	47.3%	63.0%	63.0%
+ Demographics	+6.0%	−3.8%	+3.4%	−6.3%
+ Aggregate wage levels	+6.1%	−1.0%	+3.9%	−1.4%
+ Inequality of wages	−2.0%	+0.2%	−1.8%	−0.3%
+ Work patterns	−2.3%	−1.6%	−2.8%	−1.6%
+ Government benefits	−16.5%	−24.8%	−11.4%	−28.0%
+ Taxes	−2.8%	+1.2%	−1.0%	+1.3%
= Poverty in 2007/8	35.8%	17.6%	53.3%	26.7%

Source: Author's calculations using Family Resources Survey; note that government benefits include tax credits.

government benefits to couples with children, which resulted in a 4.5% point reduction in relative poverty. None of the other factors, work, wage inequality, demographics and taxes, play much of a role in changing child poverty among these households. Reductions in absolute poverty are larger as it falls to 9.6%. This is largely driven again by benefit changes, with changing work patterns having little impact on child poverty.

The picture among single parent households is rather different. Child poverty rates among single parent households are much higher than among couple households. In 1997–8 a whopping 47.3% of these children were in poverty, some 1.3 million children. The Labour government made significant inroads into reducing child poverty among single parent households down to 35.8% in 2007–8, a reduction of about 300,000 children. There are a number of factors influencing relative child poverty here. Demographic changes have been working to increase child poverty by 6.0% points. This is likely to be the result of both a small increase in the proportion of children living with single parents, but perhaps more importantly the relative decline in the educational position of working single parents. Furthermore, aggregate wage growth has resulted in a 6.1% point increase. Remember that these are demographic changes and aggregate wage changes among the whole population, not just among single parents, which have probably raised the relative poverty line significantly, leading to these increases in poverty. However, we see that wage inequality changes have resulted in a 2.0% point fall in child poverty among single parents, possibly a result of the National Minimum Wage. We also now see that changing work patterns have contributed to the fall in child poverty by 2.3% points. Employment rates among single parents have increased substantially over this period, which is likely to be reflected here in poverty declines. Clearly, work has paid for some single parents in terms of raising their household incomes above the poverty line.

But the big story here is once again benefit changes. These have led to a 16.5% point fall in relative child poverty as both in- and out-of-work benefits have become much more generous for single parents. Tax changes have also contributed to the fall by 2.8% points.

The falls in absolute child poverty are even more striking, with a huge 30% point reduction from 47.3% to 17.6% as children in single parent households are unambiguously better off in terms of real income than their counterparts a decade ago. Most of this reduction is coming about through government benefits, resulting in 24.8% points of the fall. Demographic and work changes have a small role in this reduction. The story for poverty after housing costs is essentially unchanged, even if the poverty rates are somewhat different.

Overall our results show that the reforms implemented by Labour resulted in significant increases in the real incomes of the poor, largely as a result of increases in the generosity of benefits for both those in and out of work.

Table 16.3: Distribution of working and workless poor children by household characteristics 2007–2008

	Workless poor	Working poor
Couple Household	33.94	76.47
Couple 1 child	6.20	9.36
Couple 2 children	10.13	28.07
Couple 3 children	9.07	20.48
Couple 4+ children	8.54	18.56
Couple 1 working	0.00	58.09
Couple both working	0.00	18.98
Child under 5	18.14	39.65
Single parent household	66.06	23.54
Single 1 child	15.50	6.67
Single 2 children	23.43	9.36
Single 3 children	13.15	4.14
Single 4+ children	13.98	3.37
Child under 5	30.69	6.13
% of Poor children	50.36	49.64

Source: Author's calculations using Family Resources Survey.

However, these increases in real incomes have not been translated into quite as large a poverty decline as one might expect as demographic and aggregate wage changes have raised the poverty threshold. This has had the effect of dampening down the relative poverty reductions.

So what can a future government do to reduce child poverty further? It is helpful to examine the distribution of those left in both in-work and workless poverty to assess the likely gains from trying to increase work further. Table 16.3 presents the distribution of poor children in working and non-working households by various household characteristics. Children in poverty are fairly evenly split between working and non-working households, with about 50% of poor children in each. Among the workless poor, some two-thirds are in single parent households. Significant gains have already been made in increasing employment among this group, with employment rates now up to 57% among single parents. Trying to increase this further is likely to prove more difficult, especially in a sluggish labour market.

Some three-quarters of the working poor are in couple households. Many of these children are not too far below the poverty line so there may well be potential here to reduce child poverty further. We see that 58% of working poor children are living in couple households where only one adult is in work. Household income could rise if the government can induce the second adult into work. However, we see that many of these children are living in large families; almost 40% of working poor children live in households with three or more children. Furthermore, 40% are living in couple households where the youngest child is under 5 years of age. This may prove a barrier to increasing work among these households, as the non-working adult is very likely to be looking after children. Trying to induce these second adults into work is likely to require some very significant increases in childcare support.

Conclusions

That New Labour have failed to meet their tough poverty targets is perhaps not so surprising. The underlying primary distribution of incomes seems to be on a march towards greater inequality, driven by continued increases in the demand for more skilled workers. This results in fast growth in median incomes relative to the incomes of the poor. Labour's Welfare to Work reforms have undoubtedly offset these forces. More low income households are now in employment as the tax and benefit system has made work more attractive for those previously on benefits. However, the role of work has been somewhat limited in directly reducing child poverty. The wage paid in many of these jobs for low income families is not enough alone to raise them out of poverty, even with the minimum wage. They need assistance in the form of in-work benefits to push them out of income poverty. This is not necessarily a bad thing. Increased labour market participation may not reduce income poverty on its own, but it has many other potential benefits for both parents and children in terms of attachment to the labour market, social inclusion and role modelling.

The alternative approach is to reduce child poverty through the impact of education and skills on the primary distribution of incomes. But policies designed to tackle equality of opportunity through education take at least a generation to come to fruition. Increases in cash benefits and tax credits are probably the most straightforward way to achieve the child poverty goals. The problem for a cash-strapped government facing pressure to cut debt is that a significant push to abolish child poverty over the next decade is likely to require a substantial increase in benefits to the poor.

References

Anderberg D., Kondylis, F. and Walker, I. (2008) Partnership penalties and bonuses created by UK welfare programs. *CESifo Economic Studies*, 54(1), March: 1–21, Oxford University Press.

Brewer, M., Duncan, A., Shepherd, A. and Suarez, M. (2006) Did working families' tax credit work? The impact of in-work support on labour supply in Great Britain, *Labour Economics*, 13(6): 699–720.

—— Ratcliffe, A. and Smith, S. (2008) Does welfare reform affect fertility? Evidence from the UK. IFS Working Papers W08/09, Institute for Fiscal Studies.

Dickens, R. and Ellwood, D. T. (2003) Child poverty in Britain. In: Dickens, R., Gregg, P. and Wadsworth, J. (eds.) *The Labour Market under New Labour: The State of Working Britain*. Hampshire, UK: Palgrave Macmillan Publishing.

—— —— (2004) Whither poverty in Britain and the US? The determinants of changing poverty and whether work will work. In: Blundell, R., Card, D. and Freeman, R. B. (eds.) *Seeking a Premier Economy*. Chicago: Chicago University Press.

—— Harkness, S. and Smith, S. (2009) Welfare reform and lone parents in the UK. *The Economic Journal*, 119 (535): F38–F65.

—— Waldfogel, J. and Washbrook, E. (2006) Family expenditures post-welfare reform in the UK: are low-income families starting to catch up? *Labour Economics*, 13(6): 721–46.

Gregg, P. and Wadsworth, J. (2011) Workless households. In: Gregg, P. and Wadsworth, J. (eds.) *The Labour Market in Winter: The State of Working Britain*. Oxford: Oxford University Press.

Machin, S. (2011) Changes in UK wage inequality over the last forty years. In: Gregg, P. and Wadsworth, J. (eds.) *The Labour Market in Winter: The State of Working Britain*. Oxford: Oxford University Press.

National Equality Panel (2010) *An Anatomy of Economic Inequality in the UK: Report of the National Inequality Panel*. London: Government Equalities Office.

17

Trade Unions

Alex Bryson and John Forth[1]

Key findings

- Fewer than 8 million employees are union members today compared to 13 million when membership was at its peak in 1979. The majority are women and three-fifths work in the public sector. Half of all employees have never been a union member, a proportion that has doubled in the last quarter century.
- The decline in union density has slowed markedly in the past decade compared to the 1980s and 1990s, but density continues to fall in both the private and public sectors, as does the proportion of employees covered by collective bargaining. The decline in membership has outpaced the decline in coverage, however, leading to an increase in 'free-riding'.
- These trends have led to financial disarray among unions, a problem which has not been solved by union mergers. Yet employees are increasingly likely to perceive unions as effective at the workplace. Indeed, unions continue to play an important role at the workplace: offering 'voice' to employees, which lowers quit rates; achieving a wage premium for their members, albeit smaller than in the past; and continuing to act as a 'sword of justice' by compressing wage differentials.
- Furthermore, unions are no longer associated with poorer financial performance, nor with poorer perceptions of the climate of relations between management and employees. There is thus emerging evidence that unions are gradually transforming themselves.

[1] The authors gratefully acknowledge funding from the Nuffield Foundation (grant ref. OPD/ 37358).

Introduction

This chapter analyses the continued decline of trade unions and examines the possible implications for workers, employers and unions themselves. Membership of trade unions declined precipitously in the 1980s and 1990s. The rate of decline has slowed in the most recent decade, but unions remain vulnerable to further erosion of their membership and influence. The future of British unions turns in large part on what they do—to economic efficiency, fairness and to industrial relations.

Membership and union coverage in the Noughties

Patterns of membership

In the United Kingdom, where there is no state funding of trade unions and little by way of state support for collective bargaining, unions' ability to recruit and retain members is critical to their ability to function. Union members supply the networks of lay workplace representatives, provide the funds which pay for central services, and also give the union authority and legitimacy in its negotiations with an employer. The dramatic decline in membership in the 1980s and 1990s therefore represented a crisis for trade unions. Union membership in the UK was at an historic high-point of 13.2 million in 1979, when Mrs Thatcher's Conservative government came to power. By the time that Labour returned in 1997, it had fallen to just 7.8 million. The figure now stands at 7.6 million. Trade unions have therefore managed to stem the tide to a certain degree under successive Labour governments, but they have not managed to stop it completely.

To explore the recent trends, we focus on union membership rates among employees in Britain, thus excluding members in Northern Ireland, the self-employed and those not in employment (around 0.9 million of the total). The Labour Force Survey (henceforth LFS) indicates that the total number of union members among employees in Britain actually rose from 6.7 million to 6.9 million between 1998 and 2003. The economy was expanding at the same time but, in sharp contrast to earlier periods, unions were broadly keeping pace. Union membership density had declined at an average of 1 percentage point per year between 1989 and 1998—from 38.8% to 29.9%—but fell by a total of only 0.7 percentage points in the five years between 1998 and 2003 (Figure 17.1 and Table 17.1). The hiatus was not to last, however. Whilst 200,000 members were gained between 1998 and 2003, the same number was lost between 2003 and 2008. Density fell 2 percentage points to reach

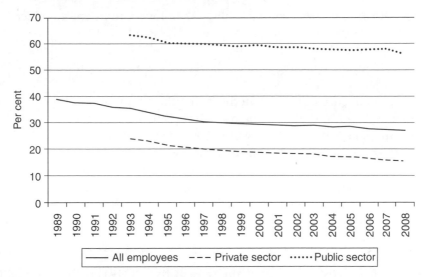

Figure 17.1: Trade union density among employees in Britain, 1989–2008
Source: Quarterly Labour Force Survey (QLFS) (Great Britain).

Table 17.1: Trade union membership density among employees in Britain, 1989–2008

	Membership density (% of employees)				Average annual change (percentage points)		
	1989	1998	2003	2008	1989–1998	1998–2003	2003–2008
All	38.8%	29.9%	29.2%	27.2%	−1.0%	−0.1%	−0.3%
Male	43.9%	31.1%	29.2%	25.5%	−1.4%	−0.3%	−0.6%
Female	32.8%	28.5%	29.2%	28.9%	−0.5%	+0.1%	0.0%
Manual	43.1%	29.9%	27.9%	25.2%	−1.5%	−0.3%	−0.5%
Non-manual	35.3%	29.8%	29.9%	28.3%	−0.6%	0.0%	−0.3%
Private sector*	24.1%	19.5%	18.3%	15.5%	−0.9%	−0.2%	−0.5%
Public sector*	63.4%	59.6%	58.2%	56.2%	−0.8%	−0.2%	−0.3%
Age less than 30	29.7%	16.6%	15.0%	14.1%	−1.5%	−0.3%	−0.1%
Aged 30–49	43.5%	35.0%	33.4%	30.1%	−0.9%	−0.3%	−0.5%
Aged 50+	43.9%	34.4%	35.0%	34.4%	−1.1%	+0.1%	−0.1%

Notes: * Series begins in 1993 rather than 1989.
Source: Quarterly Labour Force Survey (Great Britain).

27.2% in 2008.[2] The pace of decline was less than half that seen in the 1990s, but the trend was once again firmly downwards.

Membership decline has not been evenly spread (Table 17.1). In the 1990s, union membership density fell faster among men than women; faster among manual workers than non-manuals; faster in the private sector than in the

---

[2] 2008 was the latest LFS avilable for detailed analysis at the time of writing. The 2009 LFS put density at 27.0%.

public sector; and faster among younger employees than among older employees. Nevertheless, declines were seen across all of these groups. Since 1998, density has continued to fall within most of these categories. But it has remained stable among women; it has also remained stable among older workers aged 50 or more.

One consequence of these patterns is that the composition of membership has changed a great deal over the past 20 years. Union members are now less likely to be male (61% in 1989; 48% in 2008); women first outnumbered men in 2005. They are also less likely to be manual workers (50% in 1989; 33% in 2008) and less likely to work in the private sector (48% in 1993; 41% in 2008). They are more likely to be aged 50 or over (22% in 1989; 34% in 2008) and they are more likely to be highly educated (10% had a degree in 1989, rising to 31% in 2008).

Prospects for the future

There are few signs of growth at the present time. Between 1998 and 2008, density rose in only two industry sectors: 'Education' (by 1.0 percentage points from 53.1% to 54.1%) and 'Wholesale and retail' (by 0.9 percentage points from 11.0% to 11.9%).[3] Indeed, each of the three main unions in the education sector (NUT, NASUWT and ATL) grew their membership by around 25%

Table 17.2: Membership of individual unions, 1999 and 2009

	1999		2009		1999–2009		
	Members	Rank	Members	Rank	Membership change	% change	Rank change
Unite the union*	2 715 660	1	1 952 226	1	−763 434	−28%	0
UNISON	1 272 330	2	1 344 000	2	71 670	6%	0
GMB	712 010	3	590 125	3	−121 885	−17%	0
RCN	320 206	4	393 865	4	73 659	23%	0
USDAW	303 060	5	356 046	6	52 986	17%	−1
CWU	287 732	6	236 679	9	−51 053	−18%	−3
NUT	286 503	7	374 170	5	87 667	31%	+2
NASUWT	250 783	8	313 350	7	62 567	25%	+1
PCS	245 350	9	304 829	8	59 479	24%	+1
ATL	168 027	10	208 568	10	40 541	24%	0
UCATT	111 804	11	129 065	12	17 261	15%	−1
BMA	106 864	12	138 359	11	31 495	29%	+1
Total unions	220		170			−23%	
Total members	7 807 417		7 651 561			−2%	
Members/union	35 488		45 009			27%	

Notes:
* Unite did not exist in 1999, but we assume that it did for comparative purposes. Unite came into existence through various mergers (MSF merged with the AEEU to form Amicus in 2001; this was followed by mergers with the GMPU and Unifi in 2004; Amicus then merged with the TGWU in 2007 to form Unite).
Source: Annual reports of the Certification Officer.

[3] See Table 3.4 in Barratt (2009).

between 1999 and 2009 (Table 17.2). This was in stark contrast to the fortunes of the large general unions (Unite and the GMB) who lost huge numbers of members over the same period.

The success of the teaching unions (and indeed their counterparts in the health sector, the RCN and BMA) could not disguise a more general fall in membership in the public sector, where unions have traditionally been strongest. Union density is currently more than three times higher in the public sector than in the private sector (56%, compared with 16%), but density in the two sectors has declined at roughly the same rate over the past decade. Density fell by 3.4 percentage points in the public sector between 1998 and 2008, whereas it fell 4.0 percentage points in the private sector over the same period. Two percentage points of public sector decline came in 2007–8. Such a pattern cannot be blamed, as in earlier periods, on the removal of highly unionised sections of the public sector through privatisation. There are thus notable signs of concern for many public sector unions.

Explaining the continued decline

None of the decline in union membership density since the late 1990s can be explained by changes in the types of jobs on offer in the British economy. We noted above that the propensity to be a union member dropped 2.7 percentage points between 1998 and 2008. If we control for a range of individual, job and workplace characteristics[4] in a regression analysis, the residual propensity to belong to a union declines by 2.9 percentage points between 1998 and 2008. We see a similar decline if we impute the characteristics of the population of employees from 1999 into a regression of the propensity to be a union member in 2008. Thus there was an overall reduction in interest among employees which cannot be explained by the types of jobs they were doing or the types of establishments they worked in.

A second notable feature is the rise in 'never-membership'. As shown in Figure 17.2, the percentage of all employees who have never been a union member doubled between the mid-1980s and the late 1990s, but it has continued to rise in the past decade. By 2006–8, half of all employees were 'never-members'. In contrast, the percentage of employees who have been members in the past has remained roughly constant at about one-fifth. In the private sector, the proportion of employees who are 'never-members' rose from two-fifths in the mid-1980s to three-fifths in 2006–8.

---

[4] Gender, age, age squared, qualifications (five categories), white/non-white, manual/non-manual, temporary/permanent, full-time/part-time, size of workplace (25+ employees), private/public sector, industry sector (13 categories), region (21 categories) and whether the employee is covered by collective bargaining.

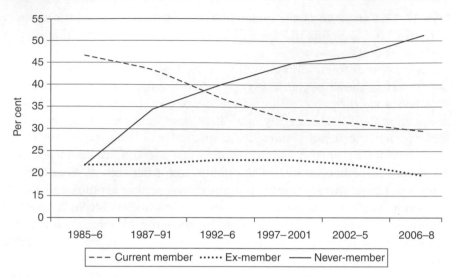

Figure 17.2: The rise of never-membership among employees in Britain, 1985–2008
Note: Employees working 10+ hours per week.
Source: British Social Attitudes Survey.

In the 1980s, it seemed that a principal cause of the fall in union density was a decline in employer and government support for union membership, most clearly evident in the decline and eventual outlawing of the closed shop (Millward et al., 2000: 145–52). In the 1990s, the principal cause of the continued decline was instead a waning of the appetite for unionism among employees (ibid.). Membership may have stabilised temporarily in the benign economic and political climate which characterised the first few years of New Labour, but enthusiasm among employees now seems to be waning once more. This is perhaps most apparent in the falling propensity of employees to belong to trade unions even when their pay is set by collective bargaining (so-called 'free-riding'). We explore this in more detail below.

Bargaining coverage

The proportion of all employees who have their pay set by collective bargaining has, in common with membership density, been in decline since the 1980s. The scale of the decline since 1979 is difficult to establish but estimates suggest that it has fallen roughly by a half, with most of the fall coming before the end of the 1990s. Coverage has been measured consistently in the LFS since 1999 and, over the ten years since then, has fallen from 36.0% to 33.5% in 2008 (Table 17.3).[5] Virtually all of this recent fall has come since 2003, with one third of the

---

[5] The 2009 LFS puts coverage at 32.5%.

Table 17.3: Coverage of collective bargaining among employees in Britain, 1999–2008

	Coverage (% of employees)			Average annual change (percentage points)	
	1999	2003	2008	1999–2003	2003–2008
All	36.0%	35.6%	33.5%	−0.1%	−0.4%
Private sector	23.1%	22.0%	18.7%	−0.3%	−0.7%
Public sector	71.7%	71.1%	69.8%	−0.1%	−0.3%

Source: QLFS (Great Britain).

2.5 percentage point decrease having occurred in the most recent year (2007–8). Unions' role in setting terms and conditions thus continues to be under pressure.

As with membership, the aggregate figure masks considerable differences between the private sector (where coverage stood at 19% in 2008) and the public sector (where it stood at 70%). However, a small decline in coverage has characterised both sectors over the past decade. De-recognition has played a relatively minor role. Instead, a key determinant of the patterns seen in the private sector has been the inability of trade unions to gain recognition for collective bargaining in newly established workplaces. Increasing product market competition appears to be have been an important factor in employers' decision-making: the decline in coverage in the private sector has been less pronounced in more profitable industry sectors than in those where profits were either historically small or have been squeezed (Brown et al., 2009). The introduction in 1999 of statutory support for union recognition has had little effect simply because there are so few non-recognised workplaces where unions have, or can attract, the support of large numbers of employees, as is necessary to trigger the statutory procedure. In the public sector, it is the gradual replacement of collective bargaining with independent pay review bodies that has been the dominant cause of declining coverage.

Recognition for collective bargaining has always gone hand in hand with union membership, and so the decline in coverage should be a notable cause for concern among unions desperate to retain their membership base. This is even more so because the securing of recognition by a union no longer serves to guarantee a certain level of membership support in the way that it did even ten years ago. Membership density has actually remained stable (at around 11%) among non-covered employees since 1999; instead, the fall in overall membership density since 1999 has all occurred among covered employees (from 66.9% in 1999 to 63.2% in 2008) (Figure 17.3). In 1999, a covered employee was 30 percentage points more likely to be a union member than a non-covered employee, after controlling for other factors; by 2008, this figure had declined to 26 percentage points. The result has been a marked increase in 'free-riding'.

There has been a particularly notable increase in free-riding in the private sector: 63% of covered private sector employees were union members in 1999,

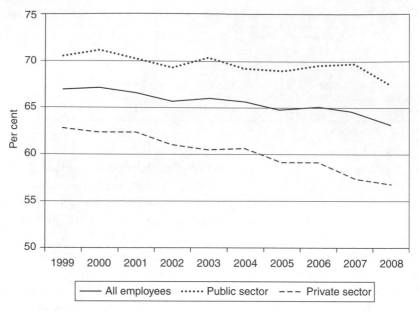

Figure 17.3: Union membership density among employees covered by collective bargaining in Britain, 1999–2008

Source: QLFS (Great Britain).

but this had fallen to 57% by 2008. In the public sector, there was virtually no change between 1999 (71%) and 2007 (70%), but then a sharp drop (to 67%) between 2007 and 2008. If one examines the propensity to free-ride in 2008, after controlling for a range of employee and job characteristics, this is greater among women than men (by around 2 percentage points) and greater among non-manuals than manuals (also by around 2 percentage points). It is also unsurprisingly much greater among temporary staff than permanent employees (by 21 percentage points) and among part-timers than full-timers (by 11 percentage points). It is 10 percentage points greater among private sector employees than among public sector employees.

As with membership, none of the overall rise in free-riding can be explained by changes in the types of jobs and employees that are covered by collective bargaining. After controlling for employee and job characteristics, the residual propensity to be a union member when covered by collective bargaining declined by 4.6 percentage points between 1999 and 2008 (compared with an actual fall of 3.7 percentage points).[6] Consequently, the rise in free-riding would actually have been greater had it not been for compositional change.

---

[6] Again, we see a similar decline if we impute the characteristics of the population of employees from 1999 into a regression of the propensity to be a union member in 2008.

There are currently almost 3 million free-riders among the 8 million covered employees in Britain. Converting the free-riders into fee-paying union members, whilst still holding onto and servicing their 6.7 million existing members, are two crucial challenges facing the union movement at the present time. Their ability to do so will ultimately depend upon what they have to offer.

Unions' response

As we have shown above, structural change in the economy and its workforce accounts for little of the decline in union density, suggesting that employee demand for union membership may have dropped. Yet a sizeable percentage of employees in non-union workplaces say they would join a union if one was available to them. According to the British Social Attitudes Surveys (henceforth BSA), one in seven employees in non-unionised workplaces say they would be 'very likely' to join a union if asked and another quarter say they would be 'quite likely'. This demand for union membership remained constant over the period 1998–2005. These estimates of the demand for union membership may be an upper bound since respondents may not have accounted fully for the potential costs of union joining. Nevertheless, they suggest there is a sizeable untapped market for union representation. This begs the question whether unions are in a position to meet this demand.

There does indeed appear to be a serious problem with unions' organisational capacity which has arisen for three reasons (Willman and Bryson, 2009). First, their finances are in a parlous state due to declining membership subscriptions. Second, the 'off balance sheet' resources provided through lay representation and employer-provided support have also been declining (ibid.). Third, individual grievance representation has become increasingly important as a union servicing activity. This is particularly resource-intensive. Unions' initial response was to fight for market share through mergers and acquisitions. As Table 17.2 showed, the number of unions fell by one-quarter in the decade to 2009. The average size of the remaining unions grew. The very large conglomerate unions suffered particularly large membership losses and have not reaped the cost savings that merger and acquisition usually imply in the corporate world (ibid.). In contrast, smaller occupation or industry-specific unions such as those representing teachers and nurses have gained members. These gains have occurred for a variety of reasons such as the growth in the public health sector, and the demand for professional indemnity insurance in the case of teachers. But it does seem that the industry- or occupation-specific unions have been more successful in growing membership than the 'mega-unions'.

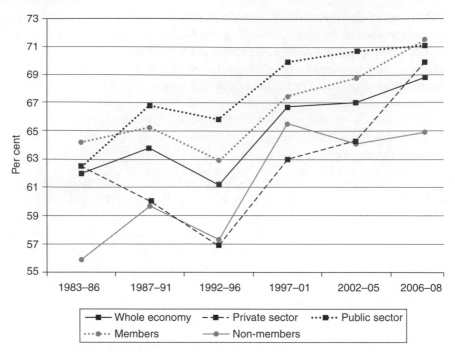

Figure 17.4: Percentage agreeing union doing its job well, 1983–2008
Note: Employees working 10+ hours in unionised workplaces.
Source: British Social Attitudes Survey.

Against this backdrop of declining membership and organisational disarray, what direct evidence is there of unions' ability to deliver benefits to their members and reach out to employers whose support they are increasingly reliant upon? One notable finding is that the percentage of employees in BSA who say the workplace union is doing its job well has been rising since 1997 so that, by the late noughties, seven in ten employees thought unions were doing a good job. The trend is apparent among union members and non-members (Figure 17.4). Below we go on to consider unions' effectiveness in more detail by considering three specific issues: their ability to give effective 'voice' to employees' concerns; union wage effects; and unions' impact on workplace performance and productivity.

Voice at work

In 2008, 45% of employees in BSA said they had no 'say' in decisions regarding changes to their job, a proportion that has remained roughly constant since the late 1980s. The same percentage wanted 'more say' over decisions affecting their work. Unions can offer employees 'voice' in the workplace and, because it is collective in nature, unions can overcome incentive problems that individual employees face when considering whether to invest in 'voice' to obtain procedural justice and other public goods. This traditional role for unions, first identified by Freeman and Medoff (1984), has come under challenge due to changes in the provision of 'voice' at workplaces with non-union forms—particularly direct two-way communication between management and employees—replacing union forms of voice (Willman et al., 2009).

If voice permits employees to solve problems at work, it should reduce the propensity of employees to quit voluntarily (Freeman and Medoff, 1984). It is arguable that if voice mechanisms do not reduce quit rates relative to instances in which employees have no voice, then it is ineffective. Gomez et al. (2009) show that workplaces with worker voice mechanisms still have lower quit rates than those without voice, but only where that voice is union voice.

In voicing employee concerns about problems in the workplace and by threatening industrial action if problems remain unresolved, unions may contribute to a more conflictual climate of employment relations than that which exists in the absence of unions. If this process leads to lower quit rates among dissatisfied employees, this can also contribute to a poorer climate in unionised workplaces than in non-unionised workplaces, where the dissatisfied may simply quit. In the 1980s, the climate of employment relations was less likely to be rated positively by employees in unionised workplaces than by their counterparts in non-unionised workplaces, even after compositional differences had been accounted for through regression analysis (Table 17.4). However, the regression-adjusted difference (net of compositional effects) disappeared in the mid-1990s. This is consistent with Blanchflower and Bryson's (2009) findings for workplace managers over the period 1980–2004. It would seem, therefore, that unions are now able to lower employee quit rates without endangering the climate of employment relations at the workplace.

Table 17.4: Climate of employment relations, 1985–2008

Year	1985–1986	1987–1991	1992–1996	1997–2001	2002–2005	2006–2008
All unionised workplaces	3.03	2.99	2.90	2.96	3.01	3.03
All non-unionised workplaces	3.35	3.31	3.14	3.20	3.26	3.23
Raw gap	−0.32**	−0.32**	−0.24**	−0.24**	−0.25**	−0.20**
Regression-adjusted gap	−0.11*	−0.12**	−0.04	−0.02	−0.03	−0.03

Notes:
1. Employees are asked to rate how good relations are between management and employees, with responses recorded on a four-point scale from 'not at all good' (code 1) to 'very good' (code 4). Rows 1 and 2 show mean scores.
2. ** = statistically significantly different from zero at 1% level; * = statistically significantly different from zero at 5% level.
3. Regression-adjusted gap based on model with following controls: union membership; gender; ethnicity; age; qualifications; part-time employment; social class; region; sector (public, manufacturing, construction with private services as reference); establishment size.

Source: British Social Attitude Surveys, 1985–2008.

Wage premium and wage dispersion

Historically, one of the principal benefits for union members in Britain has been the delivery of a wage premium over similar non-members through unions' collective bargaining activities. It is often assumed that declining union membership and collective bargaining coverage imply a lower union wage premium. This is not necessarily so, as it will depend upon whether those instances of union organisation that have disappeared were weaker or stronger than the average; logic might suggest the former. However, the increase in free-riding is one factor that points towards a weakening of union power in organisations where they remain present and, indeed, the consensus is that the union wage premium declined in magnitude during the 1980s and 1990s, as it did in other countries such as the USA (Blanchflower and Bryson, 2003). We update the picture for Britain using the LFS. Table 17.5 shows that the decline has continued in the most recent decade. Having stood at over 10% in the mid-1990s, the premium enjoyed by union members (after controlling for other characteristics) hovered around 8–9% between 1997 and 2002, but has since fallen to just 5%.

Female union members have typically enjoyed a larger wage premium than their male counterparts, and this continues to be the case as the union wage

Table 17.5: Union wage premium, by year and gender

	All employees		Male employees		Female employees	
	Raw wage premium	Regression adjusted	Raw wage premium	Regression adjusted	Raw wage premium	Regression adjusted
1994	28.8	13.9	21.3	9.7	34.6	17.3
1995	26.6	9.0	18.7	6.2	32.2	12.0
1996	28.4	12.3	22.0	9.8	33.3	14.8
1997	25.9	8.8	17.6	6.6	33.3	11.7
1998	24.4	8.3	15.0	4.2	33.3	12.4
1999	22.7	7.8	13.9	5.4	31.1	11.1
2000	22.4	8.5	15.3	6.8	29.0	10.9
2001	22.4	9.2	16.9	7.3	27.2	12.0
2002	21.1	8.6	15.4	6.9	26.9	10.4
2003	22.3	8.1	15.4	6.3	28.8	10.5
2004	21.3	7.0	15.4	5.5	27.4	9.0
2005	22.4	6.9	15.2	2.9 (ns)	30.7	10.7
2006	20.6	6.6	13.6	3.5	28.9	9.9
2007	20.9	6.7	14.8	3.2	28.2	9.9
2008	18.3	5.2	11.6	1.4 (ns)	25.9	8.7

Notes:
1. Regression-adjusted gap based on models with following controls: gender, age, age squared, qualifications (five categories), white/non-white, manual/non-manual, temporary/permanent, full-time/part-time, size of workplace (25+ employees), private/public sector, industry sector (13 categories), region (21 categories) and whether the employee is covered by collective bargaining.
2. ns = not statistically significantly different from zero.

Source: QLFS (GB).

premium has all but disappeared among men. Female union members continue to enjoy a wage premium over female non-members of around 9% (down from around 11% in the late 1990s), whereas among male employees the premium has fallen from around 7% to just 1% over the past decade and is no longer statistically significant from zero.

Studies have nevertheless shown that some of the change over time in the magnitude of the wage premium can be accounted for by the changing fortunes of the economy (Blanchflower and Bryson, 2003). Specifically, the wage premium in Britain appeared to rise and fall in line with unemployment over the 1980s and 1990s, perhaps because unions may have been more successful than non-union workers in resisting downward pressure on wages during the downturns. One corollary is that the downward trend in the size of the premium seen in the past ten years or so may be reversed when data allow one to examine the recent period of recession. This will, however, depend upon the extent to which the strategies pursued by unions in this most recent recession compare with those taken in previous downturns. There has, for example, been considerable evidence of wage restraint among unions as a means of securing jobs.

In addition to the historic presence of a wage premium for union members, it has also long been observed that wages in unionised jobs are less widely dispersed. This lower dispersion arises both because unions raise the wages of the lowest paid and also because they encourage the use of more objective criteria in pay setting. The decline in the coverage of union wage setting has thus contributed to a general increase in wage inequality (Card et al., 2003). But do unions still narrow the dispersion of wages where they are present?

One means of assessing this is to regress hourly wages on a standard set of employee, job and workplace characteristics (as above), and then to compare the dispersion of the unexplained portion of the wage (the residual) for union and non-union employees. This can be done using the LFS for the period 1994–2008. The results show that, in 2008, the dispersion in the residuals among employees who are not members of a union was 11% larger than the dispersion found among union members (Table 17.6). This figure has remained reasonably consistent over the past decade and a half. So although the advantage that union members hold over non-members in terms of their overall average rate of pay has declined, the 'sword of justice' effect, whereby unions compress pay differentials, remains.

Finally, it is worth asking whether the union premium seen in respect of wages also extends to other terms and conditions. One issue of concern to most workers is their entitlement to paid holidays. New analysis of the LFS shows that, in 1998, just after the introduction of the Working Time Regulations (WTR), union members received paid holidays equivalent to 9.5% of

Table 17.6: Relative wage dispersion among union members and non-members, by year and gender

	All employees		Male employees		Female employees	
	Raw data	Regression residuals	Raw data	Regression residuals	Raw data	Regression residuals
1994	21.1	10.7	31.9	14.5	6.1	8.0
1995	22.9	16.4	30.9	18.8	11.2	15.6
1996	25.2	16.9	39.0	22.8	8.7	12.3
1997	23.3	10.2	29.5	12.8	11.4	7.2
1998	25.9	12.7	35.8	18.9	9.9	7.1
1999	24.0	11.5	29.9	13.3	10.6	9.4
2000	21.0	7.7	25.4	5.9	11.2	8.3
2001	24.1	13.7	30.3	16.6	14.9	11.8
2002	20.9	12.1	24.8	11.9	12.8	12.4
2003	20.0	11.9	22.2	16.8	12.9	8.7
2004	19.9	13.2	27.4	19.0	8.4	8.3
2005	19.3	9.0	30.0	20.5	4.7	0.1
2006	17.8	7.5	21.0	9.4	9.1	5.9
2007	21.7	11.2	24.7	12.1	13.8	10.5
2008	20.3	11.4	28.8	22.1	8.0	3.0
Average 1994–2008	21.8	11.7	28.8	15.7	10.3	8.6

Notes:
1. Cells show the ratio of the standard deviation of log gross hourly earnings among non-members to that among union members.
2. Regression-adjusted gap based on models with following controls: gender, age, age squared, qualifications (five categories), white/non-white, manual/non-manual, temporary/permanent, full-time/part-time, size of workplace (25+ employees), private/public sector, industry sector (13 categories), region (21 categories) and whether the employee is covered by collective bargaining.
Source: QLFS (GB).

annual working hours whilst non-members received the equivalent of just 7.0% (a difference of around 6 days). After controlling for our standard set of employee, job and workplace characteristics, the union premium falls to around 3 days. The unadjusted union premium then fell to around 4.5 days and the adjusted premium to just under 2.5 days in the first half of the present decade, this presumably being at least partly the result of the gradual implementation of the WTR. In 2008, union members received 4 days additional paid leave, on average; a figure which falls to just under 2 days after controlling for other factors. A 'holiday' premium is thus apparent, although it has declined in magnitude over the past decade.

Other evidence suggests that union members also benefit in terms of greater access to family-friendly working arrangements, greater access to training and better levels of health and safety at work. Union membership therefore does still lead to better terms and conditions for the average employee, although the size of this advantage appears to have diminished recently.

Labour productivity and workplace performance

If unions raise wages without a commensurate rise in productivity, financial performance will suffer. Where product markets are uncompetitive, this might imply a simple transfer from capital to labour with no efficiency effects but, in an increasingly globalised and de-regulated marketplace, reduced profitability is liable to result in lower investment rates, making unionised firms vulnerable to closure or takeover.

Empirical evidence for the last quarter century indicates that the negative effect of unionisation on workplace performance was last evident in the 1980s: the regression-adjusted gap was not significant from 1990 onwards (Blanchflower and Bryson, 2009). There are a number of potential reasons for this change. First, the union wage premium has fallen somewhat, thus lowering the labour costs associated with unions. Second, unions have negotiated away many of the labour demarcation practices which inhibited labour flexibility in the past. Third, unions helped managers innovate through the adoption of productivity-enhancing high-involvement management (HIM) practices such that, by the early noughties, they were just as common in union workplaces as they were in non-union workplaces (Wood and Bryson, 2009). Perhaps the chief obstacle to unions continuing to deliver improving workplace performance is their own organisational capacity at the workplace: regression analyses of the 2004 Workplace Employment Relations Survey indicate a strong correlation between a range of union effectiveness measures and managers agreeing with the statement 'Unions help find ways to improve workplace performance' (TUC, 2010).

Unions' prospects

Hand in hand with the decline in union membership, union density and union bargaining coverage in British workplaces has gone a diminution in the stature and status of unions in society. Their place at the top table of political power, seemingly assured in the 1960s and 1970s, has gone. Any thought that New Labour would usher in a new era of 'beer and sandwiches' at Number 10 was no more than a mirage. Instead unions are just one of many interests jockeying for position in the hope of defending what is now often characterised as a sectional interest—that of workers. This fundamental change in the role of unions is reflected in perceptions of how much power unions are perceived to have in society. In the mid-1980s the percentage of employees who thought that unions had too much power in society out-numbered those saying they had too little by a factor of 5:1 (53% against 10%, BSA), with only one in twenty being unsure. According to the latest figures in 2007, the situation has been reversed: those saying unions have too little power outnumber those saying they have too much by a factor of 2:1 (24% against 13%). A further 20% said they could not decide, perhaps reflecting greater uncertainty about precisely what unions do today now that they are far less prominent than they used to be.

There is a rather old and tired debate in industrial relations, both here and in the US, regarding the prospects for union revival. Underlying this debate is a preoccupation with the power unions once wielded. It juxtaposes prospects for a 'Second Coming' for unions in which they rebuild their political and industrial power on the back of new organising strategies, and the prospect of terminal decline leading to near-annihilation. This debate rarely touches on a third scenario, namely unionisation in a guise, form and status similar to that which it enjoys currently. Trade unionism still constitutes the largest voluntary organisation in Britain; it represents 7 million employees; negotiates on behalf of one-third of employees; still dominates workplace employment relations in the public sector; and continues to influence important aspects of working life in the private sector as well. But the challenge for unions today is to prevent further weakening of their position. It appears that unions are 'upping their game'. Whether they are doing enough remains to be seen.

References

Barratt, C. (2009) *Trade Union Membership 2008*. London: Department for Business Enterprise and Regulatory Reform.

Blanchflower, D. and Bryson, A. (2003) Changes over time in union relative wage effects in the UK and the US revisited. In: Addison, J. J. and Schnabel, C. (eds.) *International Handbook of Trade Unions*. Cheltenham, UK and Northampton, Mass., USA: Edward Elgar.

—— —— (2009) Trade union decline and the economics of the workplace. In: Brown, W., Bryson, A., Forth, J. and Whitfield, K. (eds.) *The Evolution of the Modern Workplace*. Cambridge: Cambridge University Press.

Brown, W., Bryson, A. and Forth, J. (2009) Competition and the retreat from collective bargaining. In: Brown, W., Bryson, A., Forth, J. and Whitfield, K. (eds.) *The Evolution of the Modern Workplace*. Cambridge: Cambridge University Press.

Card, D., Lemieux, T. and Riddell, W. C. (2003) Unionisation and wage inequality: a comparative study of the US, the UK and Canada, NBER Working Paper No. 9473.

Freeman, R. and Medoff, J. L. (1984) *What Do Unions Do?* New York: Basic Books.

Gomez, R., Bryson, A., Kretschmer, T. and Willman, P. (2009) Employee voice and private sector workplace outcomes in Britain, 1980–2004. Centre for Economic Performance Discussion Paper No. 924.

Millward, N., Bryson, A. and Forth, J. (2000) *All Change at Work? British Employment Relations 1980–1998, As Portrayed by the Workplace Industrial Relations Survey Series.* London: Routledge.

TUC (2010) *The Road to Recovery: How Effective Unions Can Help Rebuild the Economy.* London: Touchstone Pamphlet.

Willman, P. and Bryson, A. (2009) Accounting for collective action: resource acquisition and mobilization in British unions. *Advances in Industrial and Labor Relations*, 16: 23–50.

—— Gomez, R. and Bryson, A. (2009) Voice at the workplace: where do we find it, why is it there, and where is it going? In: Brown, W., Bryson, A., Forth, J. and Whitfield, K. (eds.) *The Evolution of the Modern Workplace.* Cambridge: Cambridge University Press.

Wood, S. and Bryson, A. (2009) High involvement management. In: Brown, W., Bryson, A., Forth, J. and Whitfield, K. (eds.) *The Evolution of the Modern Workplace.* Cambridge: Cambridge University Press.

18

Public and Private Sector Labour Markets

Peter Dolton and Gerry Makepeace

Key findings

- In 2009, the public sector employed about 6.1m people, comprising 21% of the workforce. This fraction had been growing especially because of employment rises in the NHS, police and education.
- Over the last ten years the rate of growth in private sector earnings settlements has, on average, matched—more or less exactly—the rate of growth in the public sector.
- On average, earnings are higher in the public sector than in the private sector, but this comparison is misleading as public sector workers are, on average, better qualified and more experienced.
- After controlling for different characteristics, male public sector workers earned about 1% less than comparable private sector workers in 2009. Women working in the public sector enjoyed a premium of about 6% in 2009.
- In the current recession, there is substantial 'sector envy', with more private sector workers thinking their public sector counterparts are better off on a whole range of dimensions.

The public sector

Employment

The public sector employed about 6.1m people in 2009, mainly working to provide services such as health, defence, social security, social services, police and education through national or local government. Its workforce comprises frontline workers such as doctors and nurses, soldiers, policemen and teachers, as well as the staff required to administer their activities. Public corporations such as the Royal Mail are part of the public sector although they operate as private companies. Employment in the public sector fell from 5.9m in 1992 to 5.2m in 1998 before growing to a peak of 5.9m in 2005 and reaching 5.8m in 2008. Its share of total employment followed a similar pattern, accounting for about 21% of total employment in 2009 compared with 23% in 1992 and 19% in 1999. Although employment remained at 5.8m during the recession, it fell slightly from 2006 to 2008 with a slightly falling share of total employment before increasing by 0.3m in 2009. Partly as the result of policy initiatives to move employment to less favoured areas, the public sector share of total employment varies across the country from 17–18% in London, East Anglia and South East, to 23–24% in the Northern region, Wales and Scotland and to 29% in Northern Ireland.

The industries covered (with their contribution to public sector employment in 2008 in parentheses[1]) are NHS (26%), Education (24%) and Public

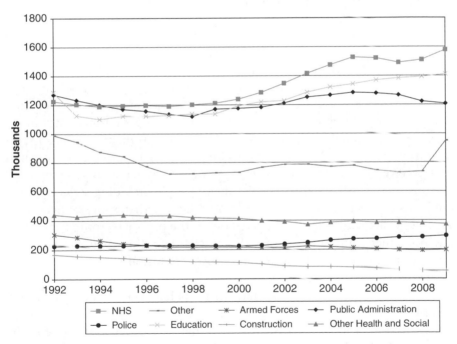

Figure 18.1: Public sector employment by industry (thousands of workers)
Source: Series C9LD, C9LG, C9LH, C9LF, C9LB, C9LC, C9LA, C9LJ available on the ONS website.

---

[1] We have chosen 2008 because there is a large jump in the 'Other' category in 2009 which seriously affects the shares.

Administration (21%), followed by Other Health and Social Services (7%), Police (5%) and the Armed Forces (3%). Construction (under 1%) and a residual 'Other' category account for the remaining workers. The composition of the workforce has varied considerably over time, mainly as a result of the privatisations in the 1980s. Railway privatisation took place in the mid-1990s and, during the current recession, failed financial organisations have joined the public sector. More recently, there has been a move towards contracting out services to the private sector.

Figure 18.1 shows the numbers employed by industry for the period. The two main drivers of employment growth were the NHS and Education where the headcount grew by 0.37m and 0.27m respectively from 1999–2009. Over this decade, the rate of growth of police numbers (30%) matched that of the NHS (30%) and exceeded that of Education (24%). The numbers in Public Administration grew by 0.1m from 1999 to 2005 before falling to record a modest growth of 3% for 1999–2009. By contrast, employment in the Armed Forces and Health and Other Social Services fell over the same period by 10%. The size and structure of public sector employment has reflected political objectives as well as demographic and social trends. A Conservative adminis-tration oversaw the initial contraction in public sector employment, although the subsequent Labour government waited before implementing its own plans to expand particularly the National Health Service (NHS) and Education.

The Office for National Statistics (ONS) provides the official definition of the public sector: those workers who are employed by an organisation that is financed by the government and for which the government has direct financial responsibility. All other individuals work in the private sector. This definition places some institutions in the private sector, such as universities that receive large amounts of public money, together with self-employed persons such as GPs. It also excludes many people providing services to the public sector, such as many cleaners in hospitals. Further, some services, such as refuse collection, will be contracted out to the private sector in some areas but not others. Although we use the official definition, it understates the direct impact of the public sector and causes confusion in data sets that ask individuals about their sector of work.

The ONS website provides the statistics for public sector employment used here. ONS is also responsible for the Annual Survey of Hours and Earnings (ASHE) and the Labour Force Survey (LFS) that we use. ASHE is the officially preferred source of earnings data for employees because of its sample size and method of collection directly from firms. LFS has smaller but still very large samples summarising responses obtained from individuals. The data in LFS, particularly about sector of work, may differ from that in ASHE, but ASHE contains little information about the characteristics of workers, so our detailed analysis of differences between the sectors relies on LFS.

274

Public sector workers

Workers in the public sector differ in many ways from other workers. They are more likely to be female, to have higher qualifications, to be older and to be a union member. In 2008 and 2009 about two-thirds of the public sector workforce was female, compared to just over two-fifths of the private sector's. In 2008 over a third of public sector workers had a degree or its vocational equivalent, compared to a fifth in the private sector, while a twentieth of public sector workers had no qualification, compared to a tenth in the private sector. The fraction of graduates increased in both sectors from 2008 to 2009, but by more in the public sector. The typical age of a man (44 years) working in the public sector was about two years more than that in the private sector and he was around four times more likely to be a union member.

An overview of public sector pay

The recession has created a funding crisis, the resolution of which has focused attention on public sector pay. In December 2009, the 'pre-Budget Report 2009' proposed 'a one per cent cap on public sector pay settlements in 2011–12 and 2012–13', while the shadow chancellor proposed a freeze on earnings above £18,000 in 2011 at the 2009 Conservative conference. Parts of the media have no difficulty in identifying the public sector with excessive pay. Certainly the median gross weekly pay in the public sector in 2008 was £412.0, 7.5% greater than that of employees in the private sector. Moreover, the gap increased to 12½% in 2009 as public sector pay grew more quickly.

These figures hide the overall pattern of public and private pay settlements over recent years. This is provided in Figure 18.2 for the last ten years. We see that periods of public sector pay growing faster than private sector pay roughly match the amount of time private sector pay growth has outstripped that in the public sector. Indeed the per-period difference in the two series is only 0.02%—negligible indeed. Perhaps the most striking thing about this graph— and clearly what has caused all the recent consternation—are the dramatic events since March 2008 when private sector pay rises plunged to become negative, whilst public sector pay continued to rise. However, this does not take into account the way the swings and roundabouts have moved over the previous ten years. Taken over the whole 1998–2009 period, there is no difference between public sector and private sector pay rises. By the end of 2009, there was already an indication that private sector pay had bounced back.

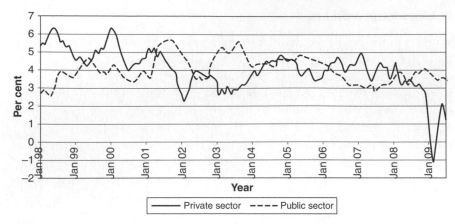

Figure 18.2: Public/private sector earnings increase, 1998–2009

A further basic piece of analysis is performed by looking at the overall distribution of earnings in the public and private sectors presented in Figure 18.3 for 2009. Here we see that the overall distribution of public sector earnings looks like a straightforward right shift to the private sector earnings distribution. We will see below that this reflects the differences in the educational qualifications, occupational and regional compositions and gender difference in the two groups.

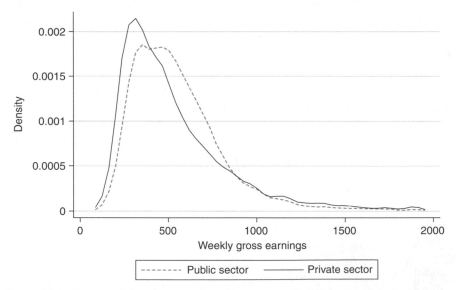

Figure 18.3: Estimated distribution of weekly earnings in 2009

Source: LFS. Full-time workers. Earnings are adjusted for monthly inflation using the Retail Price Index.

Closer inspection reveals significant differences between men and women. Since there is a penalty for part-time pay and relatively more women work part-time, we consider full-time gross weekly pay. The medians for the different groups in 2009 are: £591.2 (male, public), £508.7 (male, private), £496.3 (female, public), £373.2 (female, private). The corresponding pay differentials are 16% in favour of the public sector for men and 33% for women, illustrating that women do comparatively better by working in the public sector. One consequence is that the gender differential is smaller at 19% in the public sector compared with 36% in the private sector.

These comparisons ignore the many differences between the sectors that might account for the differences in pay. Some insight can be gained by examining differentials by occupational group. We compute occupational differentials as the ratio of the median of gross weekly earnings for a public sector group to that of the whole private sector. The calculation is done separately by gender for individuals working 30–70 hours a week. The premiums received in 2008 by the following groups are shown in parentheses (with the male premium first, followed by the female.): Primary School Teachers (41%, 77%), Secondary School Teachers (42%, 85%), Nurses and Midwives (16%, 55%), Practices Allied to Medicine (PAMs) (Radiographers, therapists etc. 28%, 57%), Medical Practitioners and Dentists (192%, 160%), Prison Officers (10%, 28%), Police Officers (57%, 82%) and the rest of the public sector, excluding the Armed Forces (–2%, 8%). All these occupational groups recorded a mark-up over the private sector, with the exception of the residual category for men who were underpaid on this metric. The mark-ups are noticeably higher for women, with the exception of Medical Practitioners. They vary quite considerably across occupation for each gender, with increased levels of education, responsibility and disagreeableness generating higher returns or compensating differentials.

Figures 18.4(a) and 18.4(b) plot the corresponding differentials over time. Medical Practitioners are omitted because their differentials are sufficiently large to distort the scale; the smallest values were 112% for men in 1995 and 160% for women in 2008. The differentials are stable enough to define three sets of occupations. Secondary and Primary Teachers and Police do relatively better than Nurses and Midwives, PAMs and Prison Officers, while the omitted Medical Practitioners clearly do best of all. All do better than the private sector, thus contributing to the public sector pay premium discussed above. Private sector earnings are typically larger than in the residual public sector group for men, but lower for women. The 'other' public sector premium for women was about 4% on average, reaching 8% of the private sector median in 2008, but almost disappearing in 2001. Men received a modest penalty of about 2%, although it did increase to 6% in 2002 and was positive in 1993–4. There are no strong trends apparent in these differentials.

(a)

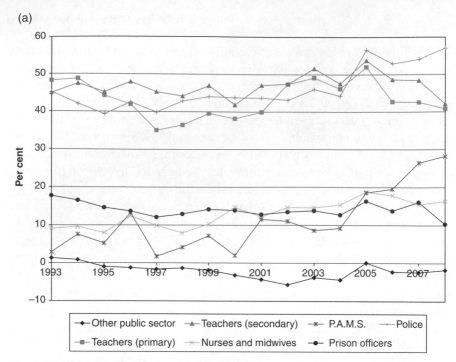

Figure 18.4(a): Occupational earnings premium as percentage of private sector earnings (men, ratio of medians of real weekly earnings)

(b)

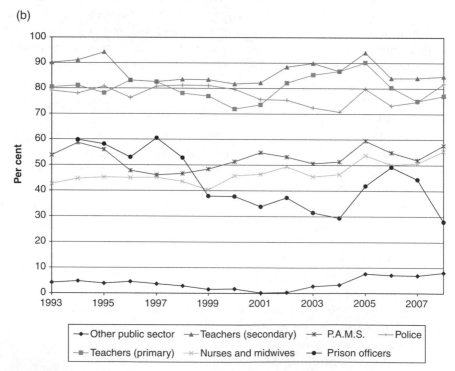

Figure 18.4(b): Occupational earnings premium as percentage of private sector earnings (women, ratio of medians of real weekly earnings)

Source: Annual Survey of Hours and Earnings.

Explaining pay differentials

Market dynamics explain pay differentials in terms of variations in demand and supply conditions. The notion of an employer motivated by profit is not widely applicable across the public sector, although some public sector firms (for example, the Royal Mail and financial institutions) sell products in well-defined markets, while many services such as bus travel, cleaning and maintenance are now supplied by contractors, some of which are owned by public sector institutions. There is an important argument about what activities should be run by the government and how the government should intervene. It is taken for granted that the government should provide schooling and health services, but there is already substantial private sector provision of these activities. Nor does government funding preclude methods of delivery that place more emphasis on markets. There is continual discussion of introducing alternative schooling methods that would make the UK system more market driven by providing parents with vouchers to purchase tuition from a school of their choice. Much activity in the NHS has involved changes in the role of market solutions. While the delivery of (free) medical care in some countries allows for more explicit markets through, for example, insurance. In practice, public corporations account for a relatively small amount of government employment (6.2% in 2008 and 9.5% in 2009) in the UK.

The lack of market constraints gives considerable scope for political factors to at least partly determine outcomes. An antipathy to certain sectors such as social work and defence, while favouring others such as the NHS and education, can lead to redistributions of expenditure, stimulating certain markets and restricting others. As noted above, many commentators feel it is possible to make general statements about pay policy without reference to the peculiarities of the markets concerned. We would also note the pressure for the public sector to be a model employer. Profit-maximising firms will seek to minimise the costs of compliance with the numerous rules and laws concerning employment, but public sector bodies are under greater pressure to follow the spirit as well as the letter of the law. One example is gender equality, where gender earnings differentials are smaller in the public sector.

Since Adam Smith in the eighteenth century, economists have argued that wages should vary according to the 'disagreeableness' of occupations. These compensating differentials accommodate differences in costs of acquiring skills and qualifications (an individual's human capital) and the degree of stress and risk, as well as the value of non-pecuniary benefits. Wages should increase with the amount of education to compensate for the implicit cost of foregone earnings and leisure and other more direct costs such as fees and study materials. Thus graduates should be paid more than individuals with A-levels, who in turn should be paid more than those with no qualifications. This earnings gradient undoubtedly underlies the differences between highly qualified public sector occupations such as teachers and the private sector. Wages should also increase with the level of stress resulting from increased responsibility or working in less pleasant conditions. This may partly explain the relatively high earnings of doctors, prison officers and police.

Compensating differentials can be negative. The public sector offers greater job security, better conditions of service and a well-defined pension. A successful career in the private sector may additionally involve job changes and greater planning, but a chance of large rewards. Indeed, the possibility of non-pecuniary benefits such as cars and medical insurance in the private sector is often ignored. A further dimension is that of public service. Teaching and nursing are often described as vocations, but the point may be more widely applicable in the public sector. Wages will be lower in the public sector to compensate for the non-pecuniary benefits.

Labour market outcomes depend on the institutional structure. Public sector wage determination is complex, but the authorities are the major or, in some cases, the sole employer in certain labour markets, giving them a high degree of monopsony power and enabling them to exert a downward pressure on wages. The public sector is much more unionised than the private sector (see Bryson and Forth, Chapter 17), so there is some countervailing upward pressure on wages. The picture is further complicated because over 2m public sector workers are covered by Pay Review Bodies (PRBs) or similar arrangements (e.g. police). PRBs receive evidence from different parties, but do not engage in pay negotiations, instead making recommendations on the appropriate pay award. A further twist is that wages are determined nationally, so, in principle, a teacher in Kent is paid the same as one in Newcastle, despite the different costs of living.

Efficiency may explain why public sector pay policies differ from those in the private sector. It may be more difficult to monitor employee performance in the public sector because the output is less well defined than in the private sector, or it may be more difficult to ensure good performance because of less demanding employment policies. In which case, other devices may be used. In particular, the age-earnings profile may be structured so that wages are low at the start of an individual's career and increase over time. Similarly, a pension can be interpreted as deferred pay. The basic idea behind delayed compensation is that the worker keeps working hard in order to qualify for the higher pay and pension associated with long service. Disney et al. (2009) argue that the earnings profiles of men with high education working in the public sector reflect this effect. Further they show that public sector workers are far more likely to have defined benefit pension schemes (that relate pensions to earnings at the end of one's career and length of service with an employer) than those in the private sector and the schemes are likely to be more generous. The argument here is that such wage-pension policies may be more efficient.

Imperfect monitoring defines a standard principal–agent problem where the principal (the employer) cannot observe fully the performance of the agent (the worker). One aspect to the problem is that in the public sector there are often several possible measures of performance. When an agent has multiple goals, it is unclear how to direct effort, although it has been shown that the agent will have an incentive to divert effort away from the less accurately measured task. If the principal wishes the agent to allocate effort towards a task that is not easily measured, then incentives on the measurable tasks must be weakened. Another feature of the public sector is that it has multiple principals. As a consequence, the actions of, say, an individual teacher (agent) could be affected by many other people (principals) who are in a position of influence. For example, the wishes of parents, head teachers, teacher unions, local authorities, taxpayers, employers, religious and ethnic pressure groups, governors and even pupils may influence the actions and decisions of individual teachers. The existence of several principals makes the overall incentives for the agent much weaker. This weakening of incentives occurs because each principal will seek to divert the agent's effort to his most preferred dimension. If the principals have competing interests, the incentive structure for the agent will become less clear as the number of principals increases. These results mean that it is difficult for the public sector to adopt performance related-pay practices or write contracts that induce the best effort of public sector workers.

Measuring pay differentials

Controlling for differences by sector

The previous discussion indicates that pay should vary between the sectors to reflect their different characteristics. Since some of these characteristics can be observed, we can investigate how much of the pay differential can be explained by observable differences. We can interpret this comparison as a 'benchmark' of public sector wages against those in the private sector, with the implication that large remaining differentials indicate possible inefficiencies.

The standard methodology estimates an earnings equation that relates pay to observable characteristics such as qualifications and age. The resulting equation can be used to compare the predicted earnings of individuals with the same attributes but working in different sectors, for example, the earnings of 50-year-old graduates working in the private and public sectors. In its simplest form (used in this chapter), the remaining systematic unobservable differences between the sectors are captured by a variable measuring whether or not an individual works in the public sector. We estimate these differences using LFS data and report them as percentage mark-ups of public sector pay over private sector pay. This analysis differs from our previous comparisons because we are making like-for-like comparisons of individuals in the two sectors. To increase the similarities we therefore take samples of full-time employees. The data is described further in Dolton et al. (2008) and the results here complement their analysis.

Table 18.1 reports the public sector pay differentials as a percentage of private sector pay. Consider the figures for 2009: 11% for the 'raw' specification indicates that public sector pay was 11% higher than private sector pay when the only adjustment made is for hours worked. Human capital refers to the skills and knowledge that a person has and is measured by qualifications and age (acting as a measure of experience); -1.7% for the human capital specification means that public sector pay was 1.7% lower than private sector pay when an adjustment was made for the level of human capital. The final value (-1.2%) shows that public sector pay was 1.2% lower when region of work was also taken into account. It is placed in parentheses to denote that the estimate was insignificantly different from zero and in statistical terms is likely to be zero.

The figures in the table indicate the importance of taking account of the differences between the sectors. The raw mark-ups give a misleading impression of the earnings differentials between the sectors. In the case of men, a substantial differential becomes negative once allowance is made for the differences in measurable characteristics. A similar change occurs for

Table 18.1: Adjusted public sector pay differentials by gender (% gap relative to private sector weekly earnings)

	Men			Women		
	Raw	Human capital	All	Raw	Human capital	All
2001	8.3	−3.3	−2.7	18.2	(0.9)	2.6
2002	8.9	−2.6	−2.2	17.9	1.5	3.0
2003	9.9	−2.1	−1.8	20.7	4.3	5.6
2004	10.2	−1.9	−1.6	20.1	3.3	4.7
2005	10.1	−1.3	(−1.1)	21.2	4.3	5.3
2006	12.1	(−1.3)	(−0.9)	21.2	4.4	5.8
2007	9.4	−2.4	−2.2	19.7	2.8	4.1
2008	9.9	−2.2	−1.6	20.8	3.7	5.2
2009	11.0	−1.7	(−1.2)	21.4	3.9	5.7

Notes: The values in the table show the difference in gross weekly earnings as a percentage of those in the private sector. Earnings are adjusted for monthly inflation using the Retail Price Index. The log of earnings is regressed on a variable for public sector work and paid hours of work in the base ('raw') specification. The human capital specification controls additionally for five levels of qualifications and age. The final ('All') specification adds controls for the 11 standard regions. An estimate in parenthesis denotes that the value is statistically insignificant.

women, although the raw differentials are much larger and are still positive after adjustment. Table 18.1 provides no support for the view that men are overpaid in the public sector. The large premium (9–11%) in observed raw earnings can be explained by the different characteristics of men working in the two sectors. In fact, the earnings of comparable men in the two sectors were 1–2% lower in the public sector in recent years. Public sector pay after adjustment increased very slightly relative to private sector pay from 2007 to 2008 and more substantially from 2008 to 2009. Nonetheless public sector pay for men is at best only equal to that in the private sector after full adjustment has been made. The case for women being overpaid relative to the private sector is more plausible. Their raw differentials are much larger (20–21% in recent years). Although they are much smaller after adjustment, the mark-up in favour of the public sector remains substantial (4–6%) for women. The raw differential has increased from 19.7% in 2007 to 21.4% in 2009 as the recession has progressed, while the figures after adjustment have also increased from 4.1% to 5.7%.

Regional variation

The notion of an aggregate labour market for a whole nation ignores the many local markets that exist. Employment and wage rates vary substantially within Britain, but public sector rates are negotiated nationally, leading to potential rigidities across the country. A wage may simultaneously be above the equilibrium in a depressed part of the country and below in another. In some areas, the public sector may be paying more than needed to secure workers, while, in others, it experiences shortages. The importance of the regional dimension has been reinforced by an explicit policy to shift central government offices to the regions to reduce pressure in London and boost local economies. Thus the Department of Health moved to Leeds, the Benefits Agency to Newcastle, the Employment Service to Sheffield and, more recently, the ONS to Newport.

Table 18.2 reports regional pay differentials adjusted for human capital differences. To simplify the presentation, we have divided England into 'South'—comprising East Anglia, South East and London—and the 'Rest'—comprising the rest of England. Once again we notice the large reduction in the pay differential after controlling for qualifications and age. This occurs in all regions for each year and gender, confirming that not much can be deduced from raw differentials. The 'human capital' results confirm that the big difference is between London and its hinterland and the less prosperous remaining areas of Britain. Once again, working in the public sector is more beneficial for women than for men.

For men, there are small positive differentials in Wales and the Rest and smaller differentials in Scotland (of –0.6% in 2009 and 0.3% in 2007). Since

Table 18.2: Adjusted public sector pay differentials by region and gender (% gap relative to private sector weekly earnings)

	Men		Women	
	Raw	Human capital	Raw	Human capital
2005				
South	6.1	−3.2	14.1	(0.6)
Rest	12.9	(0.6)	27.8	8.2
Wales	16.2	(2.5)	27.9	9.2
Scotland	9.8	(−2.1)	23.2	6.1
2007				
South	(1.7)	−6.7	12.2	(−2.0)
Rest	14.4	(0.5)	25.3	6.5
Wales	15.9	(3.2)	27.7	8.6
Scotland	12.8	(0.3)	29.8	12.0
2009				
South	5.8	−3.0	14.3	(−0.4)
Rest	15.3	(0.1)	27.9	7.8
Wales	13.7	(1.7)	34.0	13.1
Scotland	10.1	(−0.6)	22.9	6.9

Source: LFS. See the comments for Table 18.1. 'South' is East Anglia, South East and London and the 'Rest' is North, North West, Yorkshire and Humberside, East and West Midlands, South West.

these estimates are all statistically insignificant, we will simplify the discussion by treating them as zero and concluding that comparable men are paid the same in recent years. By contrast, there is a negative mark-up for working in the public sector, in the 'South' region. The penalty has varied over time, increasing from nearly –7% in 2007 to –3% in 2009. The regional pattern is same for women, except now the differential in the 'South' is zero in statistical terms, with female public servants in the regions benefiting from large positive earnings differentials. The 2009 differentials were 7.8% in the 'Rest', 13.1% in Wales and 6.9% in Scotland. These represented a large increase from 2007 for Wales, a modest increase for the 'Rest' and a fall for Scotland.

Occupational variation

The public sector covers many disparate occupational groups and our last investigation illustrates how the pay differential varies across the public sector for the groups: Primary School Teachers, Secondary School Teachers, Nurses and Midwives, Practices Allied to Medicine (Radiographers, therapists etc.), Medical Practitioners and Dentists, Prison Officers, Armed Forces, Police Officers and the rest of the public sector.

Table 18.3 reports the estimated differentials for 2009, while Figures 18.4(a) and 18.4(b) track the differential over time. Medical Practitioners are clearly an outlier, enjoying a substantial mark-up over the private sector in 2009 of 50% for men and 56% for women. It remains large over the whole period from

Table 18.3: Adjusted public sector occupational pay differentials for 2009 by gender (% of private sector weekly earnings)

	Teacher		Nurses	PAMs	Medics	Prison Officer	Armed Forces	Police	Other public sector
	Primary	Secondary							
Men	(−1.4)	(−1.4)	−15.3	−7.9	49.5	−12.1	20.4	11.1	−8.2
Women	13.2	18.2	5.8	7.6	55.6	–	–	26.7	(0.7)

Source: LFS. See the comments for Table 18.1. The public sector variable in Table 18.1 is replaced by separate variables representing the nine occupational groups and manual occupations. The specification includes human capital and regional variables. The estimates for women prison officers and armed forces are omitted because there are insufficient observations.

2001 to 2009, fluctuating between 45% (2005) and 55% (2004) for men and between 46% (2007) and 76% (2004) for women. It is omitted from Figures 18.4(a) and 18.4(b) because it distorts the graphs.

The range of differentials is still quite big, with quite large negative differentials recorded for men working as Nurses and Midwives (–15.3%) and Prison Officers (–12.1%) and in the 'Other' public sector (–8.2%) group. By contrast, Primary and Secondary School Teachers (–1.4%) have small differentials that are not significantly different from zero, but Police (11.1%) and the Armed Forces (20.4%) receive large positive differentials. The figures for women follow the same general ranking, except that Nurses and Midwives (5.8%) swap places with 'Other' public sector (0.7, but not significantly different from zero). Although the order is similar, we notice again that women do better from working in the public sector with, for instance, the larger differentials for Primary School Teachers (13.2%) and Secondary School Teachers (18.2%). Figures 18.5(a) and 18.5(b) shows that the differentials fluctuate over time, but there is considerable stability in the ranking of occupations for both men and women. There does not appear to be any obvious general pattern to the time paths. The 'Other' public sector group differential has grown from −10.0% in 2001 to −8.2% in 2009 for men and from −3.3% to 0.7% for women. Male PAMs and Nurses also saw some improvement in their differentials over the period, although much of this took place after 2004.

Is the grass greener?

One interesting aspect of the current differences between pay and working conditions in the public and private sector is how each sector perceives the other. Some recent work by Shury of the IFF and discussed in the *Guardian* (2010) suggests there is a real asymmetry in these perceptions (see Table 18.4). Shury asked 500 private sector workers what they thought was better about the public sector and vice versa. The answers to this survey show a remarkable

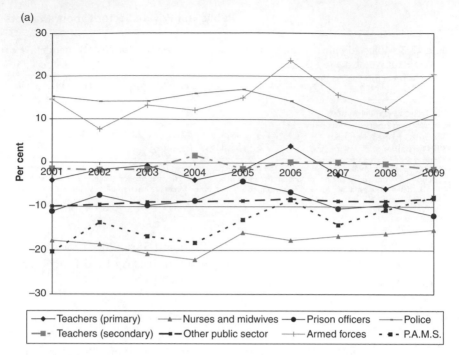

(a)

Figure 18.5(a): Adjusted occupational earnings premiums as percentage of private sector earnings (men)

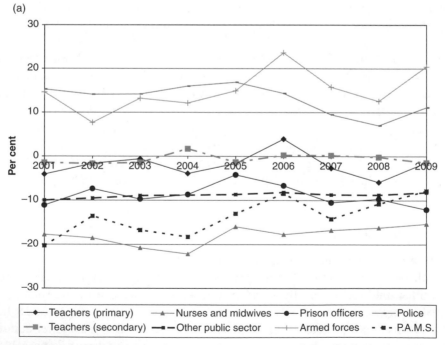

(a)

Figure 18.5(b): Adjusted occupational earnings premiums as percentage of private sector earnings (women)

Source: LFS.

Table 18.4: Is the grass really greener?

What private sector workers think is better about the public sector	What public sector workers think is better about the private sector
39% Training opportunities	45% Pay and financial rewards
36% Working hours and flexibility	23% Working hours and flexibility
33% Stress-free environment	22% Promotion and progression
33% Promotion and progression	20% Stress-free environment
33% Pay and financial rewards	18% Training opportunities
32% Job security	14% Holidays
31% Holidays	13% Job security
14% Equal opportunities	5% Equal Opportunities

Source: IFF Research in *Guardian* (2010), 'See you on the other side', 23 January, Work, p. 2, <http://www.guardian.co.uk/money/2010/jan/23/public-private-sector-grass-greener>.

asymmetry. The private sector workers think the public sector is better on: training (39%) working hours and flexibility (36%), stress-free environment (33%), promotion and progression (33%), job security (32%), holidays (31%) and equal opportunities (14%). In each category, except pay and financial rewards, these percentages were higher than the corresponding group in the public sector who were asked what was better in the private sector. In this case, 45% of public sector workers thought pay was higher in the private sector. This unusual research shows two things: first, there is much cross-sector envy—each sector thinks workers in the other sector fare better; but it also shows that—in the current recessionary time—the fraction of workers in the private sector who think all working conditions in the public sector are better, is at a very high level.

Conclusions

Public pay is and will continue to be a major policy issue as the UK struggles to recover from recession with the burden of a large public debt and a budgetary crisis. This chapter has demonstrated that recent claims that public servants are overpaid are misleading, giving rise to considerable 'sector envy', with private sector employees thinking the 'grass is greener' in the public sector. In reality, we saw that pay settlements in the two sectors over the last ten years average out to be the same despite recent falls in private sector earnings. While it is true that men and women working in the public sector typically earn much more than men and women working in the private sector, there are significant differences in the productivity-augmenting characteristics, such as qualifications, between the two groups of workers. The large differentials in the raw pay figures either disappear in the case of men or are much reduced in the case of women once allowance is made for the different attributes of workers in the two sectors. The precise values depend on the data source and the characteristics used to adjust the raw pay figures, but some feel for the argument can be obtained from the results for the regional differentials in 2009. The raw differential for men varied from 6% to 15% across the four regions considered and for women from 14.3% to 34%. After adjustment, male public sector workers earned less than comparable men did in the private sector in East Anglia and the South East including London. Men earned roughly the same in the two sectors elsewhere in the country. After adjustment, female public sector workers earned about the same as their comparators in London and the surrounding regions. Elsewhere women in the public sector enjoyed substantial premiums over similar colleagues in the private sector, although these mark-ups are much smaller than is suggested by a comparison based on the unadjusted wage data.

References

Bryson, A. and Forth, J. (2011) Trade unions. In: Gregg, P. and Wadsworth, J. (eds.) *The Labour Market in Winter: The State of Working Britain*. Oxford: Oxford University Press.

Disney, R., Emmerson, C. and Tetlow, G. (2009) What is a public pension worth? *The Economic Journal*, 119, November: F517–35.

Dolton, P., Makepeace, G. and Marcenero-Gutierrez, O. (2008) The impact of the public sector pay review bodies in the UK 1993–2008. IZA Discussion Paper No. 3373, February. Bonn: Institute for the Study of Labour.

19

The Regional Labour Market in the UK

Peter Dolton, Chiara Rosazza-Bondibene and Jonathan Wadsworth

Key findings

- While differences in regional performance narrowed prior to the latest recession, the North–South labour market divide in the UK persists.
- The North continues to have a lower employment rate and lower wages than the South.
- The North is more reliant on public sector employment than the South.
- Labour mobility between regions is at its lowest for decades and so is unlikely to foster regional convergence.
- Commuting within regions may offer the possibility of helping address differential performance within regions.

For at least 80 years there have been huge differences in prevailing economic and social conditions in the North and the South of the UK, described in some detail in Smith (1994). Ten years ago, Jackman and Savouri (1999) pondered whether the UK's long-standing regional labour market divide was beginning to weaken. They argued that the decline of geographically specific industries, such as manufacturing, mining or steel, meant that, whether by design or circumstance, regions were becoming more similar in their sectoral composition. Hence any future shocks would have a more balanced regional impact than in the past. In this chapter we explore whether the UK was indeed more regionally balanced in the past and examine some of the finer detail on this divide by looking at the UK spatial pattern of unemployment, human capital, the 'bite' of the National Minimum Wage, the pattern of public sector employment and commuting patterns by county and metropolitan areas.

Figure 19.1 and Table 19.1 track the unemployment and employment rates across three macro-regions over time. It is obvious that the 'South' has had higher employment rates and lower unemployment rates at almost all times

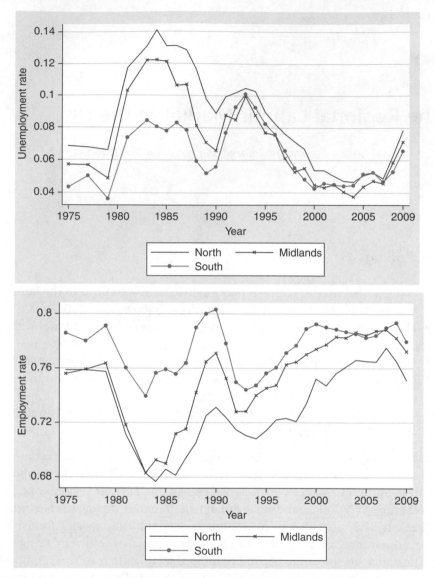

Figure 19.1: The North–South divide in employment and unemployment
Source: LFS. Authors' calculations.

over the past 35 years. The unemployment differential did narrow significantly during the recession of the early 1990s and practically disappeared over the recovery thereafter. This led some commentators to speculate that the local performance of the unemployment rate was now dominated by economy-wide factors, rather than regional factors. However, if instead the employment rate is used as the performance benchmark (Figure 19.1, lower panel), then this

Table 19.1: Employment and unemployment rate by macro-regions

	1975	1979	1986	1990	1993	2006	2009
Unemployment							
North	6.9	6.6	13.1	8.9	10.5	5.2	8.0
Midlands	5.7	4.9	10.6	6.6	10.0	4.7	7.2
South	4.3	3.6	8.3	5.6	10.1	5.3	6.6
% point gap wrt South							
North	+2.5	+3.0	+4.8	+3.3	+0.4	−0.1	+1.3
Midlands	+1.4	+1.3	+2.3	+1.0	−0.1	−0.6	+0.6
% gap wrt South							
North	+58	+82	+58	+59	+4	−1	+19
Midlands	+32	+34	+28	+18	−1	−10	+9
Employment							
North	75.9	75.8	68.2	73.1	71.1	76.5	75.1
Midlands	75.6	76.4	71.1	77.1	72.8	78.7	77.2
South	78.6	79.1	75.6	80.3	74.4	78.4	78.0
% point gap wrt South							
North	−2.7	−3.4	−7.4	−7.2	−3.4	−1.9	−2.8
Midlands	−3.0	−2.7	−4.4	−3.2	−1.6	+0.3	−0.7
% gap wrt South							
North	−3.5	−4.3	−9.9	−8.9	−4.5	−2.5	−3.6
Midlands	−3.8	−3.5	−5.8	−4.0	−3.1	+0.1	−0.9

Note: 'North' includes Scotland, North East, North West and Yorkshire. 'Midlands' includes Wales, East and West Midlands and the South West. 'South' includes London South East and East Anglia. Population of working age, excluding students.

Source: LFS. Authors' calculations.

hypothesis seems less valid. True, employment rates in the Midlands did converge toward that of the South, but the employment rate in the North lagged behind and much more so than a narrow focus on the unemployment rate would suggest. Policy makers need to be careful before pronouncing on the end of the North–South divide. This seems particularly important to stress since, over the latest recession, regional differences have widened and once again the North and the Midlands appear to have suffered more.

Typically, regional differences appear to narrow slightly in good times and widen in bad, at least as measured by the (absolute) difference in unemployment or employment rates (see Table 19.1). The latest recession is no exception. The ratio of unemployment rates is much less cyclically sensitive. If shocks to employment were evenly distributed across regions, we would expect the absolute gap in unemployment rates to be broadly the same in good times as in bad times (see Jackman and Savouri, 1999). The fact that, as Table 19.1 shows, the percentage fall in the employment rate has been greater in the North and Midlands this time round (and the absolute unemployment gap risen more) indicates that the shock of the recession was not neutral across regions. This in turn suggests a need to look at the balance of industries across regions.

Past research (Davis et al., 1998) has shown that the majority of job shedding is concentrated in downturns, while job creation is much less cyclically sensitive. This means that industries in decline, such as manufacturing, will be more sensitive to the cycle than industries which are growing. If manufacturing is concentrated in certain regions, then employment in these regions will also be more sensitive to the cycle. It is true that the share of manufacturing is now much more evenly distributed across regions than in the past. However, the decline in the manufacturing share of employment in the UK as a whole has been so large (see Gregg and Wadsworth, Chapter 1) that it is unlikely that any shock centred on manufacturing would any longer have major differential employment effects across regions. The South is now notably much more dependent on Finance. The Finance sector was the source of the downturn in both the 1990 and the 2008 recessions, albeit for different reasons. However, it is clear that the South, or indeed the Financial sector, did not suffer disproportionately in either downturn. The manufacturing sector in all regions appears to have borne the brunt of the job losses (see Table 19.2).

It is also clear that disadvantaged groups do better in more buoyant labour markets. Figure 19.2 tracks the employment rate of less skilled men—those in the bottom third of the educational distribution—in the North and the South. It is clear that the employment rate for less skilled men living in the South is consistently higher than the employment rate for less skilled men living in the less prosperous North. Once again there are signs of some convergence in good times; the employment rate appears to level off in the South, while the employment rate for less skilled men in the North continues to rise. However, when the recession arrives, convergence stops. It seems then that talk of the death of the North–South divide is, as yet, premature.

Table 19.2: Sector shares by macro-regions

	1975	1979	1986	1990	1993	2006	2009
Manufacturing							
North	34.9	34.1	26.5	24.9	23.1	14.3	11.1
Midlands	35.0	35.1	28.5	26.1	25.7	16.4	13.4
South	25.6	28.1	21.1	18.3	17.0	10.7	8.5
Finance							
North	4.6	5.3	7.5	8.9	9.5	14.1	15.1
Midlands	4.7	5.2	7.8	9.1	9.7	13.3	14.4
South	10.3	9.6	14.8	17.1	17.4	21.5	22.9
Public Admin							
North	17.6	19.3	22.8	22.2	26.2	30.6	32.1
Midlands	17.2	18.6	22.0	21.6	24.0	29.7	32.2
South	19.5	19.3	21.8	20.8	24.0	27.8	28.1

Source: ONS. Authors' calculations.

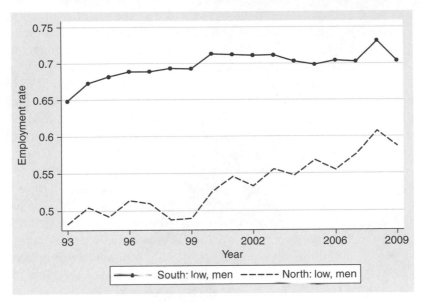

Figure 19.2: Employment rates of less skilled men across regions
Source: LFS.

However, the idea that differences in performance between regions is the only issue in regional labour markets is not true. For a long time now there has been a lot of variation in performance within regions. Around 60% of the variation in unemployment rates, measured across the 400 or so local authorities, occurs within regions rather than between regions. Figure 19.3 graphs the 2008 unemployment rate at local authority level. While it is apparent that unemployment is generally lower in the South, it is also clear that there are pockets of high employment in the North, typically in the rural periphery rather than in the industrial conurbations. Equally, there are pockets of high unemployment in the South. There is a large degree of persistence in these local area unemployment rates over time. The correlation coefficient between the 1992 local authority claimant count unemployment rate and the 2010 rate is 0.83. If we rank areas from highest to lowest unemployment rates, the correlation between 1992 and 2010 is remarkable, at 0.87. In essence, this means that the same local areas have been worst hit by the latest recession as in the previous recession. The overall average figures on unemployment for the North, South and Midlands obscure a considerable amount of important detail. Specifically, unemployment is higher in the old industrial and metropolitan areas like: South Wales, Birmingham, Liverpool, Leeds, Manchester, Teesside, the East Midlands and Humberside. London also has a high level of unemployment. The rural and remote areas in Scotland, Yorkshire, Suffolk and Cumbria have the lowest levels, in part because of the flight from the

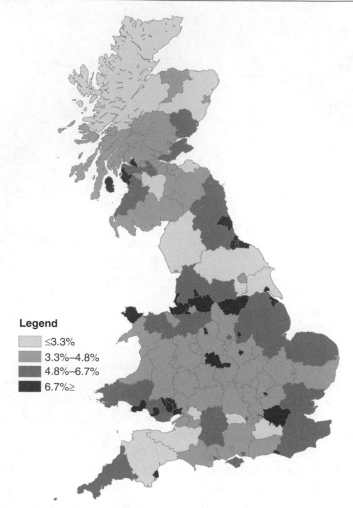

Figure 19.3: Unemployment rates at Local Authority level
Source: Annual Population Survey (APS), 2008.

country of young people looking for jobs in urban conurbations. The other low unemployment regions are the counties to the west of London, but south of the Midlands.

An important factor in the potential of any region for development must be the human capital of its inhabitants. Where graduates are trained and where they choose to live will reflect the demand for highly skilled labour and the potential of an area for regeneration. Figure 19.4 shows where those with NVQ level 4—basically degree-level qualifications— live. The spatial distribution of graduates, while skewed toward the South and especially London and the South West 'M4 corridor', does have pockets of high concentration in the

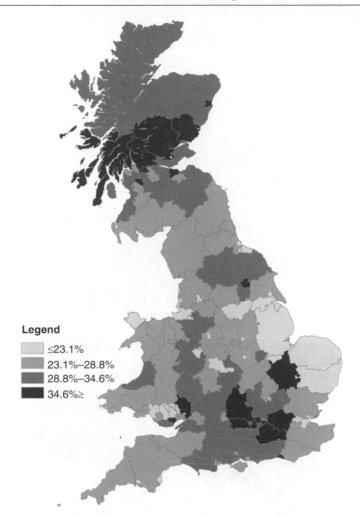

Figure 19.4: Share of graduates in the population by area
Notes: Proportion of people in working age with NVQ4 level or more in 2008.
Source: APS.

North. Most specifically, there is a higher fraction of graduates in Yorkshire, centred around Leeds and Sheffield. It is also clear that there is a high fraction of the more qualified in nearly all of Scotland and in South Wales around the capital—Cardiff. Agriculture, preponderantly important in Essex, Suffolk, Norfolk, Lincolnshire and Humberside, and the old traditional industries in South Yorkshire and Lancashire have relied less on highly qualified labour.

Some enduring features of underperforming areas with high poverty and unemployment, such as low wages, are very much features of the North. This is illustrated in Figure 19.5 which shows the fraction of workers who are in low-paid jobs that are paid at the level of the National Minimum Wage.

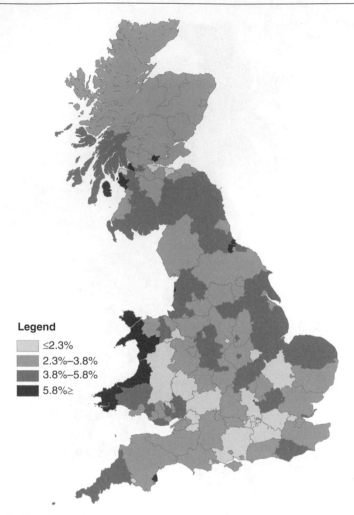

Figure 19.5: The share of minimum wage workers by area
Source: ASHE, 2008.

Unsurprisingly, this map highlights the same industrial heartlands of the Midlands, South Wales, the North West and the North East as the home of low-paid workers. However, here again, there are pockets of low pay in the South—especially Cornwall, Norfolk, East Sussex, Lincolnshire, Humberside, West Wales and East Scotland. These areas must be influenced by occasional labour markets like tourism, the service industries and traditionally low-paid jobs in agriculture. While the cost of living, particularly housing costs, are higher in the South, the idea that low pay could help encourage employment growth does not seem to be borne out by the persistent North–South employment gap. Indeed, Dolton et al. (2008) show that recent increases in the

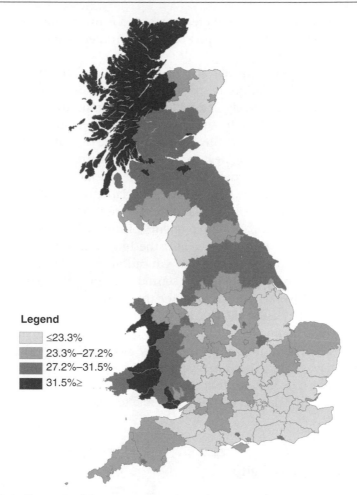

Figure 19.6: Share of public sector in employment by area
Source: APS, 2008. Authors' calculations.

National Minimum Wage, which affect areas of the North proportionately more than the South, have been associated with rises in employment in these areas relative to elsewhere.

As part of a drive to foster regional regeneration and lower central government costs, many public sector employees in central government were redeployed to the regions in the 1980s: specifically, the DVLA to Swansea, The Department of Health to Leeds, the Department of Employment to Sheffield, and the Department of Social Security to Newcastle. Recently the trend has begun anew. Following the 2004 Lyons Review, public sector relocation outside London was billed partly as an attempt to keep (wage) costs down. The Office of National Statistics (ONS) duly moved to Wales and there are more moves scheduled in the next few years, as downward pressure on public sector spending is maintained as part of the government's strategy to address the fiscal deficit.

Public sector employment has also benefited Edinburgh and Cardiff as a result of gradual devolution of political power to Scotland and Wales. Yet these policies were widely commended for helping to regenerate these areas. The question is, though—are these areas over-reliant on this political largesse? Most importantly, are these areas losing the capacity to become self-sufficient in terms of growing new competitive industries? A look at the map in Figure 19.6 gives us a partial answer to these questions. Here we see that much of Scotland and Wales, the North of England, the West Country, and parts of Yorkshire and the East Midlands and Norfolk are much more depen-dent on the public sector for employment. Clearly, when we think of this dependency, we must take into account the huge fraction of public sector workers who are in the core sectors of education, health and local govern-ment, as well as those recently moved central government departments. It is these categories of workers who are making the fraction of employed people in these areas so high. Hence, the truth is that these areas are not yet attracting new industries to complement the state and they remain over-reliant on the state for jobs. These findings must inevitably raise the issue of the degree to which Britain was right to jettison regional policy in the 1980s and the issue of whether to return to the idea that some regions of the country need central government sponsorship if they are to be able to compete with London and the South East.

Commuting and mobility

It is often mooted that a partial solution to the regional labour market division is to encourage mobility from disadvantaged to more prosperous regions. Ever since the early Margaret Thatcher government, the unemployed have been exhorted to 'get on their bike and look for a job'. The question is—is mobility a feasible strategy for regeneration and the solution to the unemployment problems of the North? Within regions, commuting is a potential response to local area differences in opportunities. Figure 19.7 gives the share of com-muters across different parts of the country. It is perhaps not surprising that commuting inside the major urban conurbations (like London, Birmingham, Leeds, Manchester, Tyneside, Edinburgh and Liverpool) is quite low. It is also clear that commuting is highest in the areas that surround these major sources of jobs. Specifically, people living in the East and West Midlands commuting to Birmingham, Leicester, Coventry and Nottingham; people in South Wales commuting into Cardiff and Newport; people in Avon commuting into

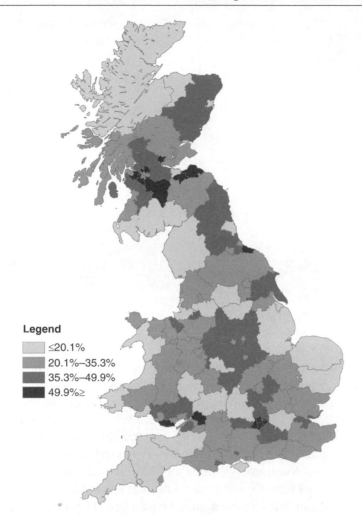

Figure 19.7: Commuting patterns by area

Notes: Sample is all individuals in work, age 16 to retirement. Commuting share is proportion of people in work living in one area and working in another area.

Source: ASHE and APS, 2008. Authors' calculations.

Bristol; people in Midlothian commuting into Edinburgh; people in the Scottish Lowlands commuting into Glasgow and people in Surrey, Berkshire, Bedfordshire, Hertfordshire and North Kent commuting into London. However commuting is also low in rural areas far away from the major conurbations—specifically in Norfolk, Suffolk, Devon, Cornwall, Lincolnshire, Cumbria, West Wales and Northern and Southern Scotland.

The pattern of mobility between regions is outlined in Figure 19.8 which graphs the fraction of the population moving regions in a given year. Mobility

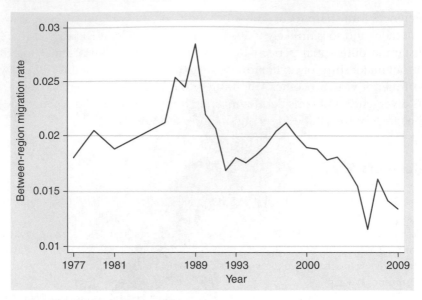

Figure 19.8: Mobility between regions
Source: LSF. Authors' calculations.

rose to a peak in 1989 and has been falling for much of the time since. The most notable thing about past recessions is that mobility fell in a downturn. So the idea that mobility could help address differential regional performance is somewhat fanciful. The unemployed are relatively more likely to move than the employed (by a factor of two to one), and marginally more likely to move away from higher unemployment regions (the correlation in 2009 between the unemployment rate in 18 regions and outmigration of the unemployed was 0.07; the correlation for 406 local authorities was 0.22). However, because the numbers in employment are so much bigger (by a factor of twelve to one), the mobility patterns over time are largely determined by what happens to people in employment. In the past decade, regional mobility has fallen further still. So mobility is unlikely to underlie the convergence in performance that was observed leading up to the latest recession.

Conclusions

Any idea that the regional differential performance that has plagued the UK economy for decades has disappeared appears to be premature. Despite an undoubted narrowing in the sectoral distribution of employment, the North of the UK continues to have much worse labour market performance than the South and the latest recession has, once again, brought these regional differences into sharp focus. Labour mobility between regions is at its lowest for decades and so is unlikely to foster any convergence. It is true that there is substantial differential performance within regions, but it seems clear that without major shifts of capital toward the North, differential performance will continue for years to come. Any future government must be made aware of this divergence and consider the most appropriate policies to regenerate the other areas of the UK besides London and the South East.

References

Davis, S., Haltiwanger, J. and Schuh, S. (1998) *Job Creation and Destruction*. Cambridge, Mass.: MIT Press.

Dolton, P., Rosazza-Bondibene, C. and Wadsworth, J. (2008) The geography of the National Minimum Wage. Report to Low Pay Commission, November, available at <http://www.lowpay.gov.uk/lowpay/research/pdf/LPC-Geography_of_the_National_Minimum_Wage.pdf>.

Gregg, P. and Wadsworth, J. (2011) The labour market in winter—the 2008–2009 recession. In: Gregg, P. and Wadsworth, J. (eds.) *The Labour Market in Winter: The State of Working Britain*. Oxford: Oxford University Press.

Jackman, R. and Savouri, S. (1999) Has Britain solved its regional problem? In: Gregg, P. and Wadsworth, J. (eds.) *The State of Working Britain*. Manchester and New York: Manchester University Press.

Smith, D. (1994) *North and South: Britain's Economic, Social and Political Divide*. Harmondsworth: Penguin.

Index

Index

self-employment 128, 139–40
sex discrimination 186–7
Sex Discrimination Act 172
Shadforth, C. 85, 93, 94
Shury 285
sickness 33
single adult households 72, 73, 78
single parents:
    and child poverty 246, 247, 248, 251
    employment rate 252
    see also lone parents
single-parent households 72, 73–4, 78–9
skill-based technology change (SBTC) 156, 165
skills 119–21
    low 22, 34, 84
    supply and demand 111, 120, 163–5, 166
Smith, D. 289
Smith, S. 59, 60, 65
social class 192–3
social mobility *see* intergenerational mobility
Social Mobility White Paper 191, 193
Spain 13, 77
state benefits:
    changes 247, 248, 249, 250, 251
    claimants 35–7, 46
    incapacity 34, 35
    welfare-to-work 35, 46–7, 67–8, 240, 253
Stewart, M. 48
Stock, W. 59
Strauss, A. 89
stress 111, 124, 125, 280
students 33, 86, 204, 209
subcontracting 122–3
Sure Start programmes 147, 200
Swaffield, J. K. 3, 4, 19, 34
Sweden 13, 163, 214

Task Discretion Index 122
task-biased technical change (TBTC) 156, 167–8
tax:
    and child poverty 247–8
    credits 35
    income 73
    VAT 9, 16
    Working Families Tax Credits (WFTC) 73, 148, 173, 241, 247
    Working Tax Credit (WTC) 147, 148
teacher quality 203, 217
technological revolution 113
Thatcher, M. 256, 298
Theodoropoulos, N. 227, 229, 230, 232, 234
Tominey, E. 30, 40
trade unions 124, 255–70
    closed shop 260
    demand for 263
    density 255, 256–8, 259
    employee voice 264–5

membership 255, 256–8
mergers and acquisitions 263
never-membership 259–60
public sector 259, 261, 275, 280
recognition 261
small 263
status in society 269–70
and wage dispersion 267–8
and wage premium 266–7
workplace role 255
Trades Union Congress 114
Trends in International Mathematics and Science Study (TIMSS) 208–9

UK Commission for Employment and Skills (UKCES) 114
under-employment 31–2
unemployment 22–38, 46–7
    across groups 28–9
    by age and gender 56–9
    impact of immigration 92–3
    and inflation 22–3
    long-term 27–8, 33
    measures of 31–2
    North-South divide 289–92
    scarring effects of 29–32
    youth 19, 28–9, 43–9
    see also youth unemployment
Unite 259
United States S 9, 15, 48, 59, 62, 63, 77, 115, 192, 242
    Current Population Survey 68
    education 203, 205
    immigrants 88, 93, 94
unskilled jobs 93, 94

Van Reenen, J. 48, 165
VAT 9, 16
Vignoles, A. 159
vocation 280

Wadsworth, J. 3, 23, 34, 74, 76, 79, 94, 129, 226, 247, 292
wage differentials 157, 159
wage dispersion 267–8
wage effect 93–4
wage gap 170, 172–3, 178
wage inequality 48–9, 155–68
    changes in 156–7, 158, 159–62
    and earnings mobility 162–3
    international comparisons 163
wage premium 266–7
wages:
    and child poverty 246–7, 248, 249, 250
    ethnic minorities 226–8, 233–4
    growth of 15–16, 17
    hourly 41, 178

private sector 272
see also National Minimum Wage
Waldfogel, J. 3, 145, 146, 147, 148, 149
Wales 217, 298
Warr, P. 130
Webb, A. 62
Welfare Reform and Pensions Act 66
welfare-to-work 35, 46–7, 67–8, 240, 253
well-being 128–42
  by employment status 134–7
  overall measures 134–7
  pro-cyclical 128, 140–1
West, A. 214
Whitfield, K. 124
Willman, P. 263, 265
Wilson, J. 215
Wise, D. 60
women:
  career advancement 179
  in the labour force 34
  with young children 146
Wood, S. 269
Work Capability Assessment 37
Work and Families 172
work intensity 111, 113, 124

work-life balance 111, 116–19
workers:
  demand for educated 163–5, 166
  discouraged 31–2
workforce strategies 16–17
Working Families Tax Credits (WFTC) 73, 148,
    173, 241, 247
working hours 13–18, 113, 116
  flexible 113, 117–18, 124; right to
    request 114, 144, 150–1, 172
  short-time 13
  young people 41
Working Tax Credit (WTC) 147, 148
Working Time Regulations (WTR) 267–8
workless households 72–83
Workplace Employment Relations
    Survey 269
Wren-Lewis, L. 162

young people 39–53
  unemployed 19, 28–9, 43–9
  working hours 41
Young Person's Guarantee 47
youth cohort size 48
Youth Cohort studies (YCS) 198